Inside Information

Inside Information

Making Sense of Marketing Data

D.V.L. SMITH & J.H. FLETCHER

JOHN WILEY & SONS, LTD

Chichester • New York • Weinheim • Brisbane • Singapore • Toronto

Other Wiley Editorial Offices

John Wiley & Sons, Inc., 605 Third Avenue,
New York, NY 10158-0012, USA

WILEY-VCH Verlag GmbH, Pappelallee 3,
D-69469 Weinheim, Germany

Jacaranda Wiley Ltd, 33 Park Road, Milton,
Queensland 4064, Australia

John Wiley & Sons (Asia) Pte Ltd, 2 Clementi Loop #02-01,
Jin Xing Distripark, Singapore 129809

John Wiley & Sons (Canada) Ltd, 22 Worcester Road,
Rexdale, Ontario M9W 1L1, Canada

British Library Cataloguing in Publication Data

A catalogue record for this book is available from the British Library

ISBN 0-471-49543-3

Typeset in 11/15pt Garamond by Mayhew Typesetting, Rhayader, Powys
Printed and bound in Great Britain by Biddles Ltd, Guildford and King's Lynn
This book is printed on acid-free paper responsibly manufactured from sustainable
forestry, in which at least two trees are planted for each one used for paper production.

Contents

Foreword

Everybody knows how to distrust statistical information – 'lies, damn lies, and statistics'. And a few people even know how misleading popular conceptions of probability are, to the extent that some can give the counter-intuitive, but correct, answer to the question 'what is the probability that two children in a class of 30 will share a birthday?' – a much higher probability than most people think.

But how many of the hundreds of thousands of people who use survey data in their work or lives, let alone how many who read survey findings in the media, have had any serious training in their analysis or interpretation? It is precisely because there is much more to the understanding and use of survey research than statistical formulae, that this book is necessary.

A very public example in recent years has been the debate on the use of focus groups by political parties in the formulation and presentation of policy. This raises two kinds of issue, each addressed by Smith and Fletcher in this challenging book.

First, the issue addressed by Chapter three of how qualitative research is carried out, when it is appropriate (and when not), and what precautions should be taken in the interpretation of qualitative evidence. Historically, most qualitative research has been widely – even mainly – used as part of the problem definition stage of a research project. Focus groups, or as they used to be called, discussion groups, were used to test how comprehensible ideas, language, or images, would be if used in a quantitative survey. Even motivation research, originally conducted by psychologists seeking to explore unexpressed motivation rather than conscious attitudes or behaviour, would commonly be reported as part of a study embracing both qualitative and quantitative data.

But the public image of focus groups, mainly triggered by political parties and their spin-doctors, has been as a short-cut to understanding of public opinion, not complementing but replacing the measurement of opinion and behaviour on political issues, among significant groups of the population, which can only be achieved by quantitative surveys. It is not just the media who over-simplify an issue of public concern: it is clear from their own accounts that those advising political parties in Britain have indeed misused focus groups, and neglected the proper use of survey research.

Dick Morris, President Clinton's spin-doctor, did not rely on focus groups to give his tactical advice to the presidential candidate in 1992, but commissioned 800 telephone interviews every night during the campaign. Not cheap, but effective. Spin-doctors to British political parties would do well to follow that example. Smith and Fletcher help to explain why.

Second, the issue of how research findings are to be used in making business decisions, which has dominated business texts on marketing research since Green and Tull. Again, the focus group controversy illuminates the issue. Too often, public reporting of research for political parties, often fed by leaks of internal documents, gives the impression that parties wish to use research, not to guide them in the presentation of policy, but as a replacement for political, social and economic analysis in the formulation of policy itself.

Perhaps they do: perhaps popularism without principle is gaining ground in our political life. But as a politician, I profoundly hope not; and as a survey researcher, both in business and in public policy, I deplore such distortion of our discipline. Survey research should assist, but never seek to usurp, the role of decision-making based on proper business or policy objectives, and in possession of all the relevant facts.

Again, this book provides practical illustrations of the dangers of misinterpretation of research findings – what the authors call the 'craft skills necessary to scan, gut, and action information'. Textbooks of market research already expound many of the rules of interpretation – caution when dealing with small sub-samples, re-percentaging when bases change (or better, avoiding changing bases), and so on: the authors rightly rehearse these rules. But in emphasising the importance of inductive reasoning, in what they call 'the seven pillars of information wisdom' they address issues which are well known to those experienced in the craft, but which have not before, to my knowledge, been suffi-ciently expounded in print.

It has always seemed to me that there are two difficult problems for those who find themselves required to commission research, or to make business or policy decisions using research findings.

The first is to remember that commissioning original research is a last resort. If effective ways can be found to use business or official statistics, or to re-examine or re-interpret existing research data, then that will be preferable to commissioning original research, which runs the twin risks of costing more than the benefit to be derived from it, or of being carried out on an inadequate budget, with the potential for untrustworthy results.

Second – and there are constant reminders of this in the book – survey research essentially provides the customer viewpoint, to counterbalance the producer bias which is inherent in business life. It does not mean that the customer is always right.

To give merely one example: for many years, economic and business researchers both in the UK and in the US devoted considerable resources and great skill to analysing the validity and reliability of anticipations data as a tool for forecasting consumer purchases. They took into account the obvious psychological truth that buying intentions will become less firm and actionable the further into the future they go; they allowed for the fact that large purchases, such as home or cars, are more likely to be anticipated than purchases of, for example, small electrical appliances; they even, eventually, caught up with the fact that anticipation of replacement purchases will follow a different pattern from first-time buying.

But what they failed to do was to recognise that other factors, themselves capable of forecasting, but necessarily unknown to the consumer at the time of interview, would influence consumer buying intentions. Without the best available forecast of trends in inflation, in consumer disposable income, in product development and pricing, anticipations data are almost certain to be misleading. Here too is a lesson from market research for public policy, and indeed for political polling.

If this book can help users of survey research, whether they be information professionals, research practitioners, or more generally people in business or public life, with the insights necessary to understand and benefit from the skills of the researcher, it will have well justified itself. It is a worthy objective.

Andrew McIntosh

Preface

In this book the authors argue that we need to develop a new information *paradigm* that provides data users and suppliers with the fresh insights and practical hands-on information skills and competencies needed to cope with the 'information explosion'. We are aware that the term *paradigm* is a much overused word. But we believe that information professionals – most notably market researchers – urgently need to put into the public domain a clear set of guiding principles about how they are currently tackling the world of marketing information in the twenty-first century. The authors – both of whom are practising market researchers – believe that this issue places the market research industry at a crossroads. The industry could stumble on pretending that many of the principles and concepts spelt out in existing market research textbooks still apply to the way they now operate. Or, as we believe, they could seize this golden opportunity to articulate the way that *New Market Research* really 'works'. This would explain how, increasingly, we are relying on more *holistic* analysis techniques than has been the case in the past. In this new Millennium market researchers must learn how to assemble a *jigsaw* of imperfect evidence using the skills of the 'bricoleur', rather than falling back on some of the more methodologically pure, but now rather stale, approaches of the past. In short, we outline what market research practitioners have been doing behind closed doors – but not articulating to the world – for a number of years. So we are not inventing new analytic techniques for the first time. But the ideas this book contains are new in the sense that this is one of the first books that make explicit what may be termed the *hidden* market research practitioners' paradigm. We believe that unless market research practitioners, and other information specialists, now start to articulate and make explicit many of their day-to-day data analysis practices, then we will not have a platform upon which to realistically debate the techniques being used to make sense of marketing data. It is a debate that is much needed if we are to develop the appropriate training for prospective information professionals.

Acknowledgements

The authors wish to thank Jo Smith and Andy Dexter for their helpful comments on the structure of the book. In addition, we are indebted to Phyllis Vangelder for her contribution to the editing process. But we are most indebted to Chris Rooke and Sandra Mead for the professionalism that they have demonstrated in typing various drafts of the book. Sandra needs a special mention for all the dedication shown in painstakingly working on the final stages of the preparation of the book.

C H A P T E R 1

Mastering Twenty-First-Century Information

Overview

This chapter:

- introduces the view that new analysis skills are needed to cope with modern twenty-first-century business information
- explains that these new skills require information to be analysed in an *holistic* way
- reviews the way this holistic approach is characterised.

ONE

Mastering Twenty-First-Century Information

'Where is the wisdom we have lost in knowledge? Where is the knowledge we have lost in information?' – T.S. Eliot

This book is about how to make sense of the data and evidence that is arriving at us from all directions in this the 'information era'. Some might think that the information era is already at its zenith. But the real information explosion is still a little way off. True revolutions are the result of changes in infrastructures, rather than just the arrival of a new invention. Thus, it was not the invention of the car that revolutionised transport, but the creation of our road network. Similarly, it was not the ability to build washing machines and other electrical labour-saving devices that changed household life, but the setting up of the National Electricity Grid. And so it is with the information era. It is not the invention of the personal computer that lies at the heart of the new information era, but the creation of the Internet distribution channel that allows information to flow from business to business, home to home and so on. And because this infrastructure is not yet quite in place – not all businesses are 'wired' with each other and not all homes are interconnected – the *full* information explosion has still not hit us. Just how far away this will be is difficult to judge. In the United Kingdom the Prime Minister has announced that the target is to ensure that everybody has access to the Internet by the year 2005.

The information paradox

The arrival of the information era brings with it an information paradox. One might have hoped that, given the busy time-pressured lives we lead and the need to master increasing amounts of information, we could now spend less time deciding on the robustness of each piece of evidence with which we are presented. But this is not the case: this is the paradox. At the very time when we have so much more information, we also have to spend more, not less, time delving into exactly what this information is trying to tell us. This is because a feature of the modern business information world is the emergence of a wide range of less than 'perfect' information drawn from a myriad of comparatively unknown information sources. In the past, decision-makers in the world of marketing have been able to rely on a small number of reasonably methodologically sound sources of marketing data. But today, increasingly, we are faced with more information, much of which will have a question mark over its robustness.

In some ways, the arrival of concepts such as Knowledge Management is helping to keep us on top of this new array of marketing information. But this – and the hope that the computer technology will come to our rescue and help us better sort, classify and even 'interpret' information – only goes so far. At the heart of the challenge facing us is recognition that we need a new set of twenty-first-century *information competencies* in order to handle this new world of multi-source, 'imperfect' data. There is talk of a high proportion of the workforce now being 'knowledge workers', but comparatively little new thinking on how to help these knowledge workers make sense of the new sources of business information. It seems that an assumption is made that individuals will, by osmosis, learn to dissect and absorb all the new information swirling around and use this for effective decision-making. But in this book we argue that these knowledge workers are going to require a new set of twenty-first-century 'information skills and competencies'.

We should stress that when we talk about applying information to decision-making, we are defining a decision as being a 'choice made between alternatives'. (The word 'decision' is derived from a word meaning 'to cut'.) And given this definition of a 'decision', in this book we will not be looking just at the way information is applied to big strategic decisions about the overall direction of an organisation, but also at the way in which information is applied to more tactically focused, day-to-day decisions.

Twenty-first-century information *craft skills*

It seems to be the case that if someone has successfully negotiated the educational system, then it is assumed that they will have automatically acquired the key *craft skills* necessary to 'scan', 'gut', and 'action' information. But the majority of people in business and commerce – notwithstanding the prowess they may have demonstrated in their chosen academic discipline – still need specific, practical guidance on how effectively to process and action modern marketing and business information to maximum competitive advantage. Specifically, we believe that there are five key skill areas that new entrants into marketing must learn if they are effectively to master the new world of marketing information.

- *The ability to instantly classify and reduce incoming information.* A clear difference between the current marketing environment and that of only 10 years ago is the need for practitioners to be able to make decisions quickly about what information to accept, reject and store. So, in this book, we will be providing a series of practical tips to help the reader keep on top of the sheer volume of incoming marketing information.

- *Getting underneath the evidence.* In today's marketing environment it is important to understand the strengths and limitations of incoming evidence from all angles. This means getting behind, and underneath, the data to identify any 'sources of error' that might have implications for their subsequent interpretation. This is an approach that squares with those who argue for data to be analysed in an *holistic*, rather than a solely statistical way. Here, by 'error' we do not mean a *mistake*, but any feature of the research process that may have introduced some form of 'bias' – something that takes us away from the 'truth'. This softer (more qualitative) assessment of data provides the platform for the subsequent, more statistically-based, interrogations of the data. In this book we will be providing the reader with a number of insights into what questions to ask about the origins of different types of evidence. In short, we will give the reader the skills needed to check out the 'full service history' of incoming data.

- *Embracing intuition.* Business history abounds with stories of individuals whose success has been founded on sparks of dazzling 'intuition'. This has been defined by Jung as the 'perception of the possibilities inherent in a situation' and Spinoza claimed that intuition was the 'royal road to truth'. And there are numerous captains of industry who will testify that the hard taskmasters of logic and rigorous analysis were only part of how they made 'big' decisions. Richard Branson tells us that his decision to go into the airline business in the mid-1980s was *a move which in pure economic terms everybody thought was mad, including my closest friends, but it was something to which I felt I could bring something that others were not bringing*. Similarly, Sir David Simon, ex-boss of BP, is on record as saying: *'you don't have to discuss things. You can sense them. The "tingle" is as important as the intellect'*. Thus, in this book we will be arguing strongly that the market research and market intelligence process needs large doses of intuition in order to realise their true potential.

Psychologists tell us that we are conscious of only a small part of what we know, pointing out that intuition allows us to draw on our unconscious knowledge – everything that one has experienced or learned, either consciously or subliminally. But this does not make intuition a 'mystical' phenomenon. If we arrive at a solution by intuition this simply means that we have got there without consciously knowing *exactly* how we did it. It does not mean that we have not been following a 'process'. It means that things are happening automatically, at high speed, without conscious thought, in a difficult-to-define process. A Grand Chess Master considers far fewer alternatives when making a move than an amateur player. The Chess Grand Master has incorporated into his/her implicit memory, knowledge of the probability of the success or failure of different moves. This provides a rich reservoir of knowledge which means the Grand Master does not formally have to search through all the alternative moves. The Grand Master can quickly eliminate the unworkable, and focus only on the potentially winning moves. For this reason, intuition has been called *compressed expertise*. Of course, the idea of attempting formally to codify and make explicit 'tacit intuitive knowledge' is a paradox. But, in this book, the authors – in pursuing their belief in the value of the 'holistic' analysis of data – provide various frameworks that help ensure that in any decision-making process intuitive insights take their rightful place alongside the more formal explicit evidence.

- *Bricolage.* Another key twenty-first-century information skill centres on the importance of being able to look at the way data, when inter-woven with other evidence, can create 'shapes and patterns' that begin to tell a story. It is helpful to think of this analysis as a form of 'bricolage'. This term refers to the practice of using a combination of different analysis techniques to understand – and weave together – a variety of evidence into a co-ordinated picture that provides a strong 'directional indication' as to the meaning of the assembled 'jigsaw' of evidence. This multi-faceted analysis and cross-weaving of different weights and hues of evidence – drawn together from an eclectic array of sources – is analogous to archaeological method. It seeks to understand the way in which fragments of evidence fit 'horizontally' with other pieces or clusters of evidence collected at that same time. But it also seeks to understand evidence 'vertically'; that is, in the context of the knowledge we have, not only about the point in time in which the evidence has become 'embedded', but also in relation to what we know about what went before and what happened after.

- *Building conceptual models.* It is also important in the modern world of marketing information to develop the skills needed to build 'conceptual frameworks and models' that explain about how parts of the marketing world 'work'. It is going to be increasingly difficult for us to absorb the many different incoming isolated pieces of information unless we locate these data into some form of 'model'. After all, this only reflects the way in which *physical* scientists have traditionally made sense of the world by looking at the connections between one phenomenon and another, thereby allowing them to build a theory or model to explain these inter-relationships. *Pure* scientists seek to find out how a change in one thing will affect others closely connected with it: they look for the far from obvious and totally unexpected. And, the holistic data analysis skills we are arguing that those in the business world now need to acquire, simply build on these well-established scientific prin-ciples. Of course, the way in which one examines a connection between events in the world of social sciences – psychology, sociology and economics – will differ from the way the natural sciences, such as physics, operate. But, importantly, there is a commonality across the two approaches. Both pure and social scientists need to feel comfortable about drawing together the 'jigsaw' of available evidence and information, and embarking on the 'bricolage' technique in order to identify critical 'shapes and patterns' that explain how the world 'works'. The main point of difference is that pure scientists, working with a manageable number of variables, can realistically aim to develop a *predictive* model that reliably explains connections and likely future events. But in the far more complex world of business and marketing, the best that the data analyst can hope to achieve is the *reduction of uncertainty* in our judgement and decision-making.

A new holistic way of evaluating information

Thus, in this book we seek to help individuals working in the world of marketing, to develop more confidence about using a range of 'hard' and 'soft' techniques, in an holistic way, in order to better understand business information. We believe this is going to reduce much of the frustration currently experienced by those using market research data and marketing intelligence when trying to solve business problems. It is claimed that three-quarters of the 'knowledge' that top managers apply in decision-making is 'implicit', difficult to codify, evidence. Yet, paradoxically, many senior managers still continue to claim that key decisions should always be 'backed up by statistics'. In this book, by providing analysis frameworks for drawing together implicit and explicit evidence, we provide some new insights into how to cope with twenty-first-century marketing information. We should point out that although there are a number of new ideas in this book, it has to be accepted that many market research practitioners will have been informally using the techniques we describe in this book for a number of years. But we believe that this book is a 'first' in the sense that it seeks to make explicit many of these industry practices, and formally defines for the first time the holistic data analysis process in a way that will allow the industry to debate and advance these methods and approaches. This book seeks to plug the yawning gap between what newcomers to the market research industry can read about in the textbooks and what actually happens in practice in agencies and client organisations.

About this book

This book will be particularly valuable to those who use market research data to make commercial decisions. But, market research practitioners – those who *supply* data – will also benefit from reviewing some of the new ways of analysing twenty-first-century marketing information explained in this book. In addition, those on the edges of marketing – those who use more general business, rather than specific marketing research, information – should also benefit from our insights and guidance on how to interpret and make sense of data in an holistic fashion.

Achieving our goal of providing the reader with a guide to the 'new' holistic-based information competencies that will be required in order to understand the new genre of multi-source, imperfect marketing information in a *single volume* is a challenge. It has to be accepted that attempts to provide the reader with insights into how better to understand incoming marketing research and marketing evidence in a single volume, means that we are working on a big canvas. It means we must tell our story in fairly broad strokes. This approach inevitably will mean that specialists in many of the areas we cover may accuse us of 'vulgarisation' of their respective disciplines. But we remain unrepentant because we believe that there is urgent need for users, and suppliers, of market research to have access to a *single* volume text that provides them with insights and practical tips on how to look at marketing data in this new information era.

This book is a 'practice-led', not 'methodological-theory-driven', book. It is based on practical experience in information-based business problem-solving. However, this of course is not to dismiss the value of 'methodological theory'. This is clearly vitally important because it sets the boundary within which practitioners must operate. Thus, our book, although applied and practical, is grounded in a solid understanding of what academic-based methodological writers are telling us about information management, qualitative and survey research, data analysis and business decision-making. But this does not mean that the book will be necessarily welcomed with open arms by *both* practitioners and academics. Our approach to analysing the new world of imperfect, multi-source information takes us into relatively uncharted waters. In so doing, we will undoubtedly be making generalisations that will attract the wrath of many methodological purists. Similarly, with many of our practical guidelines, no doubt there will be practitioners who do not share our particular view of the world. But, we believe that this first attempt to articulate the holistic data analysis approach, in a single volume, will generate debate and lead to further texts that will provide us with even better ways of looking at modern marketing data.

This book starts by providing the reader with some basic insights into the fundamental nature of marketing information, and also provides some advice on how to absorb and digest the incoming tide of information. We follow this with a review of the nature of qualitative evidence: when using 'softer' evidence, what does the decision-maker have to be alert to? This is followed by an examination of how better to understand what survey data are really saying. What are the questions to ask about surveys in order to ensure you only take from them the most robust evidence. We then put the spotlight on what decision-makers – having decided that *existing* information is not providing the answers they require – need to know about commissioning new research. This is followed by a guide to holistic data analysis: the new approach that we believe is needed to handle the incoming plethora of multi-source, marketing information. We will then, in the final chapter of the book, provide guidance to the reader on how effectively to apply qualitative and quantitative marketing information to the decision-making process.

C H A P T E R 2

Acquiring Effective Information Habits

Overview

This chapter:

- outlines seven pillars of information wisdom: insights about the very nature of the way we reason and arrive at a conclusion based on information
- reviews the robustness of different types of information, ranging from clues, anecdotes and archetypes, to formal qualitative evidence, to quantitative survey evidence and finally analytical conceptual models
- provides guidance on how to develop a 'personal information strategy' for handling the tide of incoming information
- provides a 12-point checklist aimed at helping establish whether a piece of incoming information is sufficiently robust for decision-making
- provides a guide on how quickly to get to the 'storyline' behind both qualitative and quantitative marketing evidence.

TWO

Acquiring Effective Information Habits

'We are what we repeatedly do. Excellence, then, is not an act but a habit' – Aristotle

Coping with the next generation of marketing information calls for a new set of information habits. In the past, it may have been acceptable for the market research specialist to rest on his/her laurels as a technical/ methodological specialist. But, in today's multi-source, imperfect information world, it is important for market researchers to supplement these technical skills with a wider appreciation of the whole process of information-based decision-making. In this chapter we will be looking at five areas where we believe a wider, more visionary, more holistic-based approach to information, will pay dividends. First, we look at some key *insights* about the very nature of the way we reason and arrive at conclusions based on information. Secondly, we flag the importance of understanding how particular genres of marketing data fit into the wider jigsaw of all the types of data that may exist on the topic under investigation. Thirdly, we highlight the importance of individuals developing a *personal information strategy* in order to keep on top of the relentless tide of incoming marketing information. Fourthly, we believe it is important for individuals to carry in their heads a set of 'tools' that will enable them instantly to check the *robustness* and veracity of incoming information. And finally, we argue that today's information specialists need to have a clear 'game plan' as to how they will 'hook up' incoming information with different types of *action*: the days where silos of information were built up for decision-makers to dip into at a later date are gone. Today, there now needs to be a much tighter connection between the incoming information and the decision-making process. So, in this chapter, we look at each of these above issues.

The seven pillars of information wisdom

There is a considerable body of rich philosophical evidence on what constitutes sound, methodological reasoning and practice. But very little of this material finds its way into the day-to-day practice of busy marketing research practitioners. This is disappointing because we believe that it is important for today's data analyst to have a perspective on some of the fundamental aspects of the way we make sense of marketing information. So, at the risk of high vulgarisation and trivialisation of a vast topic, below we have outlined seven key *insights* about the nature of reasoning and data. We believe these provide food for thought for any analyst embarking on the task of analysing marketing information. We feel that these insights form a bedrock upon which subsequent, more practical information-handling techniques need to be based.

Insight 1: all knowledge starts with prejudice

 This insight tells us that the way many people make sense of the world will not be based solely on 'scientifically-driven' reason. Understanding often starts by taking an initial – possibly prejudicial – view and then working through a less than perfect 'scientific' process of re-visiting our initial starting point, eventually ending up somewhere close to the 'truth'.

The ideal of a research investigation entirely free from any presuppositions about the world is an illusion. All knowledge builds on previous beliefs – however flawed they may be. It is sometimes claimed that research operates inductively: grouping observations together into general theories. However, there is growing evidence that we are not, by nature, inductive thinkers; rather, we instinctively very quickly develop a theory or hypothesis that gathers together our initial observations, and then use it to organise our subsequent observations. For example, Pasteur's discoveries about the role of micro-organisms in human disease and his development of the crucial techniques of vaccination and pasteurisation were driven by his belief in the doctrine of 'Vitalism' – the belief that living things are fundamentally different from mere non-living chemicals, as the former contain a mystical *élan vital* or living spark. This view, now rejected by science, nevertheless led Pasteur to look for 'living things' where previously scientists had looked for 'chemicals'. It was an approach – albeit flawed – that ultimately resulted in major breakthroughs in the understanding and treatment of disease. Thus, the further we want to advance our learning beyond what we already know the bolder we have to be in our initial conjectures. These conjectures may be single hypotheses, or may be more fully developed theories or models comprising a number of interlocking hypotheses. The latter is preferable because breakthroughs in our understanding are more likely to occur if we branch out on a number of various and unexpected fronts. Therefore, the more 'working hypotheses' with which we arm ourselves to tackle our problem – however provisional – the more likely we are to have to hand the one we need to crack the problem.

Insight 2: investigation is a circular not a linear process

 This insight tells us that investigation is a process of continually shuttling between where you have just arrived and the new emerging ideas that are now beginning to influence your thinking. Market research is a process that requires tenacity, a willingness to 'agonise' over the meaning of data and a preparedness to work in what many will consider is an uneven, 'messy' way.

If our prejudices (or refined prejudices in the form of hypotheses and theories) are an essential start-point for investigation, they must, nevertheless, be modified (often out of all recognition) if we are to end up providing useful and accurate representations of the world. As we have already seen, we find it difficult to observe and then generalise a theory from our observations. Rather, we tend to start with a theory (however crude and partial), make observations in light of this theory and then modify our theory in the light of these observations. This requires us constantly to shuttle between our theory and our observations as we seek to perfect the fit between our theory and the aspect of the world it is intended to describe. It is a process that is more circular than linear. Our theories become adapted to the situation we are attempting to describe or explain, developing in complexity as they do so. But merely shuttling between theory and observation, adapting the former in light of the latter, is not sufficient to guarantee that the theory is a reliable guide to the world. To ensure the theory's fitness we need genuinely to exercise it – not merely stretch it over any new observations or facts which can be made to fit it. We can do this in two ways:

1. Try to disprove our theory – or better still, given our weakness for favouring our own theories, get others to try to disprove it.
2. Try to prevent our theory from becoming a fully developed picture before we have incorporated all our relevant information and knowledge into it.

We can also impose this discipline on ourselves as we develop our theories or interpretations. The main threat to truth from theory seems to come from the temptation to organise the data we are looking at from too narrow a conceptual base – one that is inappropriate to the data. To a certain extent we can avoid this pitfall by ensuring that we have a mental toolkit of concepts and models appropriate to the data we are considering. But we cannot always be confident that we have all the relevant experience and learning needed to make correct interpretations of information of a particular kind – especially if the area is very new to us or has never before been the subject of research. Ensuring that market researchers do not impose an artificial structure on a problem is critically important. Central to this thinking is the work of Glaser and Strauss. They developed a technique for generating sociological and psychological theory that would reflect the observations that researchers made rather than distorting these data to fit an inappropriate predetermined theory. Called 'Grounded Theory' their approach was to develop a range of narrow, concrete, low-level categories out of qualitative data. As each new observation is made so the researcher has to compare it with the categories he has currently developed and decide whether it fits any of them, and if not what new category it might come under. Glaser and Strauss's stated aim with this approach was to maximise what they termed the researcher's 'theoretical sensitivity' – his or her ability to 'conceptualise and formulate a theory *as it emerges from the data*' – by providing a framework or discipline for building narrow concrete categories (what they termed 'substantive' theories) into more abstract (or 'formal') theories.

Insight 3: context is everywhere or the panorama principle

 In everyday life we naturally interpret what people are telling us and how they are behaving in the wider context of why this person may have elected to say what, or behave like, he/she did. But we are often less willing to adopt the same approach when interpreting data – tending to place a more literal interpretation on what is in front of us. Thus, this next insight is a reminder of the need for continual vigilance, when interpreting data, in establishing the context in which the original item of evidence was collected and subsequently interpreted.

One of the reasons why it is difficult to make sense of incoming marketing information is that data are not always *nested* in their appropriate context. We are all aware of politicians claiming that a comment they have made has 'been taken out of context'. Raise your hand in a classroom and it means that you want to go to the washroom: do the same thing in an auction room and it means you could be the proud owner of a Rembrandt!

Let us take a more marketing-specific example of the importance of understanding the context in which the original data were collected. A Fragrance House has undertaken market research with the aim of deciding how its customers decide between using their company or its competitor for their soaps and toiletries and so on. Here, there are three quite important contexts that it is important to clarify in order to make sense of the responses that any one customer will provide in a survey for the Fragrance House. In the first situation, the Fragrance House in question could be the *incumbent* supplier to the customer being interviewed. In the second situation, the Fragrance House could be a *challenger* to the incumbent. And in the third situation, we could have an interview with a customer who has a fairly *promiscuous* pattern in terms of being supplied by different fragrance houses. It will be clear that the way in which an interview would unfold in each of these 'incumbent', 'challenger' and 'promiscuous' situations is a vitally important context within which to understand what it is the customer is saying in the interview.

And just one more example to drive home the importance of context in analysing a situation. Imagine arriving at Northampton Railway Station and seeing an advertising poster with the name 'Northampton' (written to look like the official (then) British Rail Northampton station name). Then in brackets after the name Northampton we see the word *probably*.

People in on the joke would look up to see that opposite the railway station is the Carlsberg Brewery. In this wider context, everything would suddenly become clear. (In the United Kingdom there is a well known advertising campaign in which Carlsberg is referred to as being '*probably the best lager in the world*'.) But, someone arriving from foreign parts, unable to contextualise the word *probably* could be totally bemused about the rather tentative railway station naming policy operational in Britain!

The reason why many market research investigations fail to capture the wider critically important contextual picture is because one of the principal objectives and methods of science is to understand the world by breaking it down into simple parts which can then be manipulated and their effects on each other tested in a controlled way. By isolating and stabilising events and understanding their interactions with each other we can predict and control events, learn which signs to look out for to help us anticipate events, and which 'levers' to pull to make things happen. Much effort in the natural sciences is devoted to ensuring that important phenomena have been completely isolated. However, this sound scientific discipline can, when transferred to the social sciences, lessen, not strengthen, our understanding of what is happening. There are essentially two ways of overcoming the problem of context in the human sciences:

1. Study, as far as possible, human activities in their normal contexts. The purest form of this is observation of the actual behaviour in its normal context. However, we often need to disrupt these contexts by intervening in them, for example to ask questions about what someone is doing. In this case we need to understand what effect this intervention is likely to have. More commonly, there is a practical, or methodological, need to remove people from the contexts they are talking about (in interviews or group discussions), in which case the contexts need to be reconstructed as far as possible. This is the approach taken by most qualitative research and by quantitative research which attempts exhaustively to model all the variables that might affect an individual's behaviour.
2. The other main way of overcoming the problem of context is to take measurements, as far as possible, across all contexts in which the behaviour we are studying is likely to occur and aggregate our

findings across all these. This is a large-scale quantitative technique and typically requires observations to cover a wide geographical area and be extended over time to ensure that all significant differences or changes in context are captured.

Clearly, these two very different approaches will be suited to different marketing problems. The former depends on attempting to understand contexts and causal factors in these contexts in detail, whilst the latter generally eschews tight causal explanation in favour of identifying the overall pattern of the relationships that exist between different events.

Insight 4: everyone knows more than they think they know: or 'the iceberg principle'

 This insight tells us that there is a danger of placing too much reliance on formal explicit evidence to the exclusion of more informal, intuitive, implicit knowledge. The key in making many judgements and decisions lies in striking the right balance between explicit and implicit knowledge.

The majority of our knowledge about the world is implicit; that is to say it subsists below the waterline of our conscious awareness. We can view knowledge as being rather like an iceberg, where the amount of knowledge and reasoning ability we are able, at any one moment, to summon to mind and express verbally, belies the much larger mass of knowledge that lies more deeply in our mind, out of reach of ready verbal expression. This has the paradoxical disadvantage that we are not always aware of what we know and can very often overlook how much we already know about a situation. Contrary to the old saying about things being easier said than done, many things, 'perhaps most things', are easier done than said! Once getting home becomes a habit and we no longer have to think about the landmarks we pass, explaining the route can be quite difficult. How many times have you been given directions only to discover that a roundabout or a set of traffic lights or some other vital detail has been omitted? This can present problems in business.

It is quite common for business managers to become pressurised by the 'management science industry' into believing that what they themselves know about their business is somehow secondary to all this *science*. This problem is exacerbated by the fact that much intimate understanding about a business is, indeed must be, implicit in nature and therefore is difficult to express in a form that is comparable with the explicit 'scientific' formulations of researchers and consultants. But, whilst explicit information and learning are vital in business, they could be positively damaging if they obliterate valuable implicit understanding about the business. Thus, the key to the successful use of marketing information is knowing how to weigh incoming explicit knowledge against existing implicit knowledge. This lies at the heart of the successful *holistic* analysis of marketing data.

Insight 5: data are dumb: beliefs are blind

 This insight reminds us that data *alone*, without the organising benefit of prior belief and theory, are of limited value. But equally, our interpretation of the data and its context could reflect belief structures that are themselves flawed.

Imagine you are given a marketing problem to solve – say, what would be the optimum brand of lager to launch on the UK market? To help in this task, you are presented with a table of figures without a title or any headings. You can look at these data for as long as you like, but they will not yield anything of value. Adding a title and headings to reveal that the data relate to, say, the spending patterns of UK consumers breathes a little life into the figures: the descriptions of the rows (such as 'bottles of premium lager purchased in the last week') and the headings over the columns (such as 'male', 'female', '18–24 years old' and so on), will start to engage our beliefs – in this case about the drinking behaviour of different types of people. Prior knowledge, concepts and assumptions about the different drinking habits of men and women, young and old, and so forth will be activated by the combination of descriptions, headings and figures. Some of these beliefs will be confirmed and others affected by the data actually shown. But the table will start to tell you something. However, if tables of figures are added, relating to other aspects of drinking behaviour – such as brands of lager that are drunk, prices of the different brands and so on – the task of working out what the data are saying and what you should do, paradoxically, starts to become more difficult again. In order to deal with the manifold data before you, you now need to have more appropriate, sophisticated beliefs and concepts that enable you to distinguish what is relevant data from what is not relevant and gather up all the former to shape your conclusions. The most useful 'prior beliefs' here would be those relating to like types of data for similar or analogous kinds of task. This example illustrates the fact that data, on their own, without the means to engage our beliefs about the world are 'dumb', incapable of telling us anything. Moreover, the more appropriate and sophisticated our beliefs about an issue the more value this will be in understanding the data relating to that issue. This is another way of saying that using marketing information is all about looking for 'shapes and patterns'. Someone who has conducted analysis tasks like this before and has experience of the way in which the data, and interpretations of these data, actually 'played out' when tested in practice will have two advantages over 'prior knowledge'. In looking at the data:

- they will be able to make sense of the data more rapidly, and
- their interpretations will be more correct and provide a better guide to action.

People are often surprised and unsettled by the fact that these two advantages should go hand in hand: they are suspicious of highly selective approaches to market data and feel that in some (usually unspecified) way all available data – every figure and every word – have to be considered and weighed and factored into an interpretation for them to be adjudged sound. In a sense the best analysers of data do take all information into consideration, but they know they must dismiss much of it very quickly, as irrelevant to their central task. They reorganise the data to give what is largely irrelevant an appropriate place well down the list of priorities.

However, if data are 'dumb' without beliefs, then beliefs without data are 'blind'. The history of the social sciences is a veritable graveyard of grand theories and beliefs which took little account of observed facts and as a result failed to deliver the solutions to human problems that they promised. Marxist–Leninism, Freudian analysis and the General Equilibrium Theory of economics each claimed to offer a scientific explanation of complex human activities and events from a fairly narrow theoretical base. They each developed elaborate means of accounting for contradictory evidence in the form of 'bolted-on' theoretical extensions consistent with the original theory. They each, through their power to capture people's belief, attained considerable influence in practical human affairs:

Soviet-inspired communism and, for a long time, the mismanagement of Western economies. Part of the reason why such grand theories go astray has to do with the ratio between the wide range of phenomena they attempt to explain and the narrow range of research observations on which they are originally based. Freud, for instance, developed his theories from psychiatric observations amongst nineteenth-century, middle-class, Viennese hysterics and neurotics and was soon using them to explain, amongst other things, Renaissance artists, the history of civilisations and primitive religion!

So whilst existing models and prior knowledge are vital to being able to make full use of market data, we must be careful not to over-extend our existing knowledge in attempting to interpret new information. We need to ask ourselves whether our existing knowledge is adequate to the task of making sense of the new data. Even if the data can be made to fit with our existing knowledge, are we having to stretch what we already know unduly? We cannot, to a certain extent, avoid approaching the unfamiliar through the familiar, but we must always ask ourselves whether there are other disciplines or areas of expertise with which we may not be familiar, but which could provide more appropriate models and theories for understanding the data before us?

Insight 6: two eyes good; four eyes better – or 'the triangulation principle'

 Today we are all more aware of the fact that often the 'answer' does not lie in one single source of information but in the ability to see how different pieces of less than perfect information fit together to tell the story. So this insight re-affirms the importance of cultivating the twenty-first-century skill of utilising data drawn from multiple sources, angles, perspectives and horizons.

Anyone who can use a compass will be familiar with the process of 'triangulation'. If you want to find exactly where you are on a map using a compass you need to find reasonably well-defined (natural or man-made) features in the landscape, take compass readings on these and draw the bearings as lines on the map. The first line will tell you that you are somewhere along that line on the map – but it could be anywhere. The second line will tell you where you are along that line, i.e. at the point that intersects it. And a third line will confirm whether or not you have taken your bearings correctly and identified the features on the map correctly. If it intersects at the intersection of the other two lines (the so-called 'cocked hat'), then you have done everything right and have found where you are on the map. If it is a fair way off, then one or more of your bearings is wrong and you will need to start all over again.

This is a useful metaphor for business knowledge: the more, different perspectives you get on a problem the more likely you are to avoid errors in interpreting events. At one level this can be seen as a defensive strategy. At its most basic this could be simply getting someone to check over your work – the value of a fresh pair of eyes unfamiliar with the work you have done. At a higher level this is a matter of getting a genuinely different angle on a subject, approaching it from a different perspective. If two observers approaching a building from different directions pool their observations about the building (via say two-way radio) they can learn a great deal far more rapidly than if they each had to walk around the building and see both sides of it for themselves. Science uses a whole range of technologies to gain new perspectives on the world. Telescopes, microscopes, X-rays, are all means of adding to, and extending, our perspectives.

Insight 7: the past *is* the only guide to the future

 With the advent of sophisticated market research techniques, and the growing ascendancy of the world of 'management science', there is a tendency for people to think that there are some 'black box' techniques that will allow us to gaze confidently into the future. This is not true. It remains the case that the bedrock for understanding what might happen in the future is a rigorous analysis of what we know about the past.

History is strewn with examples of predictions that were proved wrong by events. A short list of the better known ones would include the Ford Motor Company's forecast of 200 000 sales per year of the Ford Edsel (they sold 110 000 in total in the car's three short years on the market); Decca A&R Head, Dick Rowe's prediction in 1962 that four-piece groups with guitars were on the way out – his reason for not signing the Beatles; IBM's belief in the 1970s that mainframe, rather than

personal computers would continue to be the main market for computers. If mistakes can be made with such comparatively straightforward
predictions where the prophets actually have a degree of control over
what happens, what hope is there of successfully predicting major
changes where we have no control?

With this in mind, Body Shop founder Anita Roddick once described
market research 'as the view out of the rear view mirror of a moving car'
– the implication being that it told her where she had been, not where
she should be going. This is not an uncommon criticism of market
research. But it is one that *cannot* be answered by anything other than
re-affirming the fundamental fact that the only resources market
researchers have for predicting the future lie in the past. The secret lies
in what you do with these resources.

The simplest model of prediction based on the past is *extrapolation*.
The word, literally meaning to extend a line, invokes the idea of extending the line connecting a series of points on a graph representing
observations over time to a point in the future. More or less sophisticated
versions of this technique have met with notable success in the natural
sciences. We can predict the path and time of arrival of comets in our
solar system with remarkable accuracy. But even in the natural sciences
the power of prediction on the basis of past events is limited. The
problem for forecasters is that small errors in initial measurements tend to
become exaggerated quite rapidly so that events depart significantly from
predictions in the medium to long term. Chaoticians call this *sensitive
dependence on the initial conditions*, meaning that the way systems with
any more than a few variables develop over time is highly sensitive to the
precise conditions at the start of the system's evolution. Snooker players
will know the problem. It is possible to 'canon' the first ball onto the
second ball, which should then knock a third ball into the pocket. But try
pocketing a ball that relies on, let us say, the earlier *four* balls all being
'cannoned' by the preceding ball at exactly the right point. Here, we
quickly learn that the slightest discrepancy in the contact made by the
earlier balls will lead to a quite marked skewing of the ball at the end of
the sequence, such that it is unlikely to go down the designated pocket.
But with the holistic based, bricolage analysis techniques we explain later
in this book we do provide a framework for good practice in terms of the
intelligent forecasting of marketing phenomena.

Understanding the evidence jigsaw

Let us now move on to discuss the next fundamental information competency that will be required to survive the twenty-first-century world of
marketing information. This centres on developing a better perspective,
than was the case in the past, on where a new incoming piece of
evidence fits into the wider overall *jigsaw* of evidence that – courtesy of
the new information era – will now be available to us on most topics.
Given this, it is important to provide a brief whistle-stop tour of the
fundamental nature of different types of information and evidence. It is
particularly important for market researchers to break out of the trap of
thinking that the solution to a particular problem lies exclusively with the
latest survey they have just conducted and to start seeing the survey data
as fitting into a wider pattern of evidence.

In Figure 2.1 we have provided an overview of the different types of
evidence available to the marketing decision-maker, together with a brief
comment about how the analyst should start thinking about each type of
evidence in terms of its robustness.

Clues, anecdotes and archetypes

To the left of the diagram there is a reference to *clues, anecdotes and
archetypes*. The point being made here is that in any investigation there
can be isolated pieces of information that could have a bearing on the
issue with which we are concerned but that will not have resulted from a
formal research process set up to answer questions about that issue.
Clues can be purely accidental discoveries but often we intentionally
comb, or sift, a lot of potential evidence to find relevant 'clues'. Thus,
often we will find clues in information that was gathered for purposes
other than the one for which we wish to use them. Thus, market
researchers sometimes engage in data-dredging or trawling. They will
comb through subsets of, and relationships between, data to find
evidence that tells us far more than the data was originally intended to
tell us. In order to use 'clues' you need a great deal of prior knowledge.
The most famous reader of clues, Sherlock Holmes, demonstrates this
principle. Holmes' ability to make inferences from clues was based on his

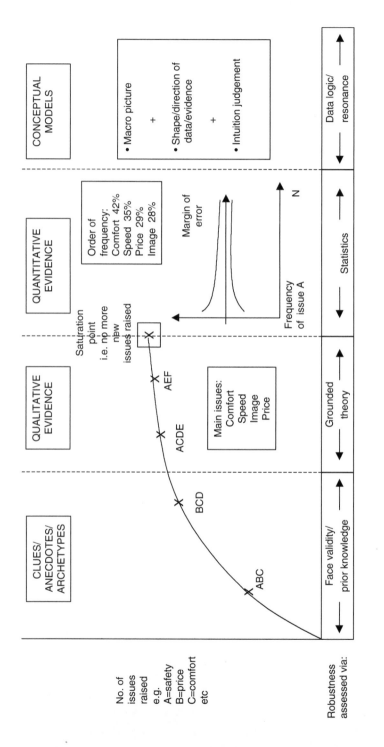

Figure 2.1 An overview of the robustness of different types of information

extensive, if rather bizarre, prior knowledge. For example, he could tell where in the country someone was from by the dirt on their shoes, having written a monograph a few years before on variations in topsoil in the British Isles!

A series of clues can build up to what we might term *anecdotal* evidence about a particular topic. Of course, this anecdotal evidence may be off-centre, and not typify the wider pattern of evidence. But in the modern information era we are beginning to learn to be less dismissive of anecdotal evidence than in the past. We should not think of anecdotes as necessarily inferior to larger scale survey evidence. So it is important to learn from anecdotes. Then as we move along our information spectrum we must start seeing the interrelationship between anecdotes and what we might call *archetypal* evidence. By archetype we are referring to evidence which, although partial in its coverage and possibly being collected from a small number of individuals, does provide a rich body of evidence in that it begins to tell us a consistently powerful story. So, one needs to be cautious of dismissing, for example, the Chief Executive Officer's account of a particular incident that, let us say, has taken place in one of his supermarkets, as 'anecdotal evidence'. Rather, we should treat the CEO's evidence as 'archetypal': a single incident true, but one that has been set in the rich, wider context of a 30-year-long retailing career.

Under the category of clues, anecdotes and archetypes in Figure 2.1, there is a reference to the way this type of evidence is assessed for robustness. We make a reference to 'face validity' and 'prior knowledge'. In essence, what we are saying is that, with type of evidence, the extent to which the points being made are logical and square with previous experience is the main way of checking its robustness.

Qualitative

In the next part of Figure 2.1 we refer to *qualitative evidence*. Later in this book we will be defining this type of research but, in essence, we are referring to a formal research process that collects information in a flexible way from small samples of the population. We can see from Figure 2.1 that qualitative research builds on the earlier process of looking at clues, anecdotes and archetypes by beginning to build a picture of the *range* of issues that are relevant on any topic. Above, when we discussed Insight 2, we made reference to Glaser and Strauss's concept of grounded theory, and it is this that provides the essential tool for looking at the robustness of qualitative evidence. As explained above, the qualitative evidence can be seen as a process of plotting the issues that start appearing on the agenda for the topic under investigation. Let us take our example of looking at attitudes towards different types of car where we have used the issues of safety, price, comfort, image and so on as being relevant to the evaluation of different brands. So, in looking at qualitative evidence we see we have a curve that shows that – as the research progresses – we gradually build up the number of issues being raised by respondents until we reach a 'saturation point' where no new issues are being generated. This 'saturation point' then leads us into the world of quantitative research, which brings us to the next part of Figure 2.1.

Quantitative

In thinking about the *quantitative evidence* essentially we are referring to information that is collected from larger samples. This moves us into the territory of measuring, rather, as is the case with qualitative research, than just identifying the range of issues. And, as we can see from Figure 2.1, we now assess robustness via techniques such as ordering the frequency with which different issues are raised and then assess this data, using formal statistics, such as establishing the 'margin of error' within which we can interpret a particular survey statistic and so on.

Conceptual models

Finally, to the far right of Figure 2.1 we refer to *conceptual model-building*. A key part of the new approach to market research will be the need for market researchers not to be overwhelmed with isolated pieces of evidence, but to start inputting this information into a pre-prepared range of conceptual models that explain how parts of the marketing world *work*. Only by having these frameworks in place will we be able to make intelligent use of all our incoming data. If we leave them as isolated data they will overwhelm us. Conceptual model-building is about locating individual evidence into the overall macroeconomic picture, and then looking at how our evidence fits into the overall 'shape and pattern' of the data available to us on that topic. This approach also requires seeing whether our new data square with existing management hunch and intuition.

So, in sum, it is important for the *new* twenty-first-century market researcher to:

- see how their piece of data can be integrated into other pieces of relevant information;
- determine what analysis tools should be used to assess the robustness of the differing types of evidence; and
- to establish how the integrated datasets can be most effectively applied to the final decisions that need to be made.

In sum, they need to carry in their heads the overall picture outlined in Figure 2.1, rather than becoming trapped in the silos of the particular study they have just completed.

Developing a personal information strategy

Claims have been made that the typical marketing manager is now faced with approximately one million words of incoming information per month. Whether or not this is true remains open to debate, but such alarming statistics about the 'information explosion' do remind us of the importance of developing 'good habits' in the way we elect to 'process' this plethora of information. Most of us are patchy and inconsistent when it comes to keeping on top of information. On some days we obsessively answer all of our e-mail messages – even though we know this is robbing us of precious time because the messages will be a combination of critical information and junk e-mail. On other days we make good 'selection' decisions: we intelligently decide what information to reject, to 'skip read', or to study more closely. All of this though does raise the question of the importance of developing our own personal incoming information strategy. Everyone is different in the amount and type of information they have to handle and the time they have available to deal with it. But an 'anything goes' approach to receiving incoming information leads to inefficiencies. In this chapter we describe an 'ideal' strategy for monitoring incoming information. This strategy is one that can be adapted to different situations in which people find themselves. The first, and deceptively simple step in the 'ideal' strategy is to 'process' information on an ongoing basis, rather than consign it to the in-tray for later review. The problem of deferring our review of incoming information is that such a review seldom actually happens. So allocating a few minutes each day to assess incoming information is a critical first step. It is important that information is not seen as an unwelcome intruder into what would otherwise have been a perfectly organised working day. Acknowledge that the ongoing absorption of information is an important (perhaps *the* most important part) of a knowledge worker's function. When receiving incoming information instead of going into 'low involvement processing mode', why not switch up a gear and energetically process incoming information in your 'high involvement' register.

Thinking outside the shoebox

We are often entreated by management and marketing writers to think 'outside the box' – a metaphor for considering options outside the normal range of ideas we are used to operating with. But when it comes to processing incoming information this injunction often needs to be taken quite literally. Detectives working on the Yorkshire Ripper case in the early 1980s gathered rooms full of shoeboxes with information about the crime, but had no mechanism for incisively identifying the key pieces of information that would have identified the murderer. Detectives interviewed the serial killer on nine separate occasions, but there was no mechanism for looking across these various potentially incriminating interview records to identify clues that would have pinpointed Peter Sutcliffe as the murderer. Detectives became overwhelmed by this store of information with no means of structuring or sorting it.

Thinking outside the shoebox means screening incoming information for its relevance before we start accumulating piles of data in which useful information is indistinguishable from useless information. The aim of the screening process is for each piece of incoming information to be allocated to one of the following categories:

- read and take action now
- file for later use
- discard completely.

Table 2.1 *Classifying incoming data*

Action	Relevance	Timing
Read and take action now	Direct	Immediate/pressing
File for later use	Indirect	Current/ongoing
Discard completely	↓ Remote	↓ Historical

The broad criteria for allocation to one of these categories are shown in Table 2.1. The outline of a framework provides us with some rules of thumb about classifying incoming information into prioritised categories. For example, if a piece of information is directly relevant to an issue and is either pressing or current/ongoing, it should be *read and acted on now*. If, however, it is directly relevant, but of only historical timeliness it should be demoted to the next category and *filed for later use*. And if it is of indirect relevance, and of immediate ongoing, or historical relevance, it should be filed for later use. Anything of merely remote relevance should be discarded. Of course the precise cut-off points for levels of relevance, or timeliness, can only be established by an individual given his or her remit. But our point is that the individual needs to establish a *predetermined* framework for making these 'read; file; discard' judgements. Whilst it is impossible to provide a universal prescription for such screening frameworks, a number of dimensions should be considered in developing an individual's particular approach. We outline these below.

Relevance dimensions

- *Saliency.* Start by examining where the new piece of information fits into the context of your overall marketing 'hinterland'. The question to ask here is: 'Does this new piece of information impact on my organisation, or is it too far removed to be of relevance?' Start at the 'outside' with information about trends and developments in the overall macro economy. Then narrow the context, moving on to the 'quasi-controllables' – what are your competitors doing and so on. Then tighten the marketing 'hinterland' further – putting the spotlight on key details of the marketing plan. Throughout the process, check for the saliency of the incoming information: will knowing this have an impact on your organisation?

- *Contribution to existing knowledge.* Next, establish the extent to which the new item of information takes you beyond what you already know. Making this assessment is not easy. Here, it is helpful to think of market research information as falling into two categories. First, there is what we might call 'instrumental information'; for example, precise details about what product features customers consider important. But there is also 'conceptual information' – data and knowledge that enrich the decision-maker's general thinking about an issue, rather than necessarily providing specific data. Remember, there could be, to reprise Jung, 'inherent possibilities' contained in the concept or idea you have just received into your information system. Information that provides fresh or up-to-date *facts* about your customers and markets, will be easy to assess in terms of its contribution to your existing knowledge. Slightly more difficult to determine – as we have already hinted – will be the potential value of ideas and more general principles. This is because your assessment of the value of new concepts and ideas will, in large measure, be contingent upon the person who will be asked to respond to this idea. As we know, an idea in the hands of some people can blossom into an insight that produces massive dividends for your organisation. But the same idea in the hands of a less creative individual may fall on stony ground. There is no easy rule here. But be confident about embracing more abstract theoretical ideas, and progressing them within your organisation.
- *Generalisability.* At one end of the spectrum an item of information could be deemed highly generalisable because, although it is only a single observation, it is, nonetheless, an entirely logically derived point where only one observation is needed to make a decision that action must be taken. (Example: *one* hotel guest having eaten the egg salad falls ill with Salmonella poisoning.) There could also be data that, although limited in scale, are also highly generalisable because they are consistent with a wider body of principles and theoretical knowledge such as, for example, the Product Life Cycle theory. At the other end of the spectrum, there could be data that seem to be extreme outliers, and as such, are of limited 'generalisable' value.
- *Impact on key scenarios.* We have already explained that good practice in information management calls for the development of

carefully thought-out criteria against which incoming information can be evaluated. As part of this, it is helpful here to think through the *consequences* of incoming information for future decisions and actions. A useful technique is 'scenario planning': mapping out different future market scenarios and the likely response of competitors to this stance. These scenarios could then provide a focus for evaluating an incoming item of information.

- *Contribution to thematic or conceptual knowledge.* An important and challenging relevance check is to see whether an item of information, when taken in conjunction with other pieces of evidence, begins to paint a picture, identify a theme or reveal a trend that starts to identify some key drivers or developments in a market. It is helpful here to look for *comparisons and connections* with other familiar situations. Does the new piece of information, when interconnected with existing knowledge, give you fresh insights? Will this information – taken in conjunction with other evidence – allow the building of a *conceptual model* of how this market works?

Timing dimensions

- *Currency.* Check when the data were collected and make a judgement about the implications of this 'currency' for the impact the data are likely to have on your business. Again, there are no hard and fast rules. On balance, the more recent the information, the more valuable it will be. But of course this is a generalisation that may not apply in all situations. A fact may go quickly out of date. But good ideas enjoy longevity: the person who provided us with our opening quotation for this chapter is still contributing! Which brings us to the last of our screening dimensions.
- *Strategic or tactical value.* It is important to establish whether the new item of information contributes towards longer term strategic issues at your company, or is of more specific, tactical relevance. For example, if you worked for Jaguar – now part of Ford – tracking developments in the US automotive sector could be considered of potential strategic importance, whereas if you were an employee of Renault, the same information may be only of tactical relevance.

Robustness checks

The following *twelve-point check list* has been prepared to help establish whether a piece of incoming information is sufficiently robust for further consideration. These checks have been ordered from the easiest to most difficult to carry out in practice.

1. *The believability check.* A simple rule here is to start by undertaking a straightforward, common sense, face value, 'believability check'. Start by asking yourself: would most reasonable people, working from first principles and using basic common sense, arrive at the interpretation that has been placed on the particular item of information you are examining? Put another way, do you, yourself – based on your own knowledge of this market – believe this information? Does it square with your experience and expertise? Remember what we have said about the value and power of hunch and intuition – implicit knowledge. Of course, it does not necessarily follow that information that is *believable* to you is automatically 'true'. But, in many situations, what can the receiver of a piece of information do other than fall back on whether it is 'believable'? In a straight choice between attempting to follow complex statistical interpretations of the evidence or falling back on prior knowledge (just how well the arguments being presented square with our own experience), not surprisingly, many of us will opt for the latter. Put another way, you will need a fairly convincing explanation as to why data that are apparently counter-intuitive are nonetheless the data upon which you now wish to base a decision. This could be the case, but everything being equal, in the greater proportion of decision-making cases, safety lies in having data that at the intuitive level make sense.

   The methodological purist may squirm at the above observations. The purist will probably be more concerned with the classic concepts of validity (the extent to which an item of information measures what it says it does, i.e. it is free from bias) and reliability (the extent to which an item of information is likely to hold good over time). But 'believability' does have a methodological pedigree. As we have begun to explain, the whole notion of 'grounded theory' rests on inspecting each piece of research evidence in relation to other (theoretical) information, to see whether the fresh survey information adds anything to our conceptual understanding of the issue under investigation. (The point at which we are no longer improving our understanding of the topic – the point of 'theoretical saturation' – is the point at which we should stop collecting new data and start trying to understand and explain it better!) In addition, the 'believability check' is one that many writers on information-based decision-making consider to be entirely legitimate. Gerald Zaltman, Professor of Business Administration at Harvard University and an authority on the application of information to decision-making, calls the believability check the *traditional truth test*. He argues that one should use past experiences and beliefs to identify the validity of incoming observations. Zaltman suggests that the manager might ask: 'Are the results consistent with what we have learnt in the past? Are these data compatible with existing practices or do they suggest that major changes in the company's philosophy and marketing strategy are needed?' Zaltman concedes that his 'traditional truth test' represents an effort to 'imitate what has gone before', but stresses that new ideas can still be embraced as long as they do not fly *totally* in the face of existing knowledge, ideas and values.

2. *Twyman's Law*. This tells us that any interesting data – anything that looks particularly exciting – are probably wrong! So, check any remarkable piece of information that you may be tempted to believe (perhaps because it instantly proves your point and/or refutes an arch rival's argument). It may simply be a mistake.

3. *Internal consistency checks*. This is another quick check to make sure your data are internally consistent with other data in the dataset. For example, if in a survey for an airline we find that over three-quarters of customers were delighted with the quality of the cabin service, then clearly we will be reassured to discover the 'companion' finding showing that more than 8 in 10 of these travellers plan to travel on the same airline the next time they make a journey on that route.

4. *The underlying assumptions*. It is important to evaluate closely any underlying assumptions that underpin the information being presented to you. Assumption is the mother of error. For example, the underlying assumption in the airline industry used to be that maximum marketing priority should always be given to the wealthy,

high revenue spending, *first class* passengers. But Virgin challenged this assumption. They decided not to have a first class passenger designation, but instead to focus on providing the burgeoning number of *business class* passengers with a range of added value services.

5. *The professionalism check.* The next check of the robustness – or 'truth' – of a piece of information is to establish just how much precision and attention to detail has been demonstrated by those who provided the information. One tell-tale guide to determining whether an item of information is robust is to see whether or not it displays the hallmarks of the professional data supplier/researcher. This will include high levels of precision and attention to detail; this is a characteristic of an information provider who knows his/her *craft*. If the detail is right, then you are more likely to trust the information. Try to establish how much time the person who provided the information has put into his/her report. Try to find out whether, due to limited time pressures, only a superficial research report – containing many shortcuts – has been presented. Also establish whether the person gathering information has a reasonable grounding – knowledge and expertise – in the area under investigation. There is always, of course, the chance that a highly pertinent and robust piece of information has been supplied by someone who is rather loose and cavalier in his/her approach to precision and attention to detail. But, on balance, this tends not to be the case. Invariably, precision equals robustness. So, in sum: is there any suggestion that any aspect of the information – the definitions being used, the statistics being presented, and so on – has been presented in a sloppy, loose, inconsistent way that *suggests* that this imprecision and lack of attention to detail could mean that these data have emanated from a less than robust source? If so, then this could make your decision 'unsafe'. When it comes to assessing the level of precision and attention to detail there are a number of specific checks the reader may wish to pursue:

- *Definitions.* It is important to double-check all the definitions that have been used to ensure that this is not a source of error. For example, if a research study refers to a study being conducted in the 'United Kingdom', did the originator really mean England, Scotland, Wales and Northern Ireland, or did he/she simply mean 'Great Britain', i.e. without Northern Ireland? These definitional points clearly need to be clarified.

- *Ambiguities*. Next, it is important to look for any ambiguities that may have infiltrated the information collection and interpretation process. Issues, comments and observations that are open to more than one interpretation should immediately be spotted. For example, let us take a staff attitudes survey: are the results referring to an assessment of the staff's 'perceptions' of how a new service will be viewed by customers, or the staff's 'own' personal attitudes towards the new service, or a confusing mixture of both?

- *Biases*. A report prepared by a 'professional research supplier' will pinpoint any 'biases' that may be evident in the research process. This will help the data analyst to interpret the implications of this bias in terms of the decisions he/she must make. For example, if the response rate to a survey is lower than expected, then the implications of this will be pointed out. Later in the book we review all the various biases that can creep into the survey research process.

- *Reliability*. Clearly it would be foolhardy to base a decision on information that only had 'meaning' for a brief moment in time. So we need to reassure ourselves that the data we are about to use are likely to hold good over time. (An opinion poll on attitudes towards bringing back the death penalty held the day after a vicious, brutal murder of a child will not provide a sound guide to views on capital punishment.)

6. *He would say that wouldn't he?* The next check we would recommend is the motivation check: establish exactly what was the (likely) motivation of the organisation or person who submitted the item of marketing evidence now in front of you? Ideally, you should try to establish who commissioned the study? Who collected the data? Who interpreted them? And so on. Is there any suggestion that the person who provided these data is consciously or unconsciously trying to sway your opinion? Does the person presenting you with this information have a personal stake in a particular outcome? How do

the data being provided reflect on the individual who is providing them? Does it make him/her (or his/her department) look good or bad? And remember any statistic will be distorted if it is used as a means of control! So, watch out for league tables on schools and the like. Determining the exact motivation behind an investigation is clearly important. For example, there will be a sharp difference between a survey conducted on the quality of the air in central London by, let us say, an environmental lobby group and a similar report prepared by a motoring body representing the interests of motorists. Both reports could contain the same facts, but one would expect the different commissioning bodies to place a different slant on the evidence. In sum, make sure you check the 'motives' of the person who supplied the data. If there is any suspicion that there is anything untoward in this area, then it is worth going back and revisiting this issue.

7. *Chinese whispers.* As statistics flow up and down an organisation they become *embellished.* Each manager in any hierarchy is prone to add his or her own positive embellishment, or critique, to those that have already been added before by their bosses and/or subordinates. By the time information arrives with you, it could move from the classic 'send reinforcements, we are going to advance' to become 'send three and four pence, we are going to a dance'.

8. *Spin.* In today's time-pressured world there is a tendency for evidence and information coming at us from different sources to be 'spun'; that is, presented in the most flattering way, with the maximum 'economy of the truth' and distinct accentuation of the positive. If there is any suggestion that an item of evidence only provides a partial or sound-bite view of the world, be cautious. In short, beware of 'on-message' data. Today, concentration spans seem to be getting shorter: there is less and less time to get over particular points; information is pumped out on intranets and on websites – a medium that necessitates brevity – in a way that means we must be alert for where there has perhaps been some over-simplistication of truth. This is an increasingly relevant issue. In today's highly competitive business environment there is increasing emphasis on success. As more and more people attend media courses on the 'art' of winning the argument – including how to 'spin' their data – the more difficult it becomes for the analyst to

seek out the 'truth'. Today, the slickness of the argument – the way the information is presented and spun – can often gain ascendancy over the absolute power and robustness of the evidence underpinning this gloss. There is also the related issue of how, these days, initially highly 'spun' accounts of events can gradually become reassembled into something that tells a different story. Daily newspapers have been described as a 'brief glance at history on the run'. So when we receive information 'on the hour' most of us are aware that, as the story unfolds, more facts will emerge. There is no problem here. However, if a pattern builds up whereby we consistently learn that there is a major difference between what we are told at the time of the event and what we are told later, then this could start contaminating the judgement we show when receiving information. Ever since President Nixon's 'economy with the truth' over the Watergate Affair, we have become almost programmed to look for the cynical hand of conspiracy in events (data) with which we are presented. In the past, people perhaps accepted the 'official account' of what was happening at the time as being close to the 'truth'. But in today's information climate, we are now more aware of the fact that the initial account of events may be some way from what actually happened. So, 'on the hour' we are told, for instance, that a US warship has shot down an Iranian jet fighter that started to attack it. But after a week, we learn that the US warship has in fact shot down an unarmed, airliner carrying 300 mainly Iranian women and children. And, some many years later, we learn even more details about what actually happened. In some ways, the move towards a culture that encourages us always to check the motives of the provider of information, as we have already indicated, is not a bad thing. However, it also carries the attendant danger of us lurching too far the other way and *always* presupposing an ulterior motive when none exists.

9. *Norms and benchmarks*. Another way of establishing the robustness of a piece of information is to see where it fits into the wider, normative context of what you know about this market. For example, if you were being told that 30% of coffee drinkers taking part in a survey claimed to be 'very likely' to try your new product, it would be helpful to set this in the wider context of what we know about the relationship

between *survey claims* and *actual purchase* once the new product is launched. Many fast moving consumer goods (FMCG) manufacturers will tell you that only around one-third of those who, in a survey, tell you that they will definitely buy a product will actually do so in practice. This is not because these survey respondents are trying to mislead the researchers, but simply because the marketplace is a far more competitive environment than the survey setting in which they answered the question. Once bombarded with lots of different alternatives on the supermarket shelves, not as many individuals as indicated by the survey will actually buy the product. So having *normative* frameworks – knowing about how the inter-relationships between reported attitudes and actual purchase behaviour works – is a useful tool to help the analyst corroborate a particular item of information. It is also good practice to take your incoming piece of information and see how well it fits into various *analytical and conceptual frameworks* that writers on marketing and business management have developed to seek to explain the area you are investigating. For example, does your item of evidence square with what an organisation like the Boston Consultancy Group tells us about classifying products in a market, depending on whether they are 'cash cows', 'rising stars', 'dogs' and so on? Or do your data strike a chord with what Michael Porter has taught us about competitive positioning strategies, and so on?

10. *Corroboration*. Check whether there is anything anyone else knows, or can find out from other sources, that will confirm the figure or data being presented and/or the interpretation subsequently placed upon them. This is the process of *triangulation* we discussed earlier in this chapter. It is a process aimed at establishing whether other readings on a particular event are consistent with the particular observation in front of you. For example, a word processor manufacturer that is keen to find out what proportion of the UK population has reasonably adequate keyboard skills may conduct a survey among *UK households*. This could show that 30% of the adult population can type at least 40 words per minute. Here, one way of corroborating this statistic is to inspect *UK workplace-based* surveys conducted on the keyboard skills of individuals in full-time work in the United Kingdom. This employment-based survey, as might be expected, may

show that the typing speed of those in work is higher than the population at large. But, the fact that you can corroborate the (expected and logical) relationship between the keyboard skills of the UK general household and UK workplace populations becomes an important indicator of the robustness of the keyboard typing statistic in front of you. But you could go still further with this triangulation–corroboration process. One could obtain data from the UK's Department for Education and Employment on the proportion of individuals who have undergone some form of keyboard/typing course as part of either their secondary or tertiary educational studies and, from this, make various extrapolations. What we are saying is that by taking various corroborative readings one can start making decisions about how much credibility to attach to a particular piece of information.

11. *Back to the core evidence.* To check on the robustness of an item of evidence you may want to go back to the market research evidence – the audio tapes and/or video tapes of focus groups and depth interviews – and inspect for yourself the evidence (the verbatims from the transcripts and the video clips) to really dig into any aspects of the problem of which you are unsure. For example, there could be scenarios where it will pay dividends to 'unpack' the data-collection process in order to pinpoint any possibilities of 'error' that could have crept into the process. For instance, if a decision pivots on a particular piece of research evidence being correct – for instance the levels of *spontaneous awareness* of an advertising campaign – it becomes important to be absolutely certain that there were no biases that influenced this 'spontaneous' reading. Here, it is necessary to get down to the detail of looking at exactly how the question was asked and establishing whether it was preceded by any questioning that could have given the respondent a clue as to the answer to the next question. Of course, this is not going to be a technique to use when you are trying to make a quick decision, but we place it on the agenda here to register the importance of caution where there is any doubt about the 'safety' of an item of information.

12. *Confirmation.* The final check is to see whether it is possible to feed the interpretation that has initially been placed on a particular piece of data back to the person (or organisation) who originally collected

that data to establish whether or not the originators agree with the subsequent third-party interpretation. This is an adaptation of the *Delphi* technique – an assessment technique that was originally developed by the military to assess the performance of trainees in war game exercises. This involves an event, or item of information, initially being assessed by different 'experts'. The *range* of these different expert opinions are then fed back to each member of the expert panel to see whether they wish to revisit their initial assessment in light of what their fellow experts are saying. This could result in a number of different scenarios. There could be, for instance, a situation in which – if there are ten experts on the panel – nine all broadly agreed on one interpretation of the evidence and there is just one *outlying* view. This could lead to a scenario where, in light of subsequent feedback from fellow experts, the single 'outlier' expert reviews his/her underlying assumptions and comes to the view that his/her initial opinion was flawed. An alternative scenario would be one in which this process of re-inspecting underlying assumptions leads to the 'outlier' expert hardening up on his/her view, resulting in the other nine experts – having also now learned that their tenth colleague is, in fact, a world's authority on this particular issue – all deciding to re-adjust their views.

Often there can be a difference between the 'ivory tower' and 'on the street' view of events. So it is always worth seeking out confirmation from the 'horse's mouth'. For example, in the world of weather forecasting this process of seeking confirmation of what your information system is telling you is called 'ground truthing'. It makes perfect sense: before you announce to the world that according to your computer projections a hurricane is about to hit the Shetland Islands, it would be prudent to phone up someone who lives there and ask them to look out the window and tell you whether or not it is getting a bit windy! And if we want to find out what happens in war, we should not rely on the rather lofty, macro accounts provided by the generals and writers of classical military campaign textbooks. We should seek confirmation of what it was really like from those in the trenches. This is why Tolstoy's graphic research-based accounts of the Napoleonic Wars in *War & Peace* tell us much more about war than the official, rather bland, military reports of the day.

Getting to the storyline

It is good practice to get into the habit of pushing yourself to identify the main *storyline* in any incoming piece of information in *real time*, rather than brushing the information aside, on the grounds that later you will be able to assess what the data, based on a detailed analysis, are telling you. Of course, some information will simply be so extensive and/or complex that it will need to be put to one side for later more rigorous analysis. But the 'good habit tip' here is to process the 'storyline' of incoming data in real time. This immediate analysis of what information is telling you will, in the long haul, pay dividends. Below, we provide some 'tools' to help develop some good 'instant' data analysis habits.

Understanding summaries

We are all aware of Pascal's now famous postscript to a long letter he wrote to a friend. He apologised for its length, explaining to the receiver that he 'did not have enough time to make it shorter'. This immediately alerts us to the importance – but also the difficulty – of summarising information. These days, more and more managers are copying the Churchillian 'one page summary' technique developed in the Second World War. Churchill insisted that all incoming information was presented to him on one page of foolscap. On the face of it, the fact that data providers now usually offer a *summary* of their evidence should make the decision-maker's task more straightforward. But, there can still be difficulties. One of the potential problems is that there is often considerable variability in what constitutes a *summary*. Here we are not just talking about the quality of the way in which a particular summary has been written up, but the fact that there are fundamentally different interpretations of what form a 'summary' should take. There is, of course, no right or wrong way of summarising a document. But it is important for information receivers to be alert to the different approaches (and where appropriate to intervene to ensure they get the type of summary they expect). Below we provide a review of some of the variations in 'summaries' of data and/or reports that you may come across.

- *Abstract*. This is a short description of the overall content of a piece of information written in a way that is unlikely to provide any specific actionable points. Typically, the language of the abstract is: 'In the last section of this document a range of information is provided about the UK second-hand car market . . .'.

- *Review of the evidence*. In its most pedestrian form this would be a list of all the key evidence in the form of the 'answers' to the various survey questions. At its most helpful, this type of summary could be a selection of evidence adjudged by the data analyst to have particular relevance to the decisions that must be made. But with the latter, there is the issue of whether the selection decisions made by the data analyst are the ones that the decision-makers themselves would have made.

- *Interpretation of evidence*. Here a review of evidence would be accompanied by an interpretation of how this evidence should be interpreted. Thus, such a summary could take the form of saying: '38% of UK garages sell second-hand cars', possibly adding supplementary, qualifying or contextualising comments along the lines of 'this is an increase of 5% on last year'.

- *Conclusions*. Conclusions usually focus on 'answering' the research objectives by summarising the supporting evidence, and then commenting on the *business* implications of this information. For example, the 'conclusion' of a study conducted to establish whether short haul, low budget airlines should provide 'free' or only 'paid for' in-flight drinks might read: '90% of passengers in the survey said that they were prepared to pay for refreshments provided they were guaranteed the lowest possible fares'. This could then be followed with the 'conclusion': 'this seems to suggest that the current policy of charging for drinks is appropriate'.

- *Recommendations*. These will, in large measure, flow from the research evidence, but could also be based on the experience of the data supplier in markets *outside* the immediate research study. For example, a survey among visitors to the Millennium Dome might show that they were dissatisfied with the catering arrangements. This could then be followed by recommendations about how to improve the catering that are, in part, based on the Dome research, but also on wider experience of researching Disneyland and other theme parks.

Clearly, the provision of recommendations has its place. But in some situations certain decision-makers may feel anxious about not always having recommendations supported by a clear statement of the exact source of the evidence that led to these suggestions being made.

- *Action points*. Given recent concerns about many market research presentations and reports not being sufficiently 'actionable' there has been a (welcome) growing tendency for market researchers to conclude their presentations and/or reports with a summary of the key 'action points'. This has the advantage – like 'recommendations' – of sharpening the decision-makers' focus on the issues addressed in the report. But the 'action points' may, in fact, only provide a partial summary of all the potentially helpful information generated by the study simply because only issues that clearly pointed towards clear-cut *action* will appear in such a 'summary'. This could result in other less clear-cut – yet potentially valuable – information being left out of an action-orientated approach to summarising data.

- *Decision outcomes*. Market researchers have always specified, at the outset of their projects, the *research objectives* (for example 'what proportion of customers are satisfied with Automatic Teller Machines (ATMs)?'). But today, there is a welcome trend towards also providing a statement of the *business decisions* the research is expected to answer on the conclusion of the study. (For example, on conclusion of the study, the research will be used to decide whether or not to increase the number of ATMs and to close some of the face-to-face counters in branches.) Given this, one type of summary of a research study would be a presentation of the evidence that helps to answer each of these possible *decision outcomes*. A summary that addresses head-on the decisions to be made at the end of the study is clearly to be welcomed. It certainly increases the chances of the research being actionable. But, again, from the standpoint of the information receiver, it is important to ensure that summaries that focus exclusively on the decisions do not do so at the expense of excluding other useful contextual information that could provide important clues for the decision-makers.

For the sake of exposition, above we have listed out different types of 'summary' as if they were mutually exclusive, discrete categories. But, in practice, most summaries will be a (varying) *combination* of these different styles. Thus, a common approach is to have a 'review of the key evidence', coupled with 'conclusions'. Other scenarios include providing a review of the key research evidence, together with an examination of the 'decision outcomes'. Where does this leave us? What is the point we are making here about summaries? The first point to stress is that there is no single correct way to summarise a document. It is 'horses for courses'. Different types of *summary* will each have their merit. At one extreme the 'abstract' could be the preferred option if what is required is a good *contextual overview* of the entire body of evidence, and where there is little immediate requirement for specific action. In contrast, the *decision outcome* style could be the most appropriate approach for the busy senior executive who must quickly decide what decision(s) to take. However, notwithstanding the merit of the 'horses for courses' approach, it is important for the putative decision-maker to be aware of the range of summaries on offer so that – when attempting to use this summary to pinpoint the overall storyline quickly – he/she does not jump to naive conclusions that are more a by-product of the type of summary being presented, rather than based on what the (full) dataset is really saying.

This issue of ensuring that you have a full understanding of what the data are saying, rather than a partial account, is a problem in today's *soundbite culture*. Today, we live in a world in which many individuals' concentration span is now rivalling that of a goldfish. To illustrate the point, apparently the length of a typical *scene* in a TV soap opera has become significantly shorter over the past 10 years. This soundbite tendency raises questions about the way in which marketing information should be presented. Remember Procrustes: if visitors did not fit his bed, he would order that their legs should be cut to size. But this 'dumbing down' of complexity to make things neat and tidy paradoxically can make some things more, not less, difficult to grasp. The absence of a key context, although reducing the *quantity* of the message, may hinder our comprehension. Individuals make sense of the world by first constructing a contextual picture of what we believe and do not believe. This process is a highly inter-connected affair. We begin to understand information by positioning it in a connecting 'narrative flow'. That is to say, we attempt to link up one item of incoming information to the wider pattern of what else we know and believe. What we know and believe sits at the centre of a vast network of inter-connections that radiate out into the world. But if the wider context is stripped out of a message and it is reduced to a 'soundbite', then we have no way of connecting it up with what we already know. Therefore, paradoxically, we can struggle to understand the *short* message we have been given.

Looking to the future, it is going to be important to standardise the way in which information specialists summarise market research information. The first step towards standardisation is to get to grips with the task of laying down some guidelines to ensure that incoming market research and market intelligence reports are 'summarised' in a way that makes the task of picking off key messages quick, simple and free from misinterpretation. Something along the following lines provides a starting point.

- *Classification/housekeeping information*: title of study, which agency conducted the project, when it was carried out and other 'house-keeping' data, etc.
- *Summary of key evidence with an interpretation*: ordered such that selected critical evidence is presented aligned to the research objectives specified in the initial research brief/proposal with key pointers to how these data should be interpreted being raised.
- *Implications for decisions to be taken*: recommendations (or a review of the options open to the decision-maker), with a tight system for cross-referencing the key evidence used to arrive at these recommendations.
- *Generalisability/strategic value*: a comment from the person preparing the summary on the likely generalisable value of the information, i.e. is this information only of immediate tactical value or could it be of wider strategic value?
- *Implications for ongoing data collection*: what are the implications of the arrival of this new information, for the data the organisation will subsequently need in order to maintain a competitive advantage?

Assimilating large volumes of information

But what happens when information does not reach us in summary form? When we have to digest and master a large volume of information – a book, or a report, or broach the task of dissecting tabular data.

Psychology has devoted a great deal of effort to identifying ways of investigating human information processing and retention abilities. This work has resulted in a number of integrated techniques and strategies for marshalling large volumes of incoming information. The most comprehensive and well established of these is the *PQ4R method*. The title of the method is itself a mnemonic device – an acronym describing each of the stages involved.

Preview, Question, Read, Reflect, Recite and Review

- *Stage 1 – Preview*. In this first stage the material should be reviewed very quickly in outline only – with attention focusing on headings, sub-headings and titles, or italicised passages. Alternatively, the text can be skim-read. The purpose of this stage is to get an idea of the general issues addressed and the structure of the material. During this phase the reader is encouraged to map the structure of the document visually (imposing organisation on material is known to be an aid to the absorption and retention of information). This opening stage also arms the reader for the second stage.
- *Stage 2 – Question*. At this stage the reader should develop a list of questions to ask of the material, inspired by the initial premier reading (e.g. 'What does the phrase in sub-heading 4 mean?') or by general experience of reading documents (e.g. 'What are the main conclusions?' or 'What relevance does this have for me?'). Questions are a good way of activating our existing schemas and knowledge and provide a spur and channel for our natural curiosity – our appetite for learning.
- *Stage 3 – Read*. At this stage the document should be read through in a fairly thorough, and linear, way with a view to answering the questions emerging from Stage 2.
- *Stage 4 – Reflect*. This stage involves making connections between the new information and the existing knowledge or concepts that the reader already possesses. This may include seeking out analogies or similarities between the new material and other things we know or think: examples that illustrate key points being made in the new material. This process, known as 'elaboration', helps to activate existing knowledge further and embed the new material within it.

- *Stages 5 and 6 – Recite and Review*. To ensure the material becomes embedded it is helpful to 'Recite' key facts or passages in the new material. This can be supplemented by 'Reviewing' longer tracts of the text, such as major sections or the text as a whole. Rehearsal of this kind is one of the best ways to enhance the recall of key material.

Set out in discrete stages in this way, the PQ4R method seems rather protracted. But in practice several of these stages can run concurrently. For example, the process in Stage 4 – elaborating connections with existing knowledge – can be carried out during the main reading, Stage 3. Furthermore, the technique can be adapted to different reading tasks and circumstances. Thus, if all you have to do is identify the key points from a document then the 'recite and review' stages will not be required.

The key lesson of PQ4R is that a single, close, detailed linear reading of a text is *not* the best way to absorb new information. As noted earlier, understanding is best seen as a circular process. It is about shuttling between the emerging picture of an issue we have in our heads and the specific details of the situation we are building up until we have constructed a well-rounded picture in our minds. The same principles apply to our absorption of new information in the form of a text. Because texts (and also tables) are laid out in a linear format we are often misled into thinking that a purely linear approach is the best way to absorb such information. But, in fact, something along the lines of PQ4R will pay more dividends.

Acting on information

To conclude this chapter on the development of 'good information habits', we arrive at the question of acting on information. Of course, as we have seen in many situations, the receipt of information will not be synonymous with the act of making a decision. There will be many situations where the application of information to the decision-making process will take some considerable thought. This is the subject of a later chapter in this book. However, the reality of modern business life is that there will be situations where individuals will be called upon – *in real time* – to evaluate information and make some kind of judgement, or decision, on what this information is telling them to do *now*.

Taking responsibility when information can make a difference

It is important to develop the habit of taking a proactive stance *vis-à-vis* incoming evidence: ensure that incoming information that could make a difference to your organisation is acted upon. In cricket, some batsmen's first reflex is to step back and play a defensive shot, while others are 'programmed' to get onto the 'front foot' and attack the ball. Our recommendation here is to be in the latter, not former, category. When you receive information, first put yourself into proactive 'helicopter mode': acquire the skill of immediately setting the new information into its appropriate context. Then from this 'big picture' vantage point, you will be well placed to alert your organisation to the implications for action and decision-making on the incoming information. When it comes to new information, do not be the person who crosses to the other side of the street. Do something with it (now).

Ongoing information renewal

The counsel of perfection calls not only for 'real time' action to be taken on incoming information, but also for the recipient of the new data to make a judgement about what the new piece of evidence means for the organisation's future information needs. Thus, in an ideal world, the information receiver will take responsibility for plugging any *information gaps* that the arrival of new information throws up. For example, you may learn that the biggest player in the market is about to take over one of your competitors. This piece of intelligence should alert the organisation to a whole host of future information needs that follow from this new development in the market. Thus, the message is look at each item of incoming marketing information, not only with regard to what it means for the problem that you are dealing with now, but also in terms of the *potential* implications it has for the information you may need in the future. So our good practice tip here is to ensure that, as the information rolls in, you have a process in place for deciding what supplementary, or more detailed, information you will subsequently need. With this in mind, a number of organisations are now – with the advent of *knowledge management systems* – beginning to introduce *strategic marketing information databases* to ensure that they have a mechanism for monitoring what information they need on a 'rolling basis'.

Building on the above point is the idea of introducing *information/ decision effectiveness audits*. By this we mean the constant evaluation of whether decisions, based on particular combinations of evidence, have led to successful outcomes or not. This is the kind of evaluation that the military constantly undertakes. For example, following a decision to attack a particular target, the military will carefully evaluate the success of this action. This analysis will include looking at the degree to which the information and intelligence that they had prior to the decision to attack this target was sufficient to achieve the desired end outcomes. The purpose of these 'audits' is continually to pinpoint what information is needed to deliver successful decision outcomes. Thus, it is helpful to think of the relationship between the information provider and decision-maker as being a continuous feedback loop, whereby both parties are constantly checking whether they are 'asking the right questions' to 'provide the right answers'.

C H A P T E R 3

A Primer in Qualitative Evidence

Overview

This chapter:

- summarises the strengths and weaknesses of qualitative evidence and reviews what can be achieved with different qualitative research techniques
- reviews the main schools of qualitative research practice
- provides the decision-maker with a guide on what questions to ask about qualitative research in order to assess its robustness and safety for decision-making
- provides guidance on how to analyse qualitative data.

THREE

A Primer in
Qualitative Evidence

'Huddled in dirt the reasoning engine lies, who was so proud, so witty, and so wise' – John Wilmot, Earl of Rochester.

Qualitative research – the use of focus groups and depth interviews – can be defined in many different ways, but at its simplest it is about asking, in a flexible way, comparatively small samples of people questions about what they do and think, and listening carefully to, and subsequently interpreting, what they have to say. Given the fairly incontestable value of such an activity it is surprising to find that qualitative market research has received a comparatively bad press in recent years. Much of this centres on the way in which focus groups have been 'demonised'. It is therefore perhaps helpful to get our discussion of qualitative research underway by immediately addressing the question of focus groups, and provide some reassurances about the constructive role that focus groups, and qualitative research generally, can play in the business decision-making process.

The poor image of focus groups seems to centre on a confusion between what most would argue is the total legitimacy of using focus groups to find out what people currently think, and the totally separate issue of the degree to which such evidence should then be used to shape the policy of a political party. In other words, the focus group debate is not about technical robustness, but about whether political parties should play out their underlying philosophy, as opposed to assembling 'popularist' policies known to be flavour of the month with the electorate. We need not get into this latter issue. Here, we just need to make the point that the focus group debate has nothing whatsoever to do with the robustness of focus groups *per se*. They remain an excellent way of finding out how people behave and think (provided, of course, the group discussion technique is appropriate to the particular problem in hand). Thus, the authors' fundamental position on qualitative research is that this approach is now an integral part of the business information fabric. It is here to stay.

Softer evidence here to stay

Going back only a decade it would have been necessary to start a chapter on qualitative research with a spirited defence of the pedigree of this form of market research. A review of the literature from the mid to late 1980s reveals a number of papers that quite vehemently challenged the basic credentials of qualitative research. Unlike today, these attacks were not about comparatively superficial matters, such as the wisdom of using focus groups for policy-making, but centred on more fundamental questions about qualitative research's core validity. Is it representative, replicable, generalisable and, by inference, applicable to sound marketing decision-making? But at the start of the new millennium, in this new information era, notwithstanding the current hiccup over New Labour's love affair with focus groups, there is now a general acceptance that qualitative research is an integral part of the marketing information scene.

This reflects the fact that we now live in an era in which we must learn how to utilise an eclectic mixture of, often less than perfect, information drawn from a range of different sources. The watch-word today is synthesis. We are beginning to accept the notion of fitting together evidence, much of which may fall short of scientific purity, into the wider jigsaw that is our marketing knowledge. Given this, in this chapter we shall review what the decision-maker needs to know about the robustness of different *types* of qualitative research, but we will not detain ourselves by questioning the fundamental legitimacy of qualitative research. Quite demonstrably, qualitative research is now a key piece in the information jigsaw. This means that in this chapter we can focus on helping the decision-maker to distinguish between the appropriate and inappropriate deployment of qualitative research. We can also provide some tips on how to distinguish between 'good' and 'bad' qualitative research practice, and go on to help the decision-maker extract maximum value and insight from qualitative research evidence (see Table 3.1).

Table 3.1   *Summary of the strengths and weaknesses of qualitative evidence*

Qualitative research good for	Qualitative research less good for
• Mapping the customer's overall range of behaviour and attitudes • Pinpointing the motivations behind people's behaviour • Examining the linkages between attitudes and behaviour • Stimulating new and creative ideas • Providing a forum for fresh creative thinking	• Profiling and mapping detailed usage and behaviour • Precisely measuring consumer preferences for different products and services • Measuring the exact priorities consumers attach to different product features • Highlighting variations between different sub-groups

However, although the primary focus of this book is to help the reader decide how 'safe' it is to make decisions based on different types of qualitative research methodology, it is also important, as a precursor, to provide the reader with a brief 'Cook's Tour' of the different qualitative research techniques that are available (see Table 3.2).

Making 'faith' decisions

Decision-makers need to understand the limits and boundaries of qualitative evidence so that when they are using this type of evidence they make 'safe' decisions. There are two key lines of enquiry in helping to understand just how far it is possible to rely on qualitative evidence for 'safe' decision-making. The first centres on building the reader's appreciation of, and confidence in, decision-making from data drawn from *smaller samples* than the typical quantitative survey. The second issue concerns giving the decision-maker confidence in using evidence that is obtained via a *flexible data collection* process, where it is acknowledged that the researcher collecting the information has more autonomy than is the case in a structured, quantitative interview.

Is small beautiful?

Some people are concerned about the legitimacy of making decisions and judgements from research that, on balance, will involve relatively small

Table 3.2 *A Cook's Tour of qualitative research techniques*

Group-based research

- *Focus group discussions.* Respondents are recruited according to predetermined criteria (such as age, gender, social class, and brand usership). 'Conventional' group discussions last under 2 hours in length. Each group discussion has a moderator (or facilitator) who is trained to: guide the discussion over the relevant topics; recognise important points of view and encourage the group to expand on these; deal with group dynamic processes; seek clarification on his/her understanding of what the group is saying; and, as appropriate, use stimuli, tasks and exercises to enable the group to articulate thoughts and feelings.
- *Mini-groups.* Each group would consist of four to six people and usually last for a slightly shorter length of time than a 'full group'. This approach overcomes the problems of mixing – in a larger group – people with different skills and expertise and will also ease some recruitment challenges.
- *Friendship groups.* People who know each other are deliberately brought together into a group to offset the problems of shyness or embarrassment.
- *Conflict groups.* These are designed to highlight – and explore in depth – the differences between people. For example, a group could be constructed with people who only ever buy British cars versus those who actively prefer Japanese cars.
- *Reconvened group.* A group could be recruited for two sessions separated by one week. The first session could cover the more straightforward topics. Then during the intervening week the group is asked to conduct a number of exercises designed to sensitise the group to a particular issue. For example, group members might be asked to visit two different stores and make observations about the display of goods and the attitudes of the sales assistants.
- *Extended creativity groups.* These sessions, lasting around 4 hours, allow time for respondents to participate in tasks, such as brand mapping, and so on. This method – because time can be spent in 'forming' the group dynamics – can overcome embarrassment or political correctness getting in the way of creative thinking.
- *Sensitivity panels.* People are invited to attend a series of group discussions and explore a subject over a period of time – perhaps up to a month. During these sessions respondents are deliberately 'taught' how to access 'suppressed' thoughts and feelings via techniques such as free association, the use of metaphors and analogies, and the like.

Individual interviews

- *The individual interview.* This is a conversation conducted between a trained qualitative researcher (or depth interviewer) and a 'respondent' selected according to agreed criteria (age, gender, social class, etc.). Generally, the standard 'depth' interview is 1 hour in length and is conducted in the respondent's own home or place of work, or in an agreed venue, such as a research facility.
- *Mini-depth interview.* An interview lasting approximately 30 minutes, which is less wide ranging than a full depth interview. Mini-depths might, for instance, be conducted to put the spotlight on a specific aspect of a much wider topic. For example, in a study on user attitudes towards using computers, mini-depths could be used to look in close detail at

continues overleaf

Table 3.2 (*continued*)

the World Wide Web. Mini-depths can also be used alongside conventional survey research to add depth to the quantitative survey findings.

- *Semi-structured interview.* The interviewers follow a predetermined list of questions; that is, they do not construct their own questions. But from the respondents' point of view, the interview seems quite flexible as they can reply to the questions in their own words without 'feeling' they are being forced into *boxes.* From the researcher's standpoint, there are three ways of recording the respondent's responses. There could be pre-coded answers on the semi-structured questionnaire. The responses could be recorded on a verbatim basis on the guideline. Or a tape-recording could be made of the interview in order to have a full data record. The semi-structured interview is helpful for providing a comparatively low cost way of boosting a sample of fuller 'conventional' depth interviews.
- *Tele-depth interview.* Most depth interviews will be conducted face-to-face. However, more recently – particularly in business research – there has been a growing use of short, 20-minute interviews conducted over the telephone. The interviewer will follow a list of questions (rather like the semi-structured interview) with the respondent being allowed to reply in a flexible way. (With the respondent's permission it is possible to tape-record the interview over the telephone.)
- *Paired interview.* This is a depth interview conducted with two respondents. This approach could be helpful, for instance, in establishing how couples decide which mortgage to take out. In a business-to-business setting, this technique might involve two individuals – for example, the purchasing officer and the *end user* – both of whom influence the purchasing decision, explaining their respective roles.
- *Family interview.* Here the whole family is interviewed either separately, in pairs, or all together (sometimes in all three ways).
- *Triangular interview.* This is an interview where three respondents have been specifically chosen to reflect specific viewpoints on the subject-matter under discussion. For example, one could talk about travel in London as an inveterate car driver, one as a committed tube traveller, and the other as a cyclist.
- *Accompanied shopping.* This involves the interviewer accompanying a respondent (with his/her agreement) on a shopping trip. This observed *real* behaviour is 'compared' with subsequent attitudinal questioning. Here, one needs to be mindful of the extent to which the presence of the interviewer may influence the respondent's behaviour.

Observation methods
- *Non-participant observation.* Here the observer operates in an impartial way, simply recording details of individual behaviour. But some unconsciously selective sampling may take place. For example, the individual may subconsciously be drawn to people in a particular type of car.
- *Participant observation.* An individual may participate in a particular group in order to find out how it operates at an ethnographic level. For example, a researcher could work at a factory for a period of time. Here, there is a range of ethical issues to be considered.

samples. There are no hard and fast rules, but qualitative studies typically use around 30 respondents for a depth interview study. Similarly, typical focus group studies may involve around six to eight groups of about eight people. This scale of study places qualitative research in sharp contrast to quantitative research (discussed in the next chapter) where comparatively large samples of respondents are asked a predetermined set of questions. To get a feel for how far it is possible to rely on qualitative research evidence, given that it covers such a small part of the 'universe' under investigation, it is helpful to briefly revisit the *Grounded Theory* explanation of how qualitative research 'works' developed by Glaser and Strauss, which was discussed briefly in Chapter 2.

It is helpful to think of the task of the researcher as involving drawing samples, in as representative a way as possible from the universe under investigation, up to the point where there are no more useful diagnostic insights to be gained from talking to more people. As we have already briefly discussed, according to 'grounded theory', in a qualitative study among, let us say, owners of a particular car, we should continue discussing with motorists the respective delights and frustrations of driving a particular type of car until all the relevant issues have been exhausted. This is called *the point of theoretical sampling saturation*. The word 'theoretical' is used here because, throughout the sampling process, we will have been inspecting the observations surfacing from the sample survey against our existing theoretical and conceptual knowledge on the topic under investigation. When we reach a point where we feel we are no longer contributing to our prevailing 'theories' on the topic we are researching, we have reached the point of saturation. At this point, all subsequent issues raised by respondents would simply start measuring, rather than explaining, people's attitudes and motivations. We have already previewed the way in which grounded theory operates in Figure 2.1 when we looked at the robustness of different types of information. In Figure 3.1 we take an extract from the earlier figure and spell out in finer detail the specifics of how grounded theory operates. Thus, it can be seen from Figure 3.1 that the first research respondent may place A (comfort) and B (speed of acceleration) on the agenda. The next respondent might also mention comfort and speed, but also bring on to the agenda C (image) and D (price). With the next respondent, we find speed and image again being mentioned, but with another new issue

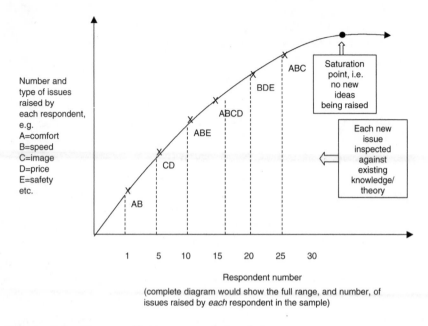

Figure 3.1 *How qualitative research 'works'*

being raised – this time E (safety). This process continues until we find that our sample of respondents is not raising any new insights or perspectives on the car under investigation. It is here that we arrive at the 'theoretical sampling saturation point'. This means that we are no longer improving our understanding of the issues that are important to motorists, and have now reached a point where – by continuing to sample car owners – we will only be measuring the frequency with which these issues are mentioned. We will not be throwing up any new insights. For qualitative studies it is at this point that we should stop our sampling.

Grounded theory and holistic analysis

The notion of grounded theory underpins the principles of holistic data analysis we have begun to unfold in this book. Hopefully, the fact that there is a solid methodological underpinning for holistic data analysis will reassure those who are perhaps nervous about using qualitative research for robust decision-making. Specifically, the above explanation of how qualitative research 'works' is a reminder that market research evidence rarely sits in a vacuum unrelated to the decision-maker's own prior knowledge, hunch, intuition and observations about the topic under investigation. As we stressed in Chapter 2, Insight 3: 'context is everywhere'. Thus, the very nature of grounded theory is that it asks the researcher to examine the extent to which each fresh sample observed contributes to our existing (theoretical) knowledge of the topic under investigation. Grounded theory tells us that qualitative research is about the process of progressing through an investigation interview by interview, inspecting each piece of fresh evidence that is brought back by the primary research team in the context of what we already know about the phenomenon under investigation.

Thus, in sum, the user can be reassured that qualitative studies, albeit based on smaller samples and using flexible data collection methods, can provide robust insights. It is not the aim of qualitative research to provide hard and fast statistical measures – $X\%$ thought this, $Y\%$ claimed this and so on. But qualitative evidence is an extremely *robust* way of gaining insights into the key issues. In short, qualitative research 'works': it is possible to use small samples to provide a fairly robust indicator of the overall direction of people's behaviour and especially attitudes. Such studies, employing all the skills of researchers who know how to operate in a flexible way in eliciting responses, can provide powerful insights into people's range of attitudes and depth of feelings on a particular issue. Let us now look at the issue of the 'objectivity' of the data collection process itself.

The main qualitative schools

Guidance on the safety of qualitative research for decision-making also means reviewing the extent to which the interventions made during the course of the research process by qualitative researchers could have influenced the evidence collected. To examine this we must accept that it is naive to think that there is just one type of qualitative research evidence. At the risk of a massive over-simplification in this primer on qualitative research, let us think in terms of there being two fundamental schools of qualitative research at work. It is important for those making judgements on qualitative research to be aware of these two broad schools of qualitative thought and practice.

The 'rational, non-participatory' school

The 'rational, non-participatory' school of qualitative research is more in the 'positivist' research tradition. It is based on the premise that there are many areas of our lives in which there are issues on which – with sensitive probing – people *will tell*. By this we mean that there are numerous issues on which people are quite prepared to communicate their attitudes. This school of qualitative research will use various sympathetic probing techniques in order to build up a picture of people's behaviour and attitudes. But the research will not be taken to any particular 'psychological depth'. The apparent lack of 'depth' with this type of qualitative research should not be a concern for the data user. There are many legitimate qualitative studies where the aim will be to go beyond the simplistic, but, given the practicalities of what can be achieved, not necessarily to take the qualitative investigation to any particular depth. In fact, the term 'depth interview' is somewhat of a misnomer. Many depth interviews, quite appropriately, will often be no more than a thorough, discursive discussion about the topic under investigation. These so-called 'depth' interviews will involve thoroughly capturing the respondents' often quite complex comments (on a particular topic), but will not necessarily involve plumbing any 'psychological depth'. Such 'in-depth' discussions stand in sharp contrast to interviews where the goal is very much to probe underlying motivations in considerable psychological depth. This concept of 'depth' is an important one. It is worth remembering that, on balance, the answer one gets in research to so-called 'deeper' questions will be more individualistic, possibly even idiosyncratic, than the answers one might expect to get from 'shallow' questions. As might be expected, we tend to find that people are much more alike in their 'shallower' feelings, and rather more different from one another in respect of their 'deeper' feelings. Thus, with quantitative research where, by design, the emphasis is on 'shallower' questioning, the results are likely to be more heterogeneous than one might find in the typical qualitative research study.

With the 'rational, non-participatory' school, the emphasis will be on 'fairly conventional' group discussions and 'standard' depth interviews. Typically, the moderator/researcher will employ a reasonably well-structured guideline and there will probably be an expectation among clients that the moderator will adhere reasonably closely to this guideline. With this type of qualitative research there will be comparatively little use of various *enabling techniques* (more of which later) designed to help 'open up' the respondent. With what we have labelled 'rational, non-participatory' research, there is *not* the expectation that higher risk, more creative questioning strategies will be employed. The quality of the output of this type of research will tend to be evaluated according to its 'independence and objectivity'.

The 'emotional and participatory' school

This school of qualitative research draws heavily on the disciplines of psychology and anthropology. In the best traditions of ethnographic research, the aim is to explore how people think and act in the context of their day-to-day lives. The emphasis is on a naturalistic approach to the subject-matter: it is about understanding the respondent's emotional agenda in the appropriate social and cultural milieu. It is helpful to think of this type of research as going into the territory where individuals are *reluctant to* or *cannot* tell; for example, eliciting information from a senior business executive, following a long period of unemployment, about his/her attitudes towards working life. With the 'emotional and participatory' school there will be quite extensive use of various enabling techniques. Thus, at one end of the spectrum, to pursue the above example, there could be fairly gentle enabling approaches, such as asking the respondent who has been made redundant how his/her 'colleagues who have been made redundant' felt about this experience. At the other end of the spectrum there could be more sophisticated approaches involving asking an individual to construct a story around a drawing of a particular scene (for example, a Chief Executive Officer in a heated debate with a subordinate).

The choice of interviewing methods that researchers in the 'emotional and participatory' school will elect to use could, in part, be driven by their alignment to a particular psychological school of thought. Thus, those influenced by the Freudian tradition argue that all of us suppress threatening feelings of which we are largely unaware, but which never-theless still have a profound influence on us. They will presumably make decisions to push well down the 'layers of consciousness' that make up the human mind in order to get at 'the truth' from the Freudian perspective. Others, as devotees of other schools of psychological thought, will let other predilections drive their choice of enabling and probing techniques. With the 'emotional and participatory' school, a combination of research methods will often be used. There could be the use of group discussions (which could often be of the extended, 4-hour variety), coupled with participant observation in retail outlets, and also individual in-home interviews. It is common for researchers using this type of qualitative research approach to use various 'story-boards' with music tracks and other techniques to convey brands in their full rounded 'emotional' form. It follows from this that clients who commission qualitative research from this wing of the qualitative research party will need to feel comfortable about the fact that the moderator/researcher will often depart from the expected and address issues that suddenly appear on the surface. In addition, researchers from the 'emotional and participatory' school – in order to progress their understanding of a situation – may make many of the meanings that they consider to be floating loosely in the heads of respondents, quite instantly explicit during the research itself.

Eclecticism

Of course, no one moderator, or no one study, necessarily neatly falls exclusively into the 'rational' or the 'emotional' camp. This will be true of some qualitative studies, but many researchers will take a fairly eclectic approach, drawing, as appropriate, from the various schools of psychological and methodological thought. The key end point to our discussions here is to register with the decision-maker the importance of being aware of whether the qualitative research in front of them emanated from what we have labelled the 'rational' or 'emotional' school, or some midway point. But either way the data user can be reassured that both schools – assuming that the research has been professionally executed – will generate evidence that will be helpful – subject to careful analysis and interpretation – in the decision-making process.

We now provide a practical guide to the kinds of questions decision-makers should be asking in order to assess the robustness of a particular piece of qualitative evidence. This guide to robustness will be helpful to the readers irrespective of whether they are looking at rational or more emotive-based qualitative research.

The quality of qualitative research

In this section we provide decision-makers with some insights into what to look for to establish the quality of the qualitative research they are considering using for decision-making. We look first at whether the research conducted was on the customer's, as opposed to the researcher's, agenda. This is a fundamental issue for any research that claims to be playing back the 'voice' of the marketplace. We then look at the quality of the researcher's group moderation and/or depth interviewing skills. We follow this with the question of whether the research was professionally managed and executed, and then look at the approach taken to, and quality of, the analysis and interpretation of the data.

Understanding the customer's agenda

Irrespective of the school of qualitative research being deployed, it is important that the data user feels reassured that the research is providing evidence that reflects the *respondent's* agenda. Important to this debate is the work of American psychologist George Kelly. It was Kelly who, in the 1950s, first registered the importance of ensuring that qualitative research *fully maps the respondents' world*. This is important because one of the criticisms sometimes levelled at market research is that it does not 'do justice to the individual's knowledge'. How many people do you know, when they talk about taking part in a market research interview, claim that they were frustrated because they felt they never had an opportunity to fully express their opinion? Kelly was keen to ensure that researchers addressed this issue. The 'Kelly Triad' technique (usually) involves placing three different stimuli before a respondent and asking him/her to decide which two are similar (and to ask why), and to then ask which one is different (and why).

This procedure is followed not because the researcher is necessarily interested in the way a respondent forms different pairs of stimuli, but in the *reasons* given by the respondent for sorting the stimuli in this way. It is the sorting process that establishes the 'constructs' (i.e. criteria) that respondents use in order to sort out the differences between different stimuli. In addition, the 'Kelly technique' also acknowledges the 'bi-polarity of attitude': the fact that the reasons for grouping two stimuli together may create one construct, but by asking why the 'odd man out' stimulus is different from the other two at a subsequent question we may create a further (different) construct. For example, respondents could be asked which two of the following three cars are most similar and why: a Jaguar, a Land Rover and a Morgan. We might expect this choice to throw up the Land Rover as being the 'different car' because it is a four-wheel drive vehicle. But, in fact, contrary to expectations, this line of enquiry may show Jaguar and Land Rover being grouped together on the grounds that they are both (now) owned by the same US manufacturer (Ford), thereby producing the evaluation criterion (construct): 'ownership'. Then, when we pursue why Morgan is different from the other two, we do *not* necessarily – following the principle of the bi-polarity of attitude – learn that the Morgan was separated out because it is British owned. We could produce, for instance, a further unexpected evaluative concept: possibly the fact that the Morgan depreciates at a much slower rate than any of the other cars. In sum, this triad sorting technique is an invaluable way of ensuring that we understand the constructs or criteria a respondent uses to evaluate a particular event. It means that we obtain the respondent's view using his/her criteria, rather than giving him/her a predetermined list of attributes, designed by the researcher, upon which respondents then comment. We have devoted the above space to what is just one of a range of interviewing techniques that qualitative researchers might elect to employ because Kelly's triad is not just a *technique*, it represents an important methodological *paradigm*. What Kelly tells us about the importance of mapping the respondent's – not the researcher's – world is an important corner-stone of market research methodology.

Moderating and interviewing quality

There is no one right interviewing or moderating style. Some moderators will use an interview guideline in a fairly ordered, disciplined way.

Others will elect to improvise around the guideline, making on-the-spot decisions about where to probe and where, given time constraints, they will have to limit their questioning. Moderators also need to make decisions, during the course of an interview, about when to apply fairly gentle 'probes', and when to use higher risk questioning techniques. The latter, for instance, could include *self disclosure*; that is, sharing with the respondent the 'moderator's view' in order to relax the respondent and encourage him/her to say how they, themselves, feel about a topic upon which they seem reluctant to express a view. The moderator will also have to make decisions about whether to go down the 'binary' (literal) as opposed to the 'ternary' (third corner, more conceptual) route in shaping questions. Let us take the example of exploring attitudes towards paying for a public school education. We all know how the binary 'you lose/I win' debate goes: 'Nobody is going to tell me how to spend my money', versus, 'Going to public school is cheating', etc. One way of breaking out of this sterile, stereotypical debate is to look at the problem from the 'third corner'. From this perspective it becomes easier to 'ladder up' the debate to a higher level of abstraction and discuss two equally honourable concepts: 'freedom of choice' and 'equal opportunity'.

However, although moderator styles will vary, from the standpoint of the data user, it is important to have some evaluative framework in place in order to assess the stance adopted during the all-important process of asking questions. Here, it is perhaps helpful to look at Table 3.3. This is a 10-point *general* framework developed in order to explain, in broad terms, how moderators gradually *ladder up* an interview. Straight away we should say that this is just an all-purpose guide. For instance, those researchers who are very much committed to the 'emotional and participatory' school, could well *start* half-way through the 10-point framework. So, it would be wrong to treat Table 3.3 as a prescription for how to do qualitative interviewing. Nevertheless, it does serve to help the data user to understand how the qualitative researcher might broach their task.

Continuing with our review of how to assess the quality of qualitative research, we now alert the reader to things that can go wrong with qualitative research. The message is: if you have any doubts or worries about any of the following issues, you should return to the provider of the research and ask the appropriate questions.

Table 3.3 *Levels to which a researcher may elect to take the questioning in a depth interview (group discussion)*

1 *Level 1: spontaneous fact-finding.* Example: what are your views on the Single European Currency? (At this level, the aim is to ask general 'catch all' questions that do not close down any particular aspect of this issue.)

2 *Level 2: expanding views by probing (but not prompting).* Example: perhaps you could say a little bit more about your views on the Single European Currency?

3 *Level 3: seeking concrete examples.* By asking for concrete examples, it is helpful to establish whether the view being advanced is based on first-hand or secondary experiences. Example: perhaps you could give me a specific example of how you, yourself, would be disadvantaged by Britain entering the Single European Currency?

4 *Level 4: prompting of specifics.* Here, the aim is to put on the agenda specific issues that you now wish to pursue, having captured people's general spontaneous views. Example: thinking specifically about travelling abroad on business, do you think having one Single European Currency will make life more straightforward, or more difficult, or make no difference?

5 *Level 5: exploring motivations.* This means drilling down to ask 'why' questions and establishing reasons for particular initial viewpoints. Here, there will be a number of different layers to which researchers could go depending on where they stand on the 'rational' to 'emotional' qualitative research spectrum.

Options
(a) Conventional probing. Example: is there any particular reason why you feel this way/have you always felt this way/what in particular is it that leads you to this point of view?

(b) Low-risk enabling techniques. Example: here is a picture of two business people talking in a queue at their local bank. What do you think person A is saying to person B?

(c) High-risk enabling techniques. Example: set up a psycho-drama where respondents play out in a small drama their feelings about an unfortunate international business experience.

(d) Creative techniques. Example: the use of brainstorming and/or synectics (the use of analogies and metaphors) to help people generate new ideas. There are also a host of other ideas including, for instance, the idea of using 'stream of consciousness' techniques. The latter are considered by some qualitative researchers to allow respondents to articulate their true views on, for example, advertising in a way that we are not simply recording post-purchase decision rationalisations of how people really felt.

• *Level 6: clarifying and feeding back.* At this point in the interview it is helpful to clarify what has been said, feed this back to the respondent, and get confirmation that the researcher is on the right lines. Example: so to summarise, what you seem to be saying is . . . Is that right?

• *Level 7: laddering up to challenge any contradictions.* The interviewer will make a decision as to whether it is appropriate to challenge any contradictions that have been made. We all know that people are contradictory in their views and this could be entirely consistent with the reality of the situation. But we can use this probing

continues

Table 3.3 *(continued)*

technique to explore the stability of a particular view, and to delve further into underlying motivations. Example: earlier you were saying that you did not feel that the Single European Currency would be a problem to your business, but just now you seemed to be showing some concern about whether, if the initial exchange rate is set too high, you may be at a disadvantage, compared with your overseas competitors. Have I understood this right?

- *Level 8: the trade-off.* The moderator *may* elect to introduce, at this point, a *trade-off* element to the questioning. Up to now, respondents may have been encouraged to talk about their views as if there were no compromises or constraints in life. But in the real world, choices may need to be made. By asking various trade-off questions, the interviewer will get an insight into how respondents are prioritising different issues.
- *Level 9: understanding the attitude–behaviour link.* In research, it is important to do as much as possible to establish the relationship that may, or may not, exist between an 'attitude' that is articulated on a particular topic, and subsequent likely 'behaviour'. There could be individuals who are attitudinally well disposed towards, say, a particular brand of motor car, but who would never ever purchase that car. Equally, there could be those who are not particularly 'attitudinally' well disposed towards the car, but who, for various practical reasons may, in fact, purchase it. Thus, towards the end of an interview or group, the moderator may sum up attitudes and ask various questions in order to establish, as far as it is possible, the likely 'link' between attitudes and behaviour.
- *Level 10: sharing the whole problem.* In certain situations the moderator may elect to ladder up the questions to share the whole problem with the respondent. In other situations, this would be inappropriate. An example of where it might be appropriate could be as follows: 'We are here this evening to help Tesco decide whether or not it should expand its operations into Australia? If you were the Chairman of Tesco, what decision would you make?' And, for those in the 'emotional' school, there remain other levels to which the moderator may go. For example, he/she may not only wish to share the initial problem, but also ask people to stay with the problem over a period of time and return to take part in a re-convened group after they have had an opportunity to talk to various people and mull over the problem.

Is qualitative research the right choice?

The first question the decision-maker needs to ask is whether qualitative research is indeed the most appropriate way of dealing with the business objectives in hand. In other words, has the correct *qualitative* versus *quantitative* decision been made? Let us say that the objective was to establish small businesses' attitudes towards e-commerce – using the Internet to do business. Here, a small-scale qualitative study of around 30 individual depth interviews and four focus groups with small businesses (possibly divided between Internet users and non-users) would be a very powerful way of gaining some key insights. But it would be imprudent to rely on qualitative research evidence if your primary objective was to establish the *exact proportion* of small businesses that subscribe to different Internet service providers.

Have the appropriate qualitative methods been chosen?

There is also the question of whether the most appropriate qualitative research method was chosen. We provide a quick overview of the rationale underpinning particular qualitative research methods (see Table 3.4).

Having established that qualitative research was the relevant approach and that the most appropriate qualitative method was chosen, we arrive at a series of other questions to ask about a qualitative research study.

The right mix of respondents?

Clearly a key question is whether or not appropriate decisions have been made about who to include in the study. For example, there will be a sharp difference between research conducted amongst people who have had a mobile phone for some years, and more recent purchasers. Then, assuming that the appropriate decisions have been made about what types of people must be included, the next question to ask is: was enough done to ensure that a representative *range* of these designated individuals were included in the study? It is also important not to think of depth interviews as each being of exactly the same 'status'. Interviewing is rather like assembling a jigsaw. The interviews gradually build up to tell us the overall picture, but each piece of the jigsaw is a different size and shape. Thus, although there may be 30 interviews all with, let us say, finance directors, these respondents will vary considerably in terms of their ability to conceptualise and think about issues in a strategic, as opposed to tactical, way. Respondents will also vary dramatically in their willingness to open up and talk freely in the interview. So the reality of interviewing is to be realistic about the varying contributions made by different types of interviewee. In sum, it is naive to think of each depth interview being of equal 'weight'. (This is particularly true of business-to-business research interviews.)

Table 3.4   *Choosing the appropriate qualitative method*

Reasons for adopting a group approach

- *Safe environment.* The group approach provides a less intimidating environment than the individual interview – people welcome the safety of numbers, and usually enjoy the excitement and energy generated by a group setting.
- *Time and cost efficiency.* Group discussions are an efficient way of obtaining customer feedback from various individuals. In addition, it is possible to understand a range of attitudes and behaviour in a relatively short time.
- *Obtaining views in the context of what other people are saying.* The fact that people are meeting in a group confers a number of constructive group dynamics. The interaction that takes place between group members can spark off new ideas. In addition, the group setting encourages people to build on each others' views, allowing them to go on to express similar or different opinions. In addition, as the group discussion progresses, individuals can re-appraise their own position. This helps them arrive at their 'true view'. This is important because an individual's attitude towards a particular topic will be a function of two factors: first, their *own* knowledge and beliefs on that particular subject, but also their *perception* of what other people are thinking. For example, our attitudes towards marriage will be shaped partly by our own experience, and partly by our perception of how society currently views the institution of marriage.
- *Client observation.* Groups can be observed through a one-way mirror or video relay system by members of the client organisation so that clients can gain first-hand experience of their customers. (But it also has to be remembered that, in certain scenarios, the fact that respondents are being viewed may inhibit the group process.)
- *Prototypes.* If there are a limited number of prototypes available, practicalities dictate that the research must be conducted via group discussions, rather than through a series of individual depth interviews.

Issues mitigating against the group approach

- *Likelihood of group conformity.* Individuals within a group may, not surprisingly, display *group behaviour*. Thus, there is the possibility of people conforming to social norms that are politically correct, but *not* ones in which privately some group members believe. For example, in a group, people may feel obliged to focus on the environmental benefits of introducing unleaded petrol and play down their true concerns about unleaded petrol lowering the performance of their car.
- *Knowledge imbalances.* People included in a group with higher levels of knowledge and understanding on a particular topic can intimidate those with less experience, and make for an unbalanced group.
- *Counter-productive group dynamics.* Notwithstanding the professionalism of the moderation and careful planning in the way a group is constructed, there can still be numerous counter-productive conflicts that take place in groups. Thus, sometimes, the hoped-for creative and constructive interaction between group members is mudded by the influence of a strong personality who continually pushes his/her views on others. This overt opinion leadership makes the frank exchange of attitudes and beliefs problematic.

continues

Table 3.4   (*continued*)

- *Sensitivities.* Today, there are few taboo topics which people are not prepared to discuss. But there could be some issues that people do not want to discuss in front of others; for example, precise details of their salary and financial circumstances.
- *Detail.* Groups are less helpful when it is necessary to record detailed purchase behaviour. This can be difficult and tedious to obtain in a group setting.
- *Awareness and knowledge.* In a group setting it is often difficult to check each individual's awareness and knowledge of particular products or markets. (Once the first individual in a group discussion has raised an issue, it becomes difficult to check, on a retrospective unprompted basis, the true awareness and knowledge of other members.)
- *Hot-housing.* For instance, small businesses may feel reasonably satisfied with the service they are receiving from their bank. But in a group setting there can be a tendency for respondents from small businesses – many of whom will work alone in Alamo-like siege conditions – to exaggerate their dissatisfaction. Once they get into the group setting with fellow 'kindred spirits', they may begin trading bank atrocity stories.
- *Reported interaction.* One of the *claimed* benefits of the group discussion is that it generates 'interaction between group members'. This is true. But this interaction is rarely reported in qualitative market research reports. Thus, many of the conceptual insights that could have been gleaned through understanding this interactive process are, in practice, lost.
- *Recruitment difficulties.* The group discussion is a poor choice of method if it is going to be extremely difficult to recruit individuals with the desired characteristics. Eight Branson-like CEOs will *not* all agree to be in the same place at the same time and stay for 2 hours.

Reasons for using individual (depth interviews)
- *Understanding the attitude–behaviour link.* Understanding the attitude–behaviour relationship is important in establishing the veracity of certain evidence. For example, someone may claim to be *pro* public transport, but his/her actual travel behaviour will tell a different story. But understanding the attitude–behaviour relationship is difficult to achieve for every single individual in an eight-person group discussion. With the one-to-one depth interview, there is more time to explore the level of congruence between attitude and behaviour.
- *Sensitivity.* Individual interviews are considered appropriate for sensitive subject-matters, such as redundancy. It also allows the exploration of less socially acceptable attitudes, such as the view that one should pay *less*, not more, attention to polluting the environment.
- *Where over- or under-claiming is likely.* Depth interviews are useful when over-claiming or under-claiming might occur. For example, people often over-claim on their use of health food, and under-claim the number of cigarettes they smoke.
- *Homework.* There could be certain areas – notably finance – where it is important for an individual to seek out various documentation – insurance policies, pension policies and so on - in order to be able to answer detailed questions.

continues

Table 3.4 (continued)

- *Researching communications.* In a group, one individual usually 'gets the joke' – the nuance or *double entendre* or play on words – in a commercial before others. This means the moderator never knows how many other members of the group have really absorbed the key message. Although the depth interview loses the important dimension of establishing how communications are viewed in a social setting, it does allow us to assess whether the key communications devices are working.
- *Recruitment.* Difficult-to-interview respondents are best interviewed individually. This can be because of: geographical dispersion (farmers); status (CEOs); or low purchasing penetration (people who have lapsed their personal pension payments in the last month). Unlike the group discussion where all eight individuals need to be available on a set day, at a set venue, at a set (non-negotiable) time, with the individual interview, an appointment can be tailored to suit the respondent.
- *Piloting.* The single interview can be used as a pilot exercise prior to a larger scale survey to ensure the questionnaire has the right vocabulary and that the attitude statements are appropriate.

Factors mitigating against depth interviews
- Time-consuming, both in terms of conducting the interview and analysing the transcripts/tapes.
- Costly (for the above reasons).

Wrong 'call' over focus groups and depth interviews
From what we have said, it is clear that the decision-maker must also look for 'bad calls' over whether depth interviews or focus groups have been used. These days there is a tendency for the depth interview to be discarded in favour of the group discussion for no other reason than it lacks 'fun' and 'entertainment value' for the client observers. There is also a reluctance among some research buyers to pay for the higher costs of depth interviews, relative to group discussions, even when individual interviews would deliver more robust insights. In other words, the criteria for choosing between the two methods will often be based on erroneous criteria, rather than on an informed evaluation of the fundamental benefits and limitations of the respective group and depth techniques.

Inexperienced group moderation and/or depth interviewing

At the beginning of this chapter we defined qualitative research in comparatively simple terms: as asking relevant questions and listening carefully to what people have to say. But, like all things simple, it requires considerable technique and skill from the moderator. We have already seen that the moderator must have in his/her head a framework that will guide him/her through the various decisions he/she needs to make about which questions to ask as a group or depth interview progresses. A good moderator will need to have high levels of self-awareness. He/she will need to know what 'personal baggage' he/she brings to the research. Moderators need to feel confident in quickly judging people in a way that is balanced and fair, rather than prejudicial. And he/she needs to be tolerant of working with people who may be less (or more) intelligent and less (or more) able than him/herself. The list goes on. One problem with using qualitative evidence as part of the decision-making process is the tendency in recent years, as qualitative research has grown in popularity, for the process to be 'mechanised'. Today, we often find individuals with little experience of the psychological and business concepts that are needed to conduct *quality* group discussions and depth interviews being let loose in front of respondents. Young people with very little experience may be thrown in at the deep end and asked to moderate a group discussion that – given the quite complex group dynamics and their level of experience – they could find difficult to manage, let alone being able to interpret what the resulting evidence means. This is not to say that younger people should not be given opportunities to undertake qualitative research. Everybody has got to start somewhere. But it is important that newcomers only *go live* when they have an appreciation of the theory and practice underpinning the qualitative research 'craft'.

The standard of recruitment

Another factor of which the user of qualitative research evidence needs to be aware is the professionalism demonstrated during the recruitment of respondents. Today, there are enormous pressures on those responsible for recruiting qualitative respondents. Sometimes these pressures are the result of the end clients who are responsible for commissioning qualitative research having no grounding in the realities of the recruitment process. This naivety can lead to requests for utterly ridiculous 'quotas'. (By this we mean the specification of the combination of characteristics that respondents taking part in the qualitative research must have.) These requests often totally ignore the low incidence of this type of individual in the population, and further ignore the chances of these individuals *all* being available on the same evening to travel to a group discussion. What happens in the face of totally unreasonable quotas is that recruiters – who are anxious to please the end client – will be 'forced' to recruit 'compliant', easy-to-access, individuals. On some projects this slight biasing of the selection of respondents may not be life-threatening. But on other projects it could have critical implications for the kind of evidence that is eventually collected.

Viewing effects

The last five years have seen a massive growth in the number of viewing facilities around the world that allow clients to observe group discussions (focus groups). On balance, viewing is to be welcomed: it gives clients the opportunity to see customers *live*. The situation is that under The Market Research Society and ICC/ESOMAR Codes of Conduct, respondents must be told at the start of a session that they are being viewed. Once such reassurances have been provided we know that many respondents are quite comfortable with the idea of taking part in a viewed group. However, it would be naive to assume that viewing does not have any affect on the group discussion process. We know from the productivity experiments conducted at the Hawthorne Electrical works in the 1930s that individuals being observed tend to behave in a different way from those who are not (this is the so-called 'Hawthorne Effect'). For example, commuters taking part in a 'viewed' focus group who have suffered at the hands of a railway company may not be able to contain some of their frustration and could 'play to the gallery'. Egged on by what they perceive to be 'cloak and dagger' one-way viewing mirror tactics, and perhaps 'sensing' that a particularly important official from the railway company is lurking behind the screen, they could turn what was supposed to be a research exercise into something close to 'scream' therapy!

The nightmare viewing scenario is where the observers behave in a frivolous manner, only partially listening to the group discussion, while discussing various non-related business matters. This 'party' atmosphere behind the screen then begins to engender anxieties in the moderator, who now feels that he/she is responsible for managing *two* sets of group dynamics: the dynamics of the group he/she is attempting to moderate, plus what he/she *senses* to be going on among the 'other group' behind the mirror. The idea of the observers behind the mirror being 'out of sight' and therefore 'out of mind' is, of course, wishful thinking. Moderators and group participants alike will pick up the 'vibes' about what is going on behind the viewing mirror. This feeling that something 'untoward' is going on not too far away can then result in some respondents behaving aggressively or posturing in order to show off in front of what the group senses is a non-*simpatico* audience voyeuristically ensconced behind the mirror.

A new trend is for some companies to insist on what might be called 'show groups' being conducted. These are group discussions that will be viewed by a senior member of the organisation to obtain a 'one-stop' insight into what his/her customers really think. Here, the pressure mounts as the client communicates to the moderator the view that it would be 'good' if there were an appropriate number of relevant 'soundbites' for the senior observer to take away. These pressures can start bringing artificiality into the research process. Instead of being an exploration of customers' views, the group becomes a type of 'live theatre'. A 'good' moderator becomes someone who can deliver to the observers memorable winning lines, and cover the agenda expected by the observer, rather than someone who is skilled at exploring the real issues that respondents want to place on the agenda.

Understanding the overall analysis approach adopted

The next area to evaluate is the approach taken by the researcher to the analysis and interpretation of the evidence. The first question to ask is whether the researcher adopted a 'top-down' or 'bottom-up' approach to the analysis.

Top-down or bottom-up?

- *Top-down theory-led*. Here, we refer to a process whereby the analyst may start with his/her own 'pet theory' of how the world 'works', and then, operating with this framework, attempt to 'fit' evidence to this overall view of the world. As we explained in Insight 5 (data are dumb; beliefs are blind) in Chapter 2, this approach has merit if the analyst's theory is informed by a rich body of normative evidence. If so, then this could be a helpful way to proceed. But if, on the other hand, the underlying guiding theory is unsubstantiated, then clearly, such a top-down approach could lead to a misrepresentation of the evidence. The reader may be surprised that we have not immediately and automatically condemned out of hand the 'top-down', theory-led approach to analysis. Why have we not argued that the bottom-up, data-led approach is *always* preferable? This is because in addition to Insight 5 there is also Insight 1: all knowledge starts with prejudice. So we have to accept that there could be scenarios where the top-down approach will have considerable merit. For example, in analysing the competition that is taking place between different brands in a particular market sector, it may be extremely helpful to start the analysis process by overlaying onto the data from a particular study what we know about this topic based on the highly authoritative work of Michael Porter on competitor analysis. These kind of top-down frameworks can add discipline and structure to the subsequent analysis of the evidence emerging from a qualitative study. Thus, it does not automatically follow that the bottom-up approach to analysis is to be preferred. But, of course, the decision-maker must be wary of an analyst who feels that his/her cranky, off-beam theories of how the world *works*, is superior to the 'data-led' approach we now discuss.

- *Bottom-up data-led.* The data-led analysis approach is where the researcher commences without any preconceived theories or informing views (although, as Insight 1 tells us, to make sense of the world, any analyst must start from some kind of perspective). Then, based primarily on a 'bottom-up' analysis of the data the analyst will start developing a 'theory'. The approach is based on the analyst painstakingly 'immersing' him/herself in the data and gradually working up to an understanding of the dataset through an extremely detailed dissection of transcripts of interviews, and so on.

- *Eclecticism.* Of course, in practice much analysis will be a combination of the above 'theory' and 'data-led' approaches. It will be a top-down *and* bottom-up analysis approach. The analysis will start with some element of 'theory' – some understanding of overarching themes. This will inform how we first come to the data. But we will then look in detail at whether the new incoming evidence supports, adjusts or adapts our initial observations. This reflects the points we have made under Insight 2 about investigation being a circular, not linear, process.

The analytical framework

We also need to clarify the particular 'analytical framework' that guided the data analyst's approach to the qualitative evidence. At the heart of the issue of which analysis framework is being employed is the need to understand the relationship between an individual's behaviour and attitude. By attitude we are talking about a *mental state of preparedness to act in a predetermined way*. There are three key dimensions to attitude. First, there is an *intellectual* component of attitude – the way we use our 'rational', left side of brain thought processes to evaluate evidence. Secondly, there is the *emotional* element: our intuitive right side of brain thinking. Thirdly, there is the *action* component (referred to as the 'conative'): because someone holds a particular (intellectual and emotional) *attitude*, this does not necessarily mean that he/she will act according to this attitude. For instance, I may feel passionate about the evils of fox hunting – an attitude driven, in part, by an intellectually based antagonism towards a sport that, in my perception, typifies the unfairness of the British class system and, in part, on a more emotionally driven distaste for small furry animals being mauled by big dogs. But notwithstanding the strength of my viewpoint, it could be the case that I do not feel moved to take any action in relation to this attitude, i.e. I cannot be bothered spending my weekends laying false aniseed trails at major hunting events when there is football to watch and there are boats to sail!

The question of the relationship between attitude and behaviour is something that psychologists have continued to explore down the years. They have tried to show how a specifically defined measurable variable 'attitude' directly relates to a specific type of 'behaviour'. Unfortunately, attempts to show a clear relationship between attitudes and behaviour have not been particularly successful. For example, there will be situations where a positive *attitude* towards a particular phenomenon (e.g. Marks & Spencer) will be backed up by affirmative purchase *behaviour* (e.g. I regularly shop there). But there will be situations where 'positive' attitudes (e.g. I am keen to help the environment) will not lead to 'positive behaviour' (e.g. I do not buy recycled paper). In addition, there will be situations in which individuals will behave on impulse, and then 'readjust' their attitudes in line with this impulsive behaviour after the event.

In this book there is not the space to do even a brief review of all of the *theories* that exist about the attitude–behaviour relationship. However, because ensuring the data user is clear on the 'analytical framework' being employed by the qualitative research analyst, it is helpful to focus briefly on one important contribution to the debate, that of Martin Fishbein. He argues that behavioural intentions are a function of two factors: a person's attitude to the behaviour in question, and the person's subjective norms about the behaviour in question. Put simply, my attitudes towards the concept of setting up my own business are partly about what number I would give this on some positive or negative scale of feeling, coupled with the subjective norm of 'do I believe that most people important to me think I should, or should not, leave my job and set up my own business next week'. Fishbein lays stress on the fact that if we wish to predict or understand a behavioural intention, we must measure attitudes to this *specific* behaviour, i.e. not attitudes to the object of the behaviour. So, it is not about doing a study to assess attitudes towards 'self-employment', but a study to look specifically at the 'act of leaving my job and setting up my own business'.

So what are the general lessons to be learnt about what we know about the inter-relationship between attitude and behaviour? Well it seems to be the case that these days attempts to explain *universal* phenomena (such as how TV advertising *works*) have been largely abandoned in favour of more localised, 'mid-range' attempts to understand likely future behaviour. For example, we seem to have a good working understanding of how public service type advertising – wear your car seat belt – works. Thus, today, for example, there would be few people claiming to have a 'model' about what exactly will happen in the UK housing market in five years time. But there will be property specialists who will have identified what might happen in different future property 'scenarios', based on making different assumptions about a host of factors, such as trends in the overall world economy, the fortunes of the euro, and so on. Thus, today in marketing, it is *not* fashionable to pursue grand predictive models of how the future will unfold outside of certain specialist areas. Today, the emphasis is on understanding how the attitude and behaviour relationship seems to work in particular market and customer scenarios.

These observations about the difficulties of understanding the relationship between attitudes and behaviour will give the decision-maker a flavour of a highly complex and much debated topic. Here, we can do no more than ensure that the data user understands a little about the main elements of: the way attitudes are shaped; their stability; and their relationship to behaviour. If, as a decision-maker, you have any doubts about your qualitative evidence, make sure you 'quiz' the researcher who is supplying the qualitative data about the 'analytical' framework he/she used to understand the attitude–behaviour relationship.

The nitty-gritty of the analysis technique

In this book it is not appropriate to delve into the detailed, often highly personalised, techniques that qualitative researchers use to make sense of the video tapes, audio tapes and transcripts of focus groups and depth interviews. This is necessary only in so far as it sets the scene for the more important task of arriving at an informed judgement about the overall rigour with which the qualitative data were analysed. The approach taken by analysts in making sense of their qualitative evidence will vary considerably. Some will directly listen to audio tapes or watch videos of the focus groups and depth interviews. Others analyse transcripts taken of depths and groups. Still others will work with a combination of tapes and transcripts. Some will do neither. Some may elect to study the evidence with a view to identifying the overarching themes quickly, which will then be followed by a subsequent more detailed analysis of the material. Some will start by conducting a detailed 'content analysis' of each individual interview, eventually building this up to the identification of more overarching themes. Some will favour treating individual transcripts as 'case studies'. These will be analysed in detail and grouped, prior to commenting on what aggregate thematic statements emerge from the various case studies.

Similarly, in terms of the actual detailed process of summarising what went on in the focus groups and depths, there will be a wide variety of techniques employed. Some will use highlighter pens on transcripts to identify the key recurring themes; others will annotate the transcript in the margin. Still others will develop quite elaborate 'post-it note' systems and/ or colour-coding schemes in order to identify the 'patterns' in the transcript. Some qualitative researchers will undertake a *content analysis* in a fairly 'loose' way, noting down key points, and so on. Others may actually carry out a classic content analysis by counting *precisely* the exact number of times, for example, criticisms of a particular feature of the car were made, and so on. Some will list out all the pertinent verbatim comments from respondents and then subsequently identify those 'quotes' they will elect to use in the presentation and report. Others – once the storyline has been established – will then simply retrospectively pinpoint some appropriate 'illustrative' quotes. Other researchers, keen to fully understand the inter-relationships within the data, will work with techniques such as 'cognitive mapping' in order to pinpoint the key drivers of attitude and behaviour and so on. Cognitive mapping is a particularly helpful technique – especially from the holistic data analysis standpoint – because it provides a graphic account of the overall context in which an individual was giving information. It is a technique that provides the basis for examining the strength of the relationship between different phenomena and can thereby help provide key insights into what makes a particular individual 'tick'. This approach is summarised in Figure 3.2.

We leave the issue of how qualitative researchers 'physically' analyse their data with an illustration of cognitive mapping, not because – in a prescriptive way – we are suggesting that it represents a 'Counsel of Perfection' yardstick against which decision-makers should evaluate the way their own qualitative data were analysed, but because it neatly illustrates the holistic approach to data analysis being advocated in this book. In Figure 3.2 we look at how to analyse data, from a depth interview conducted with a new university graduate on his/her career options.

Making judgements and decisions from qualitative evidence

We now turn to the issue of what questions the decision-maker should be asking about qualitative evidence in order to be reassured about its

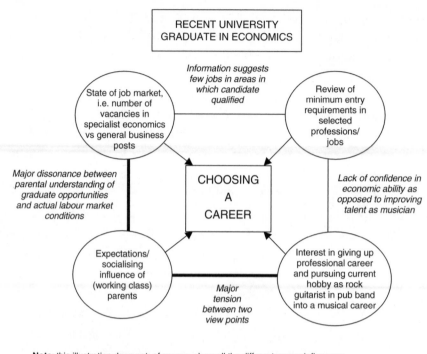

Figure 3.2 *Illustrative example of cognitive mapping*

robustness and *safety* from the decision-making standpoint. In Chapter 6 we explain ,in detail the holistic approach to the analysis of marketing data. But here, in the context of providing the reader with a guide to the safety of qualitative decisions, it is helpful to preview a few key holistic analysis concepts. Specifically, it is important to start thinking about (qualitative) data as having *weight, power* and *direction*.

Qualitative weight of evidence

The 'weight' of the evidence is related to the following two factors.

1. *The level of support for/against the proposition.* With qualitative research one will often be working with samples of around 30 observations.

Here, most qualitative researchers will be able to provide the decision-maker with confirmation about whether a particular point was supported by virtually all respondents, i.e. an overwhelming majority, or whether there was only majority or minority support. As the decision-maker, do not be afraid to ask the qualitative researcher to provide actual 'counts' of the number of individuals who support a particular initiative. Some qualitative researchers may not be comfortable with providing numbers, feeling that this is not the role of qualitative research. But having actual counts to underpin the more general statements can be helpful. Specifically, a reference to a *majority* (i.e. 25 out of 30) and a *minority* (i.e. 10 out of 30) can be useful to the decision-maker. Those in the 'rational' school will probably oblige. But those in the 'emotional' school may put up a spirited rationale as to why this may not be appropriate and/or possible. We will leave the reader to sort this out!

2. *The intensity with which views are held.* The main vehicle that will be used by the qualitative researcher to communicate 'depth of feeling' are illustrative verbatim comments. But one should not be overly influenced by the highly selective use of powerful *quotable quotes.* By this we mean a comment that has been selected, not because it is necessarily representative of the wider body of evidence, but because it is likely to stick in the decision-maker's mind and heavily influence his/her decision-making. We all know that an extremely evocative, or powerful, quote will stay in the memory irrespective of how typical this was of the overall body of opinion. How does one spot this little 'theatrical device'? A useful way of checking is to ensure that the data analyst provides a *selection* of comments to support the key conclusions of a study.

The power of different types of evidence

The 'power' of evidence involves assessing the following two elements.

1. *The nature of the formal explicit evidence.* Here you need to take into account what type of qualitative evidence is being presented. Is it a piece of data for which only one observation is needed? For instance,

apparently a Swan Vestas employee suggested removing the sandpaper on one side of the matchbox, thereby reducing sandpaper costs by 50%. Here, only one observation was needed to prompt consideration of this option. In contrast, there could be qualitative data that needs to be understood in a more contextual, normative or relative way. Let us say our qualitative study told us that when asked to comment on the product, there were virtually no complaints or criticisms. Knowing that, generally speaking, when people are asked to comment on a product – even one they like – around one-third of individuals usually offer some form of criticism is an important interpretative context.

2. *Whether the evidence squares with implicit, prior knowledge and intuition.* It is important for the decision-maker to make sure that the data analyst has, in a transparent way, mapped out the 'prior knowledge' that has been factored into his/her own analysis. Specifically, as explained at Insight 5, you need to be reassured that this prior knowledge does represent accepted wisdom within the organisation and is not based on a folklore or a quirky individualistic perspective.

The overall direction of the evidence

It is comparatively easy with qualitative evidence to look at the *internal* consistency of the evidence. If there were 30 depth interviews, does the pattern of evidence in favour of, and against, a particular idea follow a consistent pattern, or are there erratic twists and turns in the evidence that suggests some complexity that needs further investigation? This type of analysis allows us to arrive at a position whereby we have data that on a case-on-case basis consistently support the position being advanced, as opposed to data with considerable variation and irregularity. Added to this are the checks of *external* consistency. Thus, we could look at the direction of the 'depth interview' evidence in comparison with that of the 'group discussion' evidence and look for consistency in the direction of the findings from these two sources of evidence. Clearly, where we find both internal and external consistency in the direction of the data, this gives us more confidence in feeling comfortable about the robustness of the observations that the data analyst is making.

Table 3.5   *Assessing the safety of qualitative evidence*

- Qualitative research will not (necessarily) be designed to provide representative samples, but it should provide a representative reflection of the *range* of attitudes towards the topic under investigation. Check this has happened.
- With qualitative research, the moderator will – to varying degrees – interact with respondents, and as such, could be seen to 'influence' the results: this is to be expected. But have you got a fix on the degree to which the moderator him/herself has shaped the qualitative findings and are you able to factor this into your interpretation of the data?
- Was the depth interview and/or group discussion conducted in a way such that the interview was taken to the right level of 'depth' (were the right choices made about the use of enabling techniques in order to drill down for psychological depth)?
- Were all procedures followed to ensure maximum data capture, i.e. to minimise the data loss? A transcript of a tape-recorded, 1-hour depth interview will run to about 25 pages, but notes taken on the same interview will typically only run to six pages.
- Did the analyst impose a 'top-down' structure with little regard for the research findings as the basis for the analysis, or was a 'bottom-up' approach employed (possibly informed by an existing 'top-down' theory)?
- Has the appropriate and comprehensive evidence been provided – in the form of respondent comments – to support the key points in the report/presentation?
- Is the explicit qualitative research study consistent with the implicit prior knowledge, judgement, hunch and other corroborating sources of evidence on this topic?

The safety of qualitative evidence for decision-making: a seven-point checklist

To conclude this chapter we provide the data analyst with seven key questions they should ask about qualitative research before using it to make a judgement or decision (see Table 3.5 above).

C H A P T E R 4

Understanding Survey Data

Overview

This chapter:

- reviews of the key characteristics of survey-based research
- summarises the strengths and limitations of different quantitative data collection methods
- sets out the seven key checks that users of survey data should carry out prior to making a judgement, or decision, based on survey evidence.

FOUR

Understanding
Survey Data

'The question is', said Alice, 'whether you can make words mean different things.'

'When I use a word', said Humpty Dumpty, 'it means just what I choose it to mean – neither more nor less' – Lewis Carroll.

Not a day goes by without an item appearing in the media claiming that a *survey* is telling us such and such. The very word *survey* provokes a mixed response. Some – particularly if the survey findings are being presented via a prestigious media channel – will automatically think that the findings must be telling us something important. But, for others, the term 'survey' will raise hackles: the so-called 'evidence' will be dismissed as just another (questionable) survey. It is against this backdrop of our love/hate relationship with surveys that we now put the spotlight on quantitative survey data. We identify seven key areas where it is important to ask questions in order to establish the robustness of the survey evidence collected. But before we start, it is important to draw a distinction between *real* surveys conducted under the terms of the ICC/ESOMAR (including The Market Research Society of the UK) Code of Conduct, and list-building 'questionnaires'. The difference is that with the latter type of questionnaires the primary purpose is to generate lists of individuals who later – subject to permission being given – may receive direct mail appropriate to their circumstances, whereas with the *real survey* the purpose is to research the individual's attitudes and behaviour towards a particular topic and to do so in a confidential way whereby the results are only reported in aggregate, without any reference to individuals. The focus of this chapter is on real, not list-building, questionnaires.

A recap on the key characteristics of survey-based research

There are two main types of quantitative research survey: an *ad hoc* survey and continuous research panels.

1. An *ad hoc* survey. This refers to a survey that has been specifically commissioned – once it has been established that existing secondary data cannot provide a solution to the marketing problem. Some *ad hoc* surveys may be repeated at various intervals. For example, a hotel interested in measuring levels of customer satisfaction among its guests may conduct an initial *ad hoc* 'benchmark' survey to lay down a yardstick against which subsequent changes in levels of satisfaction can be measured at regular intervals. But the important point is that with '*ad hoc*' surveys, the interviews are always with 'fresh' samples of respondents.
2. *Continuous research panels.* Here we are referring to panels of con-sumers who agree to provide, on a regular – weekly or monthly – basis, feedback about, for instance, their grocery purchases and so on. The distinctive feature here is that the *same* respondents are inter-viewed each time.

In this book we look only at *ad hoc* survey-based research. Those needing to know more about interpreting continuous (longitudinal) consumer panel data will need to refer to the specialist texts. (A starting point would be Chapter 9 of the ESOMAR Handbook of Market and Opinion Research.) But this said, many of the general *ad hoc* survey principles discussed here can be universally applied to the interpretation of continuous research.

Quantitative research has three key defining characteristics.

1. *Uses larger samples.* The emphasis is on numerical measurement and subsequent statistical analysis, thereby requiring the larger numbers that are needed to look at variations by sub-groups within the population.
2. *Asks all respondents the same questions.* This allows the resulting data to be aggregated and presented in the form of summary statistics. This standardised approach means that surveys can be repeated in the future and results compared.

3. *Separates the collection of data from their subsequent analysis.* With quantitative research the data collection stage is quite distinct from the subsequent analysis. This is in contrast to qualitative research, where the collection, interpretation and analysis of data is, in part, a 'simultaneous' process.

The main ways in which quantitative research is used are as follows:

- *Profiling*: what kind of people read magazine X?
- *Measuring behaviour*: how often do people buy X magazine?
- *Monitoring change*: have sales of magazine X increased or decreased over the last three months?
- *Understanding behaviour*: why do people buy magazine X?
- *Assessing attitudes*: why do they think magazine X is better/worse than magazine Y?
- *Hypothesis testing*: is it true that more car owners than pedestrians prefer magazine X?
- *Diagnosing problems*: why are the sales of magazine X less than expected?
- *Forecasting*: how many copies of magazine X are likely to be sold in the next three months?

There are four main ways quantitative survey research can be collected: on a face-to-face basis; over the telephone; by asking individuals to complete a self-administered questionnaire (which may or may not make use of despatch and response via the postal system); and, increasingly, the use of the Internet. Below, we provide a brief overview of the strengths and limitations of each method.

 ### Face-to-face interviews

- *Plus points.* The fact that the interviewer can see the respondent gives the interviewer power, flexibility and control. The interviewer – by responding to non-verbal communications, such as eye movements, facial expressions, and body language can adapt questions to the respondent's personality. A wry smile or a shrug of the shoulders often speaks volumes. In addition, in a face-to-face interview, interviewers can make sure that concepts are released at an appropriate point in the interview. (This is in contrast to, say, a postal survey, where the respondent could turn to the back page of the questionnaire and read the last question first, thereby limiting the value of postal research for, say, checking the spontaneous awareness of an event.)

- *Limitations.* Face-to-face interviews can be considerably more expensive than telephone interviews. In addition, the face-to-face interview can suffer from what is called 'interviewer bias'. This refers to the fact that two interviewers asking exactly the same question of the same respondent might obtain different answers merely because there is an interaction between the 'personality' of the respondent and that of the interviewer. For example, a respondent – if he/she is being interviewed by an 'upmarket' interviewer – may exaggerate the frequency with which he/she eats kedgeree, as opposed to porridge, for breakfast. However, reassuringly, in large measure this type of interview bias can be avoided by ensuring that the interviewing team: receive the same detailed briefing on the project; are given clear instructions about how to ask each question; are given exactly the same definitions about the terms used in the survey; and the same, precise guidance on how to deal with queries, and so on.

 ## *Telephone interviewing*

- *Plus points.* Today, virtually all households in the United Kingdom have a telephone, which means that it is possible to interview people from all corners of the country. This is in contrast to the face-to-face interview where, for cost reasons, it is necessary to 'cluster' interviews in order to minimise interviewer travelling time. In addition, the telephone improves the chances of contacting busy respondents, and is a cost-effective way of collecting data. The telephone is also a good way of ensuring that an interview takes place at a particular point in time, e.g. within a couple of hours of a TV commercial being shown. Most telephone interviews these days are conducted via Computer Assisted Telephone Interviewing (CATI) units. These systems mean that the questionnaire is 'driven' by the computer: the reply a respondent gives to a question will automatically determine the next question this respondent should be asked. This also means that questionnaires can also be easily piloted and, if need be, changed before the start of the main fieldwork. This automatic routing of respondents – and the fact that CATI systems can monitor the interviewers – provides considerable quality control benefits over and above even the best attempts to supervise face-to-face interviewers. In particular, although there can be some 'interviewer effect' – given the different voice patterns of the respondent and the interviewer – telephone interviewing does, in large measure, minimise this phenomenon.

- *Limitations.* It is difficult to show stimulus material to respondents over the telephone (although material could be faxed or sent in advance by mail). In addition, it is difficult to ask more complex questions over the telephone. However, this can be largely offset by using the *unfolding technique* to make questions easier to follow over the phone. (For example, the interviewer says, 'I would like you to tell me whether you agree or disagree with each of these statements'. Then, after each statement has been read out, the interviewer is instructed to ask those who agreed the following supplementary question, 'Do you agree a lot, or a little?'. Those who disagreed are then asked, 'Do you disagree a lot or a little?', and so on.) Another limitation is that it can be difficult to maintain control over the telephone. However, increasingly, telephone interviewers are acquiring the skills needed in order to ensure the interviewee is paying attention, responding to the questions, and taking the interview seriously. In addition, many now argue that the anonymity of the telephone interview means that individuals are *more* likely to openly discuss sensitive issues than when taking part in a potentially more embarrassing face-to-face interview.

 ### *Self-administered questionnaires (postal research)*

Here, we look at data collection that takes place without the presence of an interviewer. The questionnaire to be completed by the respondent could be despatched and returned by post, personally delivered and collected, or some combination of these options. Poor postal research conducted is commonplace. This is because people can be attracted to the method because it is comparatively inexpensive, rather than because it is the methodology of choice. This means that postal research is often carried out as a poor second-best substitute. This type of research should be spotted and carefully interpreted prior to making decisions. In contrast, some postal research will be entirely fit-to-purpose and as such will provide extremely reliable insights.

- *Plus points.* Self-administered questionnaires, as indicated, can be conducted on a low budget. In addition, postal research is particularly helpful when asking respondents to keep a record of their behaviour on an ongoing basis: the questionnaire serves as an *aide-mémoire* – for example, for keeping a careful record of the different food micro-waved on a particular day. In addition, self-administered question-naires are suited to collecting large amounts of detailed information which would be difficult to do without looking up records, e.g. the premiums being paid on various insurance policies. There is also some evidence to suggest that self-completion questionnaires encourage honest answers on sensitive topics, on which the individual may not feel able to talk about over the telephone or face-to-face. Furthermore, there are a number of specialist applications where self-completion questionnaires play a role. For example, with employee research it is often necessary – for political reasons – to ensure that *every* employee has an opportunity to register his/her views. Thus, although a sample survey would provide a representative view, this is not pursued because some employees may distrust the results because 'they didn't ask me'.
- *Limitations.* The biggest single concern about postal research is whether or not an adequate response rate was achieved. If the response to a survey falls below around 65%, the results will need careful interpretation. The working hypothesis for a survey result based on a response rate of *less* than 65% should be that the result is *not* necessarily typical of the overall population under investigation. For example, a postal survey conducted among ex-graduates of a university on the quality of their tuition, with a 20% response, is perhaps more likely to reflect the views of those who have performed well at that institution, rather than those that have done badly, and

who therefore feel that they do not want to *rake over the past* by returning a questionnaire. Another limitation with a self-completion questionnaire, as already explained, is that respondents will read the end of the questionnaire before the beginning. This means that assessing levels of awareness of products, or services, is problematic. A postal questionnaire also limits the extent to which question *sequencing* – important in effectively constructing a dialogue with the interviewer and the respondent – can be effectively deployed. Not only does it become difficult to go from the spontaneous to the prompted, but it can also be difficult to release general concepts that are stepping stones towards the eventual release of a specific product idea. For example, with a postal questionnaire you cannot explore attitudes towards different aspects of the current Jaguar – learning lessons as you go – and then, when appropriate, open out the study to assess attitudes to the proposed new F-type. Another factor is the length of a postal questionnaire. On balance, this should be shorter rather than longer, although there are no hard and fast rules. It is generally true that shorter questionnaires obtain a higher response rate than longer ones. But the main determinant of whether a postal survey will receive a high response rate will be the *overall* professionalism with which a survey is conducted.

 ### Internet surveys

The Internet is now extensively used for survey purposes. When the goal is to obtain a sample of individuals who use the Internet for, for example, e-commerce, then this is an economical way of obtaining data. However, if the aim is to access the wider population, then we must remember that the Internet remains the preserve of a reasonably elite minority. The jury is still out on the question of whether conducting market research on the Internet will be any more problematic than was the transition from face-to-face to telephone interviews. Much depends on how the Internet will bed down as a way of buying goods and services. One hypothesis is that the Internet will simply become yet another channel of commercial distribution. Whereas in the past we would ask Mrs Smith about her purchasing experience at Tesco on a face-to-face basis, today, if this person shops over the Tesco website, then we shall simply ask her about her Tesco retail experience over the Internet. The other hypothesis is that, in certain product fields, for some people, using the Internet is a totally different purchasing experience. Some people, for example, when they are on the Internet go into a kind of 'cyber-space', almost becoming different personalities and using different names. And it is this latter scenario that poses challenges for market researchers using the Internet to research customers attitudes. So with the Internet it is a matter of watch this space while researchers find out more about how effectively to use the Internet to research customers.

We now turn to seven checks that we believe the decision-maker should take into account in interpreting the robustness of survey evidence.

Seven key checks

Below is a brief summary of the seven questions we believe every user of survey data should ask about survey evidence prior to making a judgement or decision.

1. *Were there any flaws in the survey design?* Is the overall design fundamentally flawed or has the survey been structured to answer your research objectives robustly?
2. *Was the sample representative?* Does the sample reflect the wider universe or have certain key groups been excluded and/or certain biases been introduced into the selection process?
3. *Did the questionnaire 'work'?* Have the questions been asked of the right person in the right way such that no bias or ambiguity has been introduced?
4. *Was there any interviewer bias?* Let us assume the questionnaire itself was bias free. Was the way in which the interviewer asked the questions free from any subtle forms of bias?
5. *Were there any data preparation errors?* Have any errors crept into the process of encoding the survey information, preparing the subsequent computer analysis and producing the final tabulations?

6. *Were there any presentation and/or reporting errors?* When the data were reworked, reduced and analysed prior to the preparation of the presentation (and report), did any errors creep into this process?
7. *Were there any interpretation flaws resulting in 'unsafe' decisions?* Is the interpretation that has been placed on the data likely to mislead the decision-maker into a flawed decision?

So let us move to the first of our seven checks: identifying fundamental flaws in the overall design of the survey.

✓ Check 1: are there any design flaws?

Ask the following questions to establish whether the design of a survey is sufficiently robust to meet the decision-making requirements.

- *Failure to provide fitness-to-purpose.* Is the study design commensurate with the problem? For example, evidence is being produced that will be hotly debated in the public domain by individuals with little experience of surveys, so a more robust, easy to comprehend research design is needed than when looking at low profile issues to be reviewed by survey specialists within a company.
- *Appropriate choice of data collection method.* The data collection method selected – face-to-face, telephone, self-completion and/or Internet – should be appropriate to the research study. Above we have already briefly reviewed the strengths and limitations of each method. It is important to check that the person who designed the study has not opted for a method that is going to introduce bias and/or only a partial understanding of the problem at hand.
- *Inadequate scope.* In reviewing Insight 3 (see Chapter 2) we learnt that *context is everywhere and is 'everything'*. Given this, not surprisingly it is important to take into account whether the survey data have been cast on the appropriate canvas. For example, a study about attitudes towards use of computers in the *work context* will – given what we know about the growing use of computers in the *home* and *leisure* environments – provide only a partial account of an individual's overall familiarity with, and expertise in using, computers.

- *Wrong or partial focus.* It is important to check whether the research focuses on the appropriate audience(s). Let us take the example of an evaluation of a trade exhibition about photographic equipment. Clearly, obtaining the views of those who *exhibited* is important in assessing the overall effectiveness of the event as a business generation tool. But a survey that did not assess the views of *visitors* to the exhibition will have failed to capture the opinions of a group instrumental to any assessment of the success of the event.
- *Too shallow.* In some situations a *description* of a particular market is all that is required for the decision-maker to feel that the information is of value. For instance, if an American firm that is considering entering the UK legal publishing market is provided with a comprehensive descriptive *map* of the UK market for legal books – what the key titles purchased by barristers and solicitors are – this could provide an extremely helpful start point for the company. However, such a description could be deemed too shallow for a company that is already well along the descriptive learning curve, and as such is looking for a study that goes beyond simply describing and must start to *explain* in depth some of the complex dynamics of the UK market, such as why in-house company solicitors read different books from those working in practices.
- *Too imprecise.* Another potential design flaw for a survey is for it to generate statistics that must be interpreted within a margin of error that is too broad for the decision-maker. For example, an organisation that wanted a 'steer' on whether or not to introduce a new on-line electronic weather information service for farmers would be satisfied with survey evidence saying that between 60% and 80% of farmers expressed interest. But, if the manager of a hotel was told that between 60% and 80% of his customers were satisfied with their stay, he would want to know whether the true figure was closer to the upper or lower estimate. It could be argued that if eight in ten hotel visitors were satisfied, then comparatively minor adjustments to the current service need to be considered. But if only six in ten hotel visitors were satisfied, then much more draconian action is probably warranted.
- *Lacks realism.* Studies that simply seek feedback about the 'ideal' product or service – where, at no point, is the customer asked to acknowledge the commercial realities of price, and so on – can be

naive and entirely unhelpful. In some scenarios, establishing what would constitute the 'ideal' service could provide helpful insights into developing future strategy. However, it would, for instance, be unhelpful for a parcel carrier to know that customers would 'ideally' like parcels delivered within an hour, for under £1. In this situation it is preferable to present different *trade-offs* in order to establish a *realistic* product feature or service/price offer.

- *Frame of reference.* Market research can only operate within frames of references that are familiar to respondents. Today, we can ask respondents about radio, TV, cable, satellite, DVD and other new multi-media products. But at the turn of the last century, when radio technology was first invented and used for transmitting morse code from one specific point to the other, it would have been unrealistic to expect respondents, given their existing frame of reference, to comment on the idea of 'broadcasting' news, music and sport via radio signals – this was technology they barely knew existed.

- *Causes and inferences.* The decision-maker needs to be aware of the fact that the vast majority of surveys provide *inferential* insights, rather than tightly pinpointing the exact *cause* of a particular event. It is rare for surveys to deploy experimental designs that include 'treatment' and 'control' groups in order to isolate the key variable under investigation. So beware of surveys that may be *overclaiming* what it is possible to definitively conclude by just relying on the survey data.

Check 2: is the sample representative?

The next issue to review is the extent to which the survey is representative of the wider universe it claims to represent. For example, if the aim is to discuss safety at football grounds with a *representative* sample of football supporters, then a sampling procedure that over-represented the supporters of London sides at the expense of teams in the North, would clearly be questionable. The key questions to ask are:

- What sampling method was employed? Was it a *probability* or a *quota-*based sample?
- Were the *appropriate procedures* for the preferred sampling method adhered to?

- Were appropriate decisions made about the *size of the sample*, such that the results will provide robust evidence.

We look at each of these three issues below.

An overview on the two key sample methods: probability and quota

The overwhelming majority of *commercial* research conducted throughout the world employs – for cost and practical reasons – *quota* rather than *probability* methods. However, it is helpful to understand how probability sampling works. This creates the yardstick against which to evaluate just how close the particular sampling method that was eventually employed came to this ideal.

Probability sampling This involves ensuring that each individual (or firm) in a sample has an equal (or to be precise *known*) chance of inclusion. This seems simple enough, but meeting this condition means that the researcher must follow a number of steps that are often difficult to adhere to in practice. First, the researcher must locate an appropriate *sampling frame*: a list of all the people, firms – let's call them *units* – in the population under investigation. This sampling frame must be up to date, have no omissions, be free from duplication and be freely available to the researcher. From this (best possible) sampling frame, the next task is to select the individuals (or firms) to be included in the study. With probability sampling, only the *selected* units are eligible for the study – no substitutes must be taken. Where a *unit* cannot be included, this interview would have to be declared as part of the 'non-response' to the survey. The next task is to ensure that interviews are conducted with a minimum of (ideally) 65% of the population under investigation.

Questions to ask about probability sampling:
- Was a sampling frame used whereby all the people you wanted to talk to were included in this frame?
- Was the sampling method used to select people from this sampling frame (or list) one that gave everybody an equal (or known) chance of inclusion?

- Of the people designated to take part in the survey, did 65% or more of them actually agree to take part and give an interview (if not, has an explanation been given of how the failure to reach this target level may affect the interpretation of the results?).

Meeting the above demands of probability sampling places quite heavy demands on time and budget. Identifying an appropriate sampling frame is not always easy, and it can be difficult to achieve a 65% response rate. For these reasons, in a high proportion of cases market researchers do not use probability sampling, but turn to alternative sampling methods, the most common of which is 'quota sampling'.

Quota sampling   This involves the researcher first obtaining up-to-date information about the population (or universe) under investigation. From this description the researcher sets *quotas* to reflect the characteristics of the target universe. For example, for a consumer sample this would typically involve specifying the number of individuals that are required by region, gender, age, socio-economic group, and so on. For business-to-business research, the quotas will typically be set by type of company, e.g. by standard industrial classification (SIC code); the company size (either turnover or number of employees); and geographical area. The quotas are usually *interlocked*; that is, the interviewer has to contact people with a view to finding individuals who meet a *combination* of the quota criteria, e.g. males who are aged between 45 and 54 *and* also fall into the AB C1 socio-economic groups.

Quota sampling is predicated on the idea that the *haphazard* way in which interviewers initially contact people in order to *fill* their quotas will approximate the *true* random probability procedures outlined above. With quota sampling – notwithstanding the interlocking procedure – there is always a danger of a slight bias towards respondents who are available for, and predisposed towards the idea of, a market research interview. This stands in sharp contrast to the probability method where, once an individual or firm has been randomly selected for an interview, *only* this person (or firm) can be interviewed, with no substitutes being allowed. But on a reassuring note, various experimental studies have shown that quota sampling usually produces results that approximate those that would have been obtained via the probability method. Thus, although quota sampling does not enjoy the rigorous theoretical under-pinning of probability sampling, it is regularly used by market researchers and does *work* in practice. (Subject to the caveat that the principles of professionally executed quota sampling must be adhered to.)

Questions to ask about quota sampling:

- Was an up-to-date and accurate description of the universe under investigation used to set the quotas?
- Were the quotas set the appropriate ones to ensure a representative sample? For example, if you are researching attitudes towards gamb-ling, it would be preferable to set quotas in terms of sub-groups known to be related to gambling, possibly income level, rather than just by age, gender and geographical location.
- Was the selection procedure – the way by which the quotas were applied – sufficiently rigorous such that the study did not just include individuals for whom it was comparatively 'easy' for the interviewers to encourage to take part e.g. people who do not work who are at home a lot? A rigorous study will be one that also includes harder-to-access individuals, such as young, professional workers who do a lot of international travelling.

Sampling structure

There is a range of issues associated with the way a sample is structured. This takes us into quite complex territory. Here we only touch on the key issues in broad outline. Above, we have referred to the idea of a sample statistic being accurate to within an error margin. We have explained that this error margin is largely determined by the size of the sample from which the statistic was drawn. However, this sampling error is also a function of two other key factors which we discuss below, namely stratification and clustering.

Stratification   In structuring a sample it is good practice to organise (or stratify) the sampling frame – that is the lists used to draw sample respondents – in a way that guarantees that the sample will represent key segments of the population. For example, if we know the proportion of people who live in the North East, as opposed to the South East and so on, it is sensible to organise our sample into strata (all of the individuals living in the North East or South East and so on), and then select our sample (apply the sampling interval) *within* each of these strata. By following this process for other strata – where it is possible to organise the sampling lists in this way – we can build in further guarantees about the accuracy of the sample. This means that we guarantee having the right proportion of the sample by the stratum chosen. This process *reduces* the size of the sampling error because it reduces the chances of drawing a 'fluke' sample by chance.

Clustering   The second issue is the degree to which the sample is *clustered*. Theoretically, once a representative sample has been selected, interviewers should interview all these respondents wherever they fall geographically. In practice, the extra costs associated with sending interviewers to far-flung corners of the country is often not justified by the increases in accuracy that this counsel of perfection provides. Thus, typically, in most (at least) face-to-face surveys, the sample will be structured around various sampling points or clusters. The general principle is clear. The process of moving from a totally *unclustered* sample to a more practical *clustered* interviewing design will *increase* the sampling error. Thus, the survey designer is attempting to strike the optimum balance between introducing clustering in order to save interviewer travelling costs, while at the same time not dramatically increasing the sampling error. This process of introducing stratification (which reduces sampling error) and clustering (which increases sampling error) necessitates adjustment of the sampling error estimates that would be generated by assuming we had taken a 'pure' random sample, in order to take into account these two factors. The difference between the sampling errors that would be calculated using the simple random sample formula for calculating a sampling error (based on an unclustered, non-stratified sample) and actually what happens with clustered and stratified sampling designs, is referred to as the *design effect*.

Optimum interviewer allocation   A further factor of which the reader needs to be aware centres on decisions taken about the optimum number of *interviewers* that need to be deployed on a particular survey. We have already explained about the concept of *interviewer variability* – the fact that it is possible for two different interviewers asking the *same* question of the same respondent to get slightly different answers. Given what we know about interviewer variability, on certain large-scale sample surveys, the research design should be informed by what the methodological literature tells us about the optimum allocation of interviewers for different sizes of sample.

Following the appropriate sampling procedures

A central issue to monitor is the extent to which there is any 'sample bias'.

Avoiding sample bias   Many inexperienced users of survey research consider that estimating the *sampling error* associated with a particular survey statistic – the error margin within which we must interpret the statistic – is the only aspect of survey accuracy that needs to be checked. Nothing could be farther from the truth. In most research the most critical issue is the risk of *sample bias*. There are two aspects to this.

1. *Sampling frame deficiencies.* The first possible form of sample bias centres on the fact that even when a 'pure' probability-based sampling method has been employed, it is quite possible that the sampling frame for this project contained certain deficiencies that could seriously bias the resulting data. For instance, if a sample was drawn from a robust sampling source, such as the (UK's) Electoral Registers, even this frame would be deficient in adequately researching 18-year-olds, i.e. those about to vote for the first time. Thus, if the study is for a fashion company focusing on 18- and 19-year-olds, up to one-third of young people might not appear on what, otherwise, would be an extremely robust sample source. Similarly, with quota sampling there could be biases introduced because the original sources upon which the interviewers' quotas were based were in fact out of date.

2. *Non-response.* The second – and more important – bias that can creep into the survey process is non-response bias. This is a major issue for many surveys. Many decision-makers will think that simply

because they have a large number of responses to a survey they have a robust survey. But this large number of responders to a survey could be a highly 'self-selected' sample that is not reflective of the overall universe. An example of this are the 'polls' that often appear in the 'lifestyle' magazines and TV phone-in programmes which ask the reader or viewer for a vote on who is the 'greatest musician of all time', and so on. Even though thousands – even millions – may respond, the poll could still be heavily skewed towards a particular age group, social class group, or those with a particular musical inclination. This explains why an interview survey with a million plus responses on 'Musicians of the Millennium' put Madonna ahead of Aretha Franklin (not to mention Beethoven!). Surveys of this kind – where there is such a large amount of self-selection – are extremely unsafe for (more serious) decision-making.

It is important for data users to be clear about the terms used by research suppliers when they refer to the 'response rates' on their surveys. It is an area of much confusion. Strictly speaking, the term 'response rate' should only be used for *probability*-based samples that start life with a list of respondents (or organisations) to be interviewed. In Table 4.1 we provide a description of the way in which the response rate on such a probability based sample should be presented.

We know from a body of empirical evidence that – with probability samples – response rates of 65% or more mean that the attitudes and behaviour of those taking part in a survey will reflect the attitudes and behaviour of those who have not. Another way of putting this is to say that once a response rate of 65% or over has been achieved, fairly random factors – that are unrelated to the topic under investigation – tend to explain co-operation and non-co-operation in the survey. However, as the response rate drifts down below 65%, there is the chance that those who have taken part in the survey could be different from those who have not taken part. Or to put this another way, it means that factors relating to the very issue one is trying to measure could begin to explain non-co-operation in the survey. For example, if only people who have managed to get a job after leaving college took part in a survey on what they thought about their university, the survey would provide a flattering account of what ex-students think of the university, because those who

Table 4.1 *Defining survey response rate*

● Number of individuals/organisations issued for interview	100	

● Number of individuals/organisations deemed as ineligible because no longer at address/in business	10	
● Effective sample issued	90 = 100%	

	(No.)	100 %
● Number of individuals who were not contactable	10	11
● Number of individuals who refused	20	22
● Number of individuals who were successfully interviewed	60	67

● Response rate (i.e. achieved interviews as a percentage of effective issued sample)	67%

failed to get a job will presumably vote with their feet and not bother taking part in the survey.

The above account of response rates, as they relate to *probability* samples, is comparatively straightforward. The problem starts when fieldwork companies, which have employed quota sampling methods, describe the 'success' they have had with their interviewing – their 'strike rate' – by (mistakenly) referring to this as a 'response rate'. In order to clarify this point, we have in Table 4.2 mapped out the way in which a 'strike rate' drawn from a quota sample should be presented. Hopefully this makes clear the difference in the way to calculate a *response rate* from a probability sample and the *strike rate* from a quota sample.

Why it is important to distinguish between the 'response rate' and the 'strike rate' is because, as Table 4.2 illustrates, with the strike rate (unlike the true response rate) we have a limited amount (if any) of information about the number of *contacts* that were made in order to achieve the required number of interviews. In some cases not having this information will not be important. But there will be situations where this missing information is extremely critical. For example, in a study about the mobile phone usage of business executives, not knowing that we had *not* made *contact* with a high proportion of those in the *eligible* sample is an important piece of information. This could tell us that we had success- fully conducted the required total number of interviews, but that these

Table 4.2 *The quota sample strike rate*

• Target number of interviews (set in the form of quotas)	100
• Total number of contacts made to achieve quota	Not (always) recorded
• Respondents approached but refused	50
• Respondents successfully interviewed	50
• Strike rate, i.e. total interviews as a percentage of total interviews plus refusals	**50%**

may all have been conducted with the *easy-to-interview* part of the business executive mobile phone market, i.e. those who are less transient, and are not engaged in much domestic or international travel (and, as such, are easier to interview).

What sample size do you need to be confident, within different error margins, about your results?

There are two situations of interest. First, there is the question of drawing samples of the complete, let us say, UK *population*. And secondly, there is the issue of the sample sizes that are required for analysing particular *sub-groups*.

Interpreting statistics from a sample of the total UK population To be comfortable about interpreting a survey statistic drawn from a sample of the overall UK population, as a general rule one is looking for a sample size of around *400 interviews*. This is because the sampling error surrounding any survey statistic reduces significantly, up to approximately 400 interviews. After this point the gains in accuracy to be made become proportionally less great. Thus, a survey statistic of 50%, drawn from a sample of 100, would be accurate within plus or minus 10% (at the 95% level of confidence), whereas a survey statistic of 50% from a sample of 400, at the same level of confidence, will be accurate to within plus or minus 5%. However, had we allocated more resources to increasing the sample to 1000, we would still – for a survey statistic of 50%, at the 95% level of confidence – only achieve an accuracy of plus or minus 3.2%.

Figure 4.1 *Overlapping common evidence*

Interpreting statistics from sample sub-groups   When interpreting a statistic from a sub-group of a sample there are two issues to take into account: the first centres on statistical principles and the second on the issue of taking an 'holistic' approach to understanding the data. From the statistical standpoint, a survey statistic of 50% drawn from a sub-sample of 50 will be accurate to within plus or minus 14% (at the 95% level of confidence). But, in interpreting such a statistic from a more 'holistic' perspective, the following two factors also need to be taken into account.

1. *Overlapping 'common' evidence.* In deciding on the robustness of a statistic drawn from a sub-group sample, it is important to bear in mind that although aspects of a certain sub-group's behaviour and attitude will be distinct from other sub-groups, there will be a certain amount of 'common ground'. For example, as shown in Figure 4.1, a study conducted among people who visited a theme park may show that the sub-group of parents with young children had uniquely different views on many aspects of their experience from individuals visiting the park without children. But, there could be an area of overlap where effectively the results of the two sub-groups are best analysed together, rather than separated out. For example, as indicated in Figure 4.1, this could be views on value for money. Thus, this holistic interpretation needs to be set alongside the statistical evaluation of how to interpret statistics drawn from different sample sub-groups.

2. *Prior knowledge.* In deciding on the robustness of a statistic drawn from a sub-sample, it is also important to take into account to what extent 'prior knowledge' – a wider holistic understanding of the topic

under investigation – will build confidence in interpreting the statistic. For example, statistically speaking it may be the case that the survey indicates that a fairly broad band of between 20% and 40% of mothers with young children thought that the theme park had inadequate facilities for nursing mothers. But this statistic, coupled with let us say a criticism of the facilities for young mothers registered during a recent TV holiday programme's evaluation of the theme park, would suggest that operating with the upper, rather than lower estimate of the extent of dissatisfaction, is the prudent course of action.

☑ *Check 3: did the questionnaire work?*

Most people think that an assessment of whether a questionnaire has worked or not would immediately plunge them into the issue of whether the actual questions being asked were flawed in any way. Question wording is an important area, but first it is important to understand the context in which the questionnaire will be administered and to review the overall nature of the dialogue between interviewer and respondent that is 'set up' by the interview method and questionnaire structure.

Relevance to the respondent

The first issue associated with evaluating a questionnaire centres on whether it was appropriately tailored to the scenario that is the focus of the interview. This is important because some survey questionnaires will give misleading results, not because there was anything fundamentally wrong with the questions asked, but because the subject-matter of the survey was not relevant to the respondent. This is important given what Kelly has taught us about 'understanding the respondent's world'. For example, in a survey on how businesses choose their Internet provider, an interview with an Office Manager may be of limited value because he/she may not be responsible for the decisions taken on IT networks. This may be dealt with by a higher level IT specialist. Building on this point, in researching a 'business' it has to be accepted that frequently one requires data that cannot be obtained from just one person in an organisation. For instance, the person responsible for purchasing photocopiers may not also be able to answer detailed questions about the functionality of the machine. The key issue centres on how to make sensible and pragmatic decisions about interviewing the different players within the *decision-making unit* of the organisation, i.e. those who may have an influence on the purchase decision. These could include the 'gatekeeper' who is responsible for the flow of relevant information into the organisation; it could also include various 'users' of the product to be purchased, and will include various other influencers, including the specialist purchasing personnel and the final decision-maker.

Is the questionnaire structure right?

The next issue to take into account is whether the questionnaire has an appropriate 'structure'. By this we mean does it have the right 'flow and feel'? Is it structured in a way that makes the dialogue between the interviewer and respondent seem natural? Does the questionnaire come close to emulating the way in which a conversation on the topic under investigation would really take place? Does the questionnaire introduce so many non-sequiturs, jumps and breaks that it makes the whole interview experience stilted, unrealistic and prone to error? The concepts of 'length', 'width', 'depth' and 'tone' of a questionnaire are explained below.

- *Length*. The first component of a questionnaire to get right is its length – the time it takes to administer. One needs to construct a dialogue that has a distinct introduction (beginning), core (middle) and conclusion (end). Within each of these parts of the interview, the objectives of the research that have been set have to be met. There is no such thing as a 2-minute interview, because it becomes very difficult to set up a dialogue in this time. Similarly, interviews – even if costs are available – that go beyond 30 to 40 minutes are probably beginning to ramble. (After this point, our ability to concentrate falls away.)
- *Width*. A questionnaire does not just have to have an appropriate 'length', but a manageable 'width', i.e. the number of topics to be covered must be presented in a 'logical' and understandable way. If a

'grasshopper' structure is attempted where the respondent must rapidly switch from one topic to another this may cover a wide spectrum of topics, but it will have a disruptive effect: respondents will get irritated and provide less information and of poorer quality.

- *Depth*. Every questionnaire must also be pitched at the appropriate 'depth' – striking the right balance between being too shallow or too deep. There are two ways of defining depth. One way is to regard it as the amount of technical detail required. For example, in a business interview, we might look in *depth* at the finances of a company. The second way is to see depth as a 'psychological or emotional' dimension; in this sense, 'deep' topics are those that involve exploring emotive issues and teasing out deeply-held beliefs.
- *Tone and balance*. It is also important to ensure that the questionnaire has the right 'tone' and 'balance'. By 'balance' we mean the right combination of more rigorous, detailed, in-depth questioning, as opposed to lighter, more general, context-setting questions. By 'tone' we are referring to the fact that, as people are usually freely giving their time in an interview, it is important to keep the interview interesting, engaging, with possibly even introducing an element of fun to it. In fact, making an interview rewarding and good fun is increasingly going to be a feature of interviewing. Today, more and more, busy people are realising that information carries value and, as such, are looking for some personal return from having contributed to the market research process.

To sum up, one of the key factors in determining whether a questionnaire will 'work', i.e. deliver comprehensive and robust information, centres on whether it has the right 'structure'. In short, the questionnaire must not be too long, boring, un-interesting and/or intense. The aim should be to strike the right balance between length, depth and tone. Generally speaking this will make for an engaging *dialogue* between the respondent and the interviewer. Beware of questionnaires written by someone who feels he/she has a divine right to ask a series of tedious, non-salient questions of fellow human beings, with no concession to the realities of people's level of interest, concentration and so on. In particular, beware the questionnaire that involves administering mindless batteries of attitude scales. If the questionnaire has been set up as an interesting dialogue, rather than as a chore to the respondent, then the chances are that it will produce truthful answers. But if not, your data could be quite 'flaky' in the sense that they will not really have captured the 'truth'.

Were any of the questions flawed in any way?

We now arrive at the issue of whether any of the questions in the survey were themselves flawed: were any of them ambiguous, misleading or unlikely to get to the 'truth' of the matter? Below, we provide a 24-point list of issues to 'check out' about any survey questionnaire. The format of the checklist is straightforward. We outline the key principle and then give (typically) a couple of examples of where an 'error' has been committed, which should provide ideas on how, at the design stage of a survey, these errors can be avoided. We also provide clues as to how the interpretation of the data resulting from flawed questioning needs to be interpreted to offset the biases caused by the framing of the question.

The 24 point 'ask a silly question' checklist

1. *Make sure each question falls within the respondent's frame of reference*. It is important that a respondent can immediately relate to the overall context in which the question is posed.

   Examples:
   Q. What would you do if your neighbours constantly held loud parties? [Asked of farmer with no neighbours for four miles.]
   Q. Would you describe yourself as a solipsistic primarily in the classical, existentialist sense, or as an expression of post-modern ironic comment? [Asked of West Ham supporter!]

2. *Do not cast respondents in an unfamiliar role*. There will be issues on which the respondent will be able to offer a view, but sometimes the question will cast the respondents in a totally unfamiliar role in which they have little grounded experience.

   Examples:
   Q. Car crime is at an all time high. Do you feel those that are found guilty of breaking into cars should be made to pay their victims

compensation? [Asked of a non-car owner with no experience of the success and failure of different punishments.]

Q. Do you think the UK should stop insisting on UK nationals travelling abroad carrying a passport, and instead, switch over to an identity card system? [Asked of an individual who has never travelled abroad and has no experience of the practicalities of introducing and maintaining an effective ID card system.]

3. *Avoid questions where the respondent feels they have something to prove or say about themselves.* Sometimes respondents will not be willing to give a factually correct answer to a question because he/she desires to give what he/she believes to be the 'real truth' about himself. This can happen with high interest subjects. For instance, a person who is a major business buyer of computers is asked whether he/she has bought a computer in the past month. For various unusual reasons, the exact answer to this question at this moment in time is 'no'. But this person may wish to send out a signal about his/her overall involvement in buying in computers and do this by communi-cating his/her 'usual behaviour'. Therefore, this person may elect to give a 'yes' to this question. This is not done out of perversity or malevolence, but in an attempt to be helpful. But, this would under-mine the validity of a survey estimate of the level of computer pur-chases over a typical month. (A valid estimate would be one in which the atypical monthly purchasing behaviour by one person would be ironed out by counter-balancing the atypical behaviour in the other direction by another person.)

Examples:

Q. Have you, in the past four weeks, purchased the new computer-based navigation system that can be directly linked into your Global Positioning System (GPS)? [Asked of a yachtsman who is parti-cularly interested in navigation, and although has not purchased the new system, is interested in learning more and feels that by saying 'yes' he will be led further into a topic of interest.]

Q. On the last occasion you threw out glass, beer and wine bottles, did you put them in the environmental glass disposal unit provided by the Council, or dispose of them in the household waste? [Asked of a member of the Green Party who, for a particular, unusual reason, did not, on the last occasion, use the environmental glass disposal unit, but feels they should answer 'yes' because this would better typify the kind of person they are.]

4. *Be cautious in asking hypothetical questions*. These are questions that force the respondent to answer questions to which they are unlikely to have given any prior consideration.

Examples:

Q. If the quarantine laws has been relaxed earlier so you could take your dog overseas, would you have visited Belgium last summer instead of going to the Lake District?

Q. If you had to pay £100 to cross the M25 motorway and enter London, do you think you would continue to use your car as regularly as you do now or not?

5. *Beware of politeness bias*. When taking part in a survey most people try to be 'nice'. As the following examples illustrate, the way a study is introduced will have a marked affect on the answers that are given to specific questions.

Examples:

Q. I am conducting a study on behalf of the BBC. Do you mind telling me whether or not, on balance, you prefer BBC 2 to Channel 5?

Q. I am conducting a survey on drug addiction on behalf of the Metropolitan Police. Could you tell me whether you have ever, in the course of the last five years, had reason to take any form of addictive drug? (Introducing drugs in this context is different from explaining that the study is being conducted, for example, on behalf of a Hospital Drug Addiction Unit.)

6. *Beware the devious use of pretext*. The way in which information is released *prior* to the asking of a question will affect the answers given to a particular question. This phenomenon will be well known to devotees of the television programme *Yes Minister*. In a famous sketch Sir Humphrey, the Permanent Secretary, explained to the Prime Minister how, through the use of pretext, you could 'get any answer you wanted from a survey'. The gist of the point is that if

you ask the following question: 'Are you in favour of Britain re-introducing national service for young men aged 18 to 23 or not?', you will secure different results depending on which of the following two pretexts are used to introduce the question:

> Pretext A: *it is argued that the discipline of national service could help reduce levels of crime among young people . . . are you in favour of Britain re-introducing national service for young men aged 18 to 23 or not?*
>
> Pretext B: *it is argued that forcing national service on young people will be seen as unnecessary authoritarian intervention likely to have a disruptive affect on the formative stage of young men's careers . . . are you in favour of Britain re-introducing national service for young men aged 18 to 23 or not?*

Another example of where the importance of pretext is also critical to the following question:

Q. Do you think Britain should admit immigrants into the UK or not?

> Pretext A: *most countries in the world have some kind of restriction on immigration . . . do you think Britain should admit immigrants into the UK or not?*
>
> Pretext B: *Britain has always had a liberal approach to admitting immigrants to our country . . . do you think Britain should admit immigrants into the UK or not?*

7. *Apply judgement with sensitive questions.* Delivered with the right amount of professionalism and set in the right context, there probably are no taboo questions for surveys. But if the survey has *not* been presented in an appropriate context, then some questions will be unlikely to produce truthful responses. Some examples of where the lack of an appropriate context are critical is shown below:

Q. How many times in a typical week do you take stimulants, including caffeine products designed to give you boosts of energy?

Q. Have you had a sexual relationship outside of your marriage in the last five years?

8. *Always question underlying assumptions.* Questions should not be asked if they are founded on a critical, questionable assumption.

   Examples:
   Q. Where did you buy that tie? [Assumes that the tie was purchased, not received as a gift.]
   Q. Do you think there should be more or less time devoted to sports coverage on your local TV channel? [This assumes that the respondent evaluates sport on TV purely in terms of the *quantity* of sport, i.e. it denies the respondent the opportunity to talk about *quality*.]

9. *Avoid abstract and vague questions.* People are not good at responding to questions that encourage them to generalise.

   Examples:
   Q. Would you say London is a good or bad place in which to live?
   Q. Would you say that Americans have a better, the same or less of a sense of humour than the British?

10. *Avoid leading questions.* Most people will be familiar with the leading question, i.e. one that edges the respondent in a particular direction, and therefore introduces a bias.

    Examples:
    Q. Most people thought their visit to the Tower of London was exciting. Do you agree with this?
    Q. How do you think the Liberal Democratic Party should go about exposing the Tories' failures?

11. *Avoid biased questions.* The biased question is a slightly softer variant of the more overt leading question. It is a question that will contain certain wording that could subtly lead the respondent towards a particular (desired) type of answer.

    Examples:
    Q. When you were thinking about acquiring this machine, which other brands did you consider as possible alternatives? [Assumes respondent did consider alternatives.]

Q. Do you think the Labour Party should celebrate its 100 years as a party by building a statue, or by using the money to help various good causes? [Assumes that everybody wishes formally to celebrate the 100th birthday.]

12. *Make sure your questions are balanced.* Building on the idea of avoiding asking leading questions is the issue of the bias introduced by questions not being even-handed.

Q. Do you think the UK should adopt the Single European Currency?

Should read:

Q. Do you think the UK should adopt a single European currency, *or not*?

Q. Do you like your job?

Should read:

Q. Do you like or dislike your job?

13. *Do not employ questions that sell under the guise of research.* There has been a growing tendency (in some cases quite unwittingly) for organisations to promote themselves during the course of a survey (allegedly) aimed at establishing unbiased attitudes towards their organisation.

Example:

Q. I am going to read out a series of benefits that individuals who are members of the (name Institute) receive. Would you tell me whether each of these benefits is of interest to you or not? [This question may seem innocent enough, but it is imparting key information, i.e. the benefits of membership of this body in a way that could contaminate the answers to subsequent questions.]

14. *Always ensure there is total clarity: use precise definitions.*

Examples:

Q. Does your household have a garage in which you can park a car? [Does a garage include a covered standing areas, i.e. a car port? How does the interviewer code situations where the household has a garage, but because it is being used to store other materials it cannot currently be used to park a car and so on?]

Q.   Do you, yourself, own a car? [This does not define car. Does this include the following: three-wheeled vehicles; vehicles that are currently not taxed and kept off the road; cars that are still being paid for on credit, etc.?]

15. *Avoid any ambiguous wording.* Ascertain that the interviewer and respondent are talking about the same thing.

Examples:

Q.   Do you think it should be made easier for people to get on to their local council? ['Get onto' has two meanings: 'to complain to', and 'to become a member of'.]

Q.   What was the length of your residence in Australia? [Asked of returning immigrant who gives his answer not in years, but in terms of feet!]

16. *Do not use unfamiliar words.* Many comparatively 'ordinary' words, such as 'sanguine' and 'assuage', will not be understood by a large proportion of the population.

Examples:

Q.   How much discount, if any, was given when you last made purchases of over £100 at Debenhams? [Exactly how is discount defined?]

Q.   Do you think the Highways Authority should use more chevrons to indicate sharp bends on UK roads? [Many will not know that a chevron is the term used for a set of 'sideways' arrows.]

17. *Beware of asking questions that are too detailed.* There are a number of occasions where the data required are so detailed that the respondent, however willing, will be unable to provide answers because they are too trivial or too intricate.

Examples:

Q.   What is the wattage of the electric light bulbs in each of your rooms in your house?

Q.   Exactly what time each morning of the week does your milkman deliver your milk?

18. *Avoid over-complicated questions.* In order to add precision, questions can end up being quite long-winded, resulting in the respondent being unable to grasp the essential content.

Examples:

Q. If the price of the new bendable scratch-resistant polycarbonate sheet was $10 per square metre for 5 mm thickness, $12 for 8 mm thickness, and $15 for 10 mm thickness, compared with an industry average for non-bendable, non-scratch-resistant poly-carbonate sheet (but with better transparency) of $11 per square metre for 7.5 mm thickness, how likely would you be to buy it?

Q. Does your establishment have a central reprographic depart-ment: by this I mean, a printing or copying department which services other departments in the establishment, and which has at least one full time employee, and makes at least 10 000 copies or prints per month?

19. *Do not ask two questions in one.* This is very common with attitude questions, but also occurs with factual questions.

Examples:

Q. Are your two major suppliers British? (This does not allow for one being British and one not.)

Q. Are you satisfied with the price and quality offered by the supermarket at which you regularly shop? [Price and quality are different concepts.]

20. *Avoid double concepts.* Slightly different from the sin of asking two questions in one is the error of asking for levels of agreement or disagreement with concepts that, on closer inspection, sub-divide into two quite separate elements.

Examples:

Q. Do you agree or disagree with the following statement?
    People will live longer if they do not smoke cigarettes and cigars. (Cigarette and cigar smoking carry different health risks.)

Q. Do you agree or disagree with the following statement?
    A good Prime Minister must have ideas and know how to carry them out. (This is difficult to answer for a Prime Minister who has great ideas, but is weak in executing them.)

21. *Avoid double negatives.* This always confuses even the most intelligent of respondents.

Examples:

Q. Do you agree or disagree with the following statement?
    There are no suppliers with which we would not do business?

Q. Do you agree or disagree with the following statement?
    Offenders over the age of 50 should not be allowed not to do community service.

22. *Avoid feats of memory.* It is clearly poor practice to phrase questions that defy what we know about the human memory.

Examples:

Q. How many times in the last five years have you visited Sainsbury's and spent over £25?

Q. When did your business acquire its first staple gun?

23. *Avoid arithmetic concepts.* Even respondents in business-to-business surveys can be bemused when arithmetic concepts, such as 'percentage' and 'proportions', are used.

Examples:

Q. What proportion of your weekly pay goes on your mortgage payments?

Q. What percentage of your time do you spend watching television each week?

24. *Check out any schoolperson howlers.* Silly mistakes and sloppiness can also lead to catastrophically incorrect survey results.

Examples:

Q. How likely are you to continue buying *The Guardian* if it were 1p [should be 10p] more expensive?

Q. Research has shown that black *cars* are the safest form of any air, sea or land transport. Were you aware of this fact or not? [In fact, black cars, given their lack of visibility are quite dangerous. The 'r' should have been a 'b' to produce black cabs – these are actually the safest form of transport.]

Attitude scaling There is a vast body of literature on the subject of developing and administering attitude scales in surveys. Here, we can raise a few critical issues. The first point to make is that many of the general principles explained above about questionnaire design will apply to the use of attitude scales. The second point is that, in fast moving commercial market research, there is not always time to undertake initial, qualitative developmental work that, in an ideal world, would help in developing particular attitude scales. This means that in many situations market researchers, on the basis of their experience of what has worked for them in the past, will make judgements on how a particular attitude scale should be structured. Invariably, these judgements will be reasonably well informed. Market researchers, over the years, have built up a solid understanding of when it is appropriate to assess attitudes using a five-point, as opposed to a seven-point scale, and so on. But as a data user it is worth asking the researchers supplying your data to run through the rationale underpinning their choice and format of attitude scale.

The attention to detail check   Earlier we discussed the importance of attention to detail when conducting surveys. When looking at ways to check the robustness of data we referred to the 'professionalism check'; that is, those little tell-tale signs that indicate whether or not the researcher really does know the 'survey craft'. With regard to question-naire design, there is a specific technique that can be employed to check whether or not the questionnaire was designed professionally. This is a four-point 'universal survey question check'. It involves asking, for *every single question* on the survey, the following:

- Is it clear *who* should be asked this question?
- Could you *answer the question yourself*?
- Is it clear *how the interviewer should record the answer*, e.g. write in, circle code, etc.
- Is it clear which question the interviewer *goes to next*, having asked the earlier question?

If these four questions are asked at *every* survey question, the 'mechanics' of the questionnaire will immediately be tightened up.

We now look at the next check of the robustness of the survey – whether the interaction between the interviewer and the respondent had any undue affect on the answers being given.

Check 4: was there any interviewer bias?

We have looked at the way in which a respondent's answers can be distorted by faulty memory; embarrassment about sensitive topics; a tendency to exaggerate in certain scenarios; and other biases resulting from the way in which questions are contextualised and worded. But in addition to these biases there are other features of the dialogue taking place between the respondent and the interview that can lead to bias. The fact that interviewers can influence the responses given by the respondent is, as already indicated, referred to by market researchers as 'interviewer variability'. Given this, it becomes important for those responsible for undertaking surveys to do everything they can to minimise this type of bias. On the one hand, interviewers must attempt to establish an easy, pleasant relationship with respondents. But it is also important that interviewers in (standardised) surveys do everything possible to avoid giving the respondent 'clues' about their own attitudes or expectations, or say anything about their own background.

The professional interviewer will always ask all the questions in a neutral, straightforward way and record the answers in the same way. Any (self-disclosure) of information about the interviewer could encourage the respondent to *tailor* what it is he/she is reporting to them. So interviewers are trained to encourage the interview to flow, but to be mindful of the fact that they themselves must not introduce a 'bias'. For example, as we have said, respondents' answers can be distorted by the accent and other personal characteristics of the interviewer. For instance, in normal conversation, we know that people will adjust what they tell another person according to what they think that person wants or expects to hear. Such responses are quite commonplace in smoothing social relationships. But this tendency of people to adapt what they are saying in order to accommodate the interviewer is extremely dangerous in the context of a survey interview. Thus, market researchers are trained not to get involved in extraneous discussions prior, or during, the interview about their own family circumstances, where they live, and so on. If the interviewer answers these apparently innocuous, simple questions, it is possible that this may lead the respondent to change or modify his/her subsequent answers. Similarly, if asked their views on unfamiliar subjects, respondents may often reply by asking interviewers what they think. The danger is obvious. A note of surprise or disbelief, or an over-sympathetic reaction may easily affect respondents' subsequent answers. But consistently showing no reaction – other than uniform, polite interest – requires considerable concentration and effort. Even apparently trivial reactions can affect answers. For example, following a respondent's reply with the word 'good' can introduce a bias in subsequent answers. Interviewers have to find ways of encouraging the respondent to talk without this gravitating towards a discussion of the interviewer's views or circumstances.

The good news is that the professional survey researcher can offset much potential source of bias through careful questionnaire design (and skilful interviewing). Even the most professional of surveys will not wholly counteract biases of this kind, but a lot can be done to minimise their effect.

Practical solutions   Thus, the degree to which an interviewer can affect the results given by a respondent can be largely overcome through comprehensive interviewer training and good ongoing survey practice: the use of clear, well written interviewer instructions, piloting, quality control checks and the like. There could be some deep-seated chemistry that may be set up between an interviewer and a respondent that could 'contaminate' the responses given. But, in the overwhelming majority of cases, if the interviewer goes through a proper training programme during which he/she is told how to deliver standardised questions in a fairly objective way, and how not to get involved in gratuitous conversation, to a large degree the problem of 'interviewer bias' will be eliminated. Added to this, precision when drafting the questionnaire wording – including providing interviewers with definitions about different terms – will help ensure that all interviewers work from the same 'hymn sheet'. In this way, the extent to which 'interviewer variability' will contaminate the survey results will be minimised.

☑ *Check 5: were there any data preparation errors?*

It is important that the processing of the data by the computer has not distorted the true meaning of the original data. Here, there are 12 points to check.

Twelve-point checklist of data preparation errors

1. *Table labelling errors.* Incorrect labelling can massively influence the interpretation placed on data. For example, as illustrated in Table 4.3, the failure to correctly label the exact status of 'brand awareness' – not explaining that is was *prompted, not spontaneous* – is critically important.

Table 4.3   *Incorrect table labelling*

Awareness of Fiasco supermarket		Spontaneous and prompted awareness of Fiasco supermarket	
Base	200	Base	200
		Awareness:	
Aware	80%	Spontaneous	40%
Not aware	20%	Prompted	40%
		Total	**80%**
		Not aware	20%

2. *Table legend categorisation errors.* Differences between the way information was categorised in the original questionnaire and then subsequently grouped in the computer tabulations could change our understanding of what the data are telling us. In Figure 4.2, the decisions made about how to allocate the 'fairly satisfieds' (code 3) make a marked difference to the satisfaction picture.

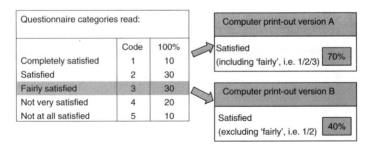

Figure 4.2   *Questionnaire and coding categorisation errors*

3. *Analysis breakdown category errors.* It is important to look at the original distribution of the data to establish whether the way an analysis sub-group has been created conceals something of importance. For example, in Table 4.4 the decision to group together 18 to

34-year-olds seems sensible, given the limited range of their views on 'Besto'. However, the decision to group individuals aged between 55 and 65+ is problematic. An inspection of the distribution here tells us that attitudes are markedly different amongst the 55 to 64-year-olds (who like this product) and the over 65-year-olds (who do not).

Table 4.4 *Cross analysis tabulation breakdown errors*

Preference for Besto		Analysis across breakdowns		
Age	%			
18–24	45	18–34	35–54	55–65+
25–34	55			
35–44	59	Range:	Range:	Range:
45–54	62	45–55%	59–62%	10–70%
55–64	70			
65+	10			

4. *Coarse open-ended coding.* A coarse approach to grouping the open-ended verbatim comments into aggregate groups for subsequent computer analysis is another potential source of misinterpretation. For example, as shown in Table 4.5, at first glance, a hotel customer satisfaction survey that shows that 87% of visitors registered a complaint about the quality of the food is a cause for alarm. But an inspection of the way in which the overall 'complained about the food category' has been derived shows us that the hotel clearly has a problem with its *room service*, but is performing acceptably with regard to its restaurant and snack bar services.

Table 4.5 *Coarse open-ended coding data loss errors*

Category on computer print out	% of all visitors		Questionnaire categories	% of all visitors
		Derived		
Complaints about food	87%	from:	• Room service	85
			• Hotel restaurant	5
			• Snack bar	4

5. *Precision in labelling who was asked a particular question.* The left-hand part of Figure 4.3 gives the reader the impression that the Quest Motor Company enjoys an excellent image. But the question labelling

flatters the support for Quest. More precise labelling tells us that these are ratings for individuals who have *purchased* brand-new cars from Quest within the last three months.

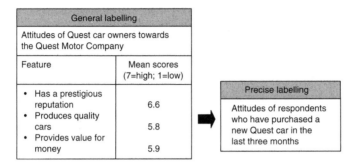

Figure 4.3   *Labelling of bases*

6. *Means without a full distribution.* In Table 4.6 we show two distributions, each with the same mean. But if the decision-maker were operating with *just the mean*, clearly he/she would get a distorted picture of what the mean score for the polarised distribution was really telling him/her. So, it is important to ensure that measures of location are accompanied by an indicator of the nature of the distribution that accompanies the central location measure.

Table 4.6   *Meaningless mean*

(a) Even			(b) Polarised		
Attitude scale		No.	Attitude scale		No.
High	7	0	High	7	80
	6	0		6	70
	5	60		5	60
	4	320		4	0
	3	30		3	60
	2	0		2	70
Low	1	10	Low	1	80
Mean		**4.00**	**Mean**		**4.00**

7. *Failure to tell the full 'don't know' and 'not answered' story.* The categorisation *not answered* is used by survey researchers when a

respondent has not been asked a particular survey question. The *don't know* category is reserved for definite confirmation that the person does not know the answer to a particular question. In some situations, differentiating between the *not answered* and *don't know* categories will not be of particular importance. But in other cases, grouping together the *not answereds* and *don't knows* could conceal an important piece of information. For example, let us assume a poll was conducted among members of the general public. Those who were aware that the Conservative Party had held a leadership contest were asked to name who was the new Tory leader. On the left-hand table in Figure 4.4, we learn that 35% fell into the *combined* 'don't knows/not answered' category, i.e. these respondents either were not aware that a leadership contest has taken place, or did not know who won the leadership contest. But on the right, when we separate out those who did not answer the question (because they were not aware of the leadership contest) and the 'don't knows' (i.e. did not know who was leader) we learn the extremely important fact that 33% of those who were aware of the election did not know the name of the current Tory leader.

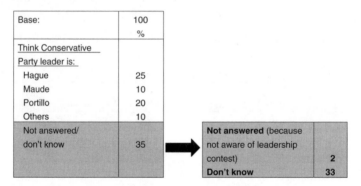

Figure 4.4   *Differentiating between 'not answereds' and 'don't know'*

8. *Capturing the depth of feeling.* In Table 4.7, by merging the top two scale positions, we increase the chance that the decision-maker will fail to understand just how strongly people felt about this issue.

9. *The suppressor effect.* The cross analysis of data of sub-groups, in the majority of cases, will produce a *refining effect*. That is, the analysis will show (comparatively modest) variations by sub-group. However,

Table 4.7   *Capturing the depth of feeling*

Full attitude scale	%	Presented as	%
Very strongly	80		
Strongly	10	Strongly	90
Fairly strongly	5		
Not at all strongly	5	Not strongly	10

in certain situations, a *suppresser effect* could be at work: important variations by a particular sub-group(s) are masked (or suppressed) and will need teasing out. The following example illustrates the point. In Figure 4.5, in part A of the table, the sub-groups suggest that we have a product that is preferred by women, rather than men. However, when we look at part B we can see that this gender breakdown 'suppresses' an age effect. In actual fact, this is a product that is liked by older people, *irrespective of their gender.*

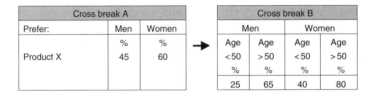

Figure 4.5   *The suppresser effect*

One way to ensure that one does not fall victim to the 'suppressor effect' is to adopt a statistical technique called 'Chaid'. The example in Figure 4.6 illustrates how this technique can be used in credit scoring or making decisions about who is likely to repay a loan and who is not. We will not explain in detail how the technique works here, but a quick inspection of the diagram will illustrate the power and essence of the technique. In the top box we can see that the sample has been classified into the 48% who are good credit risks, and the 52% who are bad credit risks (these are the rounded percentages). The technique then allows us to split the data into different sub-groups, following through a series of analyses in order to tease out how worthiness varies by particular sub-groups. We eventually arrive at an optimum analysis that alerts us to the importance of

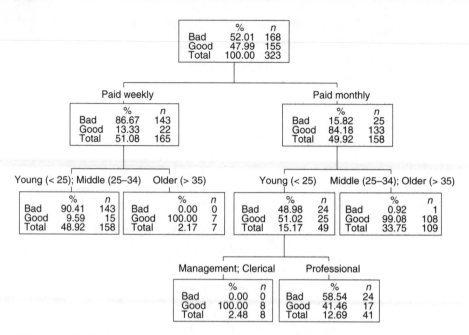

Figure 4.6 *Pinpointing the drivers of attitude and behaviour*

looking at individuals who are paid monthly, are under 25 and who are professional.

10. *Failure to detect the underlying shapes and patterns in data.* Fundamental to the holistic approach to analysing data is the identification of the overall theme(s) contained within data. Below we provide an example of how a series of statistical tests of significance on evidence A through to E might reveal that only one item of evidence is seen as 'significant'. But if we were to look at the same evidence (A to E) in terms of its 'overall (relative) direction', then we can see that these data are providing a helpful insight into which direction to head. We return to the question of analysing data in a holistic fashion later in the book. But in Table 4.8 we provide an example of the essence of this approach to data analysis.

11. *Data not set in their appropriate context.* It is important to understand the context to the answers given to individual *survey questions*. For example, the fact that only 10% of magazine readers responded to a promotional offer could be seen as 'disappointing'. But if this redemption rate is set in the context of similar coupon offers in the magazine, this places the evidence in a different light (see Figure 4.7).

Table 4.8   *Analysing in an 'holistic' fashion*

THE ISSUE: what does the evidence tell us about Sunday newspaper readers' attitudes towards a change in the design and format of their Sunday paper?

KEY QUESTIONS AND CONCLUSIONS

Exclusively statistically led analysis	The holistic approach
• *Approach.* A sample of 400 regular readers of the Sunday newspaper were asked whether they preferred the current or new design for the newspaper. This showed that 52% of the sample favoured changing to the new design and 48% staying with the existing design. • *Analysis and decision.* As there was no statistically significant difference (at the 95% level of confidence) between the two survey statistics, it was deemed reasonable to assume that there was no *preference* for the new design and a decision was therefore taken to stay with the existing design.	• *Approach.* The survey of 400 regular readers set in the context of accompanying qualitative research showed that all those who wanted a change in the paper expressed their views with considerable depth of feeling, whereas those who voted for no change reported that they would not feel at all alienated if a change was made (they would get used to the new format). • An inspection of research conducted five years ago for the same newspaper showed a similar reticence among regular readers to vote for change in a market research study. Later survey evidence then showed that, subsequently, there was a rapid endorsement of the new design, i.e. within a few weeks readers became familiar with the new format. • Also taken into account is an acknowledgement that the new design reflects leading edge design thinking in terms of newspaper design, i.e. other competitors are expected to follow. • *Analysis and decision.* Decision taken, notwithstanding the non-statistically significant survey evidence – based on the above holistic analysis – to take a calculated risk by introducing the new design.

12. *Absence of prior knowledge.* We conclude this series of checks by continuing the theme of looking at *errors of omission* in the way data are presented, rather than *errors of commission.* Below is an example of what can happen if key 'prior knowledge' is omitted from a table. In Table 4.9 we could come to the naive conclusion from Part A that companies in the North West of England (for reasons that cannot be

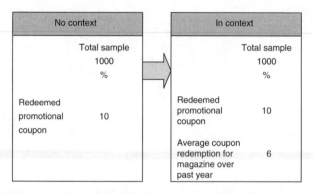

Figure 4.7 *Locating data in their appropriate marketing context*

explained) are massively more committed to the Post Office than companies in the North East. In fact, had the analyst located the relevant prior knowledge, then we could have avoided naively talking up the North West's commitment to the postal service, because we would have known that a high proportion of the UK's mail order companies are located in the North West.

Table 4.9 *Large companies use of postal services by region*

(A) Region	North West	North East	**(B)** Region	North West	North East
Mean expenditure in £s on postal services	£5000	£2000	Mean expenditure in £s on postal services		
			• All companies	£5000	£2000
			• Excluding mail order houses	£2500	£2500

☑ Check 6: were there any presentation and/or reporting errors?

We now identify the key issues that must be taken into account in making a judgement on how well the data have been interpreted, presented and reported. Below, we provide a checklist of key issues in evaluating presentations and/or the reporting of quantitative survey data.

(The first 10 issues relate to tabular survey data. We follow this with a further checklist of 10 points for evaluating graphical representations of the quantitative data.)

1. In Table 4.10, we can see that 80% of women prefer product A, compared with only 20% of men. But this does not entitle the report writer to say that *more* women than men preferred the product. This is because the sub-group base for women is considerably smaller than for men. Thus, taking this into account, in absolute terms, more men than women preferred the product. This is why writers of market research reports are quite meticulous in their use of phrases such as 'women were *proportionately* more likely to favour product A than men'.

Table 4.10 *Proportions and absolute numbers*

	Percentages		Numbers	
	Men	Women	Men	Women
	1000	100	1000	100
Prefer product	%	%	No.	No.
A	20	80	200	80
B	80	20	800	20
Total	100	100	1000	100

2. *The introduction of selective normative data.* Contextualising survey data is to be commended, but beware of the report writer who selectively introduces normative data at a particular point in an argument such that it undermines the *actual* survey result.

   Example: Although 85% of Tottenham season ticket holders thought an increase in the price of the new season ticket was bordering on the unacceptable, this has to be set in the wider context of there being two other London football clubs whose annual season tickets are more expensive than those of Tottenham.

3. *The disguised personal opinion.* Beware of the report writer who introduces what is effectively his/her own personal opinion, but 'disguises' it in rather grandiose manner.

Example: The majority of respondents enjoyed reading the new magazine, but in the opinion of the Acme Research Company this raises questions about the ability of ordinary people to professionally evaluate down-market publications.

4. *Failure to present detailed base sizes.* Another presentation (and to a lesser extent, reporting) problem is the failure to provide details of the base upon which a statistic is based. In Table 4.11 we see that in a survey of 400 individuals, 15% preferred the Audi, with 10% preferring the BMW, with the remainder opting for other makes. However, this economical presentation style conceals the true picture. Looking at Table 4.12 we see that the question was only asked of drivers who had owned *both* an Audi and a BMW during the last three years (not necessarily at the same time).

Table 4.11 *Topline presentation of findings*

	Total sample
Base for %	400
Prefer Audi	15%
Prefer BMW	10%
Other answers	75%

Table 4.12 *Clarification of bases for percentages*

Base: Total respondents	400
Have owned an Audi and BMW in past three years	25%
Base for question: all drivers who have owned an Audi and BMW in past three years	100
Preference	
Audi	60%
BMW	40%

5. *Beware of 'black box' explanations.* Be alert to reports written by someone who demonstrates only a hazy understanding of exactly how a particular statistical technique has been applied. If we take the

example in Table 4.13 of correlation analysis, one would hope that the report writer demonstrates that he/she understands in detail how the technique works (see Table 4.13, Level 3). As a minimum, one could accept a conceptual explanation of this technique (see Level 2). But a 'black box' explanation would be unacceptable (see Level 1).

Table 4.13 *Level of explanation*

- Level 1: 'black box' explanation. We fed all the numbers into our computer which then told us that A and B were correlated!
- Level 2: conceptual approach. The Pearson Product Moment Correlation co-efficient technique was employed and this established a relationship between the two sets of data.
- Level 3: the technical explanation. *The above level 2 explanation leading to* . . . the strength of the correlation is shown by a value between −1 and +1. Negative values indicate negative (inverse) correlation. Positive values indicate perfect (complete) correlation. A correlation coefficient of zero indicates the absence of correlation.

6. *The use of a powerful prefix.* The phrase '*as many as 50%* of respondents like the Ford Cortina' clearly gives a different slant from the pre-amble '*as few as 50%* liked the Ford Cortina'.

7. *Selection decisions.* The data user needs to be alert to the decisions that the report writer has made as to which survey questions will be reported. It is quite legitimate for the analyst to omit that a survey question has 'not worked'. For example, the questionnaire designer, in good faith, may have attempted to differentiate between awareness of Burton Snowboards (which makes sports clothes) and Burton (the more traditional English men's outfitters). But if respondents were confused, then it is legitimate to omit answers to these questions. However, the data user needs to be reassured that such omissions do not represent major 'data loss', thereby reducing their overall understanding of the issue under investigation.

8. *The powerful headline.* A presenter or report writer may use an extremely powerful headline to introduce the actual data. This technique is commonplace in journalism. It is also a good way to sell books. For example, we may not want to read a book that 'reviews the evidence for and against the accusation that Pope Pius XII did not do enough during the Second World War to speak out against the Holocaust'. But we might just be tempted by a book entitled *Hitler's*

Pope (written by John Cornwell). But, in the context of market research reports, such headline-grabbing techniques are largely unhelpful.

9. *Multiple and single mentions.* Some survey questions allow individuals to give more than one answer to the question. So the data user needs to be certain that the report writer/presenter has been clear in explaining the difference between 'single' and 'multiple' mentions. It can make a difference. As shown by Table 4.14, the references made by the report writer to – in this example – pet ownership, will need to be precise. Thus, although the raw data in Option One shows that 30% own a dog and 30% own a cat; it is *not* true to say that 60% of the sample own either a cat or a dog. The data would need to be *de-duplicated*, i.e. those who mentioned owning both a dog and a cat would need to be identified (see Option Two). The other option would be to set up a table of *Total Mentions*. This would create a base of 180 mentions of different pets. Then, the percentage of all these mentions that fell into the different pet categories – dog, cat and so on – would be presented as percentages of this base (see Option Three).

Table 4.14   *Single and multiple mentions*

Option One			Option Two			Option Three		
Base: Total sample			Base: Total sample			Base: Total mentions		
Pets owned	No. (200)	% 100	Pets owned	No. (200)	% 100	Pets owned	No. (180)	% 100
Dog	(60)	30	Dog only	(30)	15	Dog	(60)	33
Cat	(60)	30	Cat only	(40)	20	Cat	(60)	33
Hamster	(30)	15	Dog and cat	(20)	10	Hamster	(30)	17
Budgerigar	(30)	15	Other			Budgerigar	(30)	17
None	*(60)*	*30*	combinations/ none	(110)	55			

10. *Selective choice of data.* The choices the report writer has made in deciding on which statistics to comment upon is another issue of which the decision-maker must be aware. In the example in Table 4.15, it would be tempting for the report writer to focus on the 'top box' issue: the 71% complaining of disruption caused by *temporary*

building work. But clearly it would be a major omission not to address the fact that 31% of the hotel's staff was seen as *always* being 'rude and unhelpful'.

Table 4.15 *Spontaneous dislikes with the Faulty hotel*

Comments made	Base all respondents (%)
• Temporary building works to hotel made it difficult to sleep	71
• Staff always very rude and unhelpful	31
• Food of poor quality	18
• Car park too far from hotel	11
• Swimming pool was closed	8
• Room service was poor	7

A picture is worth a thousand words – or is it?: ten issues in interpreting graphical representations of survey data

Below is a checklist of 10 issues that need to be taken into account in evaluating survey data presented in graphic form.

1. *Mischievous use of bar charts.* By exaggerating the scale it is possible to give a dramatic, yet false, impression about the relationship that may exist between two phenomena. For example, in Figure 4.8 it is quite clear that the differences in preferences for the old and new version of a product are negligible. But the way the bar charts are presented gives the impression – at a quick glance – that A is considerably preferred to B.

Base 200	Prefer old version A	51%
	Prefer new version B	49%

Figure 4.8 *Preferences for the old and new formation*

2. *Exaggerated charting.* The idea of exaggeration can be given even more dramatic effect when applied to graphs. Below, at first glance, it

looks like variations in the Sterling/Franc exchange rate is a major driver of decisions taken by UK holiday-makers about whether or not to visit France. But, in actual fact, on closer inspection, we can see that the monthly fluctuations in visitors to France are quite modest, as are the changes in the exchange rate over the period in question. What variations exist have been heavily exaggerated by the choice of scale (see Figure 4.9).

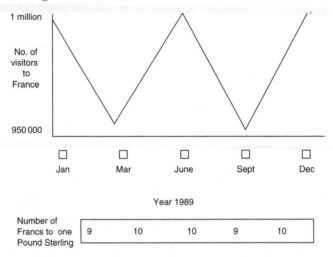

Figure 4.9   *The relationship between changes in the exchange rate and choice of holiday location*

3. *Deceiving use of perspective and three-dimensional shading.* Very small changes in the turnover of the company, shown in Figure 4.10, have been presented to provide an over-positive picture. The graphic gives the impression of a company with dramatic year-on-year increases in turnover. But an inspection of the actual scale shows that, over a three-year period, there has been only a £100 000 increase in turnover.

4. *Cavalier approach to detail.* Figure 4.11 suggests that there are some important variations in the way younger and older customers view a chain of supermarkets. But, in fact, the differences shown in the bar charts are based on extremely small base sizes.

5. *Use of impactful, yet misleading, pictograms or other graphics.* Figure 4.12 below shows the preferences among UK residents for France and Germany as a holiday destination. The graphic, at first glance,

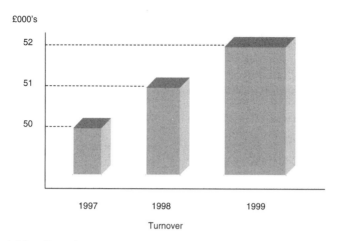

Figure 4.10   *Growth in turnover: 1997 to 1999*

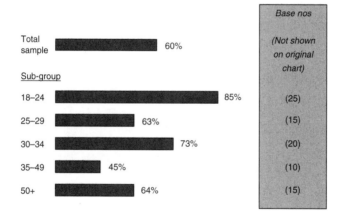

Figure 4.11   *Variation in attitudes by age group*

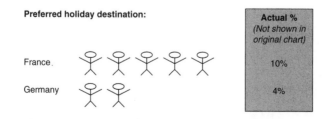

Figure 4.12   *Preference for holiday location*

suggests that France beats Germany hands down. But, on closer inspection, it is clear that as each 'stick man' only represents 2%, which means that the difference in preferences between the two countries is negligible. Here one should also be aware of the difficulties of doing follow-up statistical analysis on pictograms. You know the kind of thing: the left arm of a caricature of a Russian farmer represents 100 million tons of wheat – this is a difficult concept upon which to start subsequently, statistically dissecting the data!

6. *Inappropriate use of pie charts.* The pie chart is a popular graphic. But it should be used only when it is appropriate to the data. As shown in Figure 4.13(a), it is unhelpful to use a pie chart to show changes in the overall *size* of a market. (It looks as though the market is bigger in 1999 than in 1998 – but by just how much?) Whereas, as shown in Figure 4.13(b), using a pie chart to demonstrate how a market is segmented by customer is more appropriate.

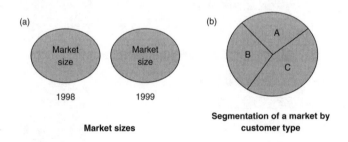

Figure 4.13 *(a) Inappropriate use of a pie chart; (b) appropriate use*

7. *A table would have told a better story than a graphic.* It does not automatically follow that a graphic is better than a well-constructed table. The availability of numerous graphic software packages has led to data analysts – on 'automatic pilot' – generating 'mindless' graphs. In contrast, the process of constructing a table (arguably) means that there is a greater likelihood that more thought has gone into the process. In Figure 4.14 we show students' attitudes towards their university, by type of course, in the form of a bar chart. Then in Table 4.16 we show how the same data can be presented in what we consider to be an easier to understand tabular form.

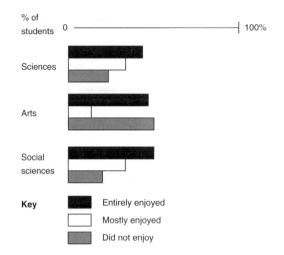

Figure 4.14 *University students' attitudes towards university by type of course – the bar chart approach*

Table 4.16 *University students' attitudes towards university by type of course – the table approach*

	Course			
Attitudes towards university	All students	Social sciences	Science	Arts
Base for %	300	100	100	100
	%	%	%	%
● **Total enjoyed**	**75**	**80**	**76**	**54**
● Enjoyed the *entire* experience	40	46	42	43
● Enjoyed *most* of my time at university	35	34	34	11
● Did *not enjoy* my time at university at all	25	20	24	46
Total	**100**	**100**	**100**	**100**

8. *Tedious use of graphics with no change of pace.* The idea of a graphic is to capture the imagination of the reader, but some data analysts simply slavishly use the same graphic throughout their presentation. Clearly, as shown in Figure 4.15, this does little to encourage the reader to pick up the 'storyline'.

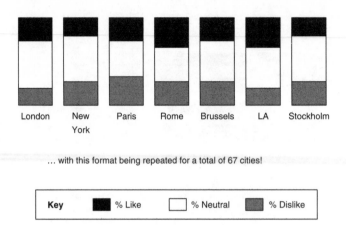

Figure 4.15 *Attitudes towards different cities*

9. *Coding pattern too complex.* As Figure 4.16 below illustrates, problems can arise when too much rides on the reader immediately being able to pick up the meaning of the different shading patterns.

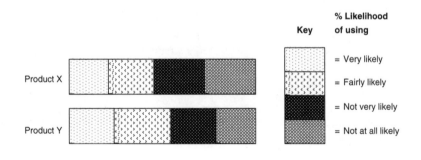

Figure 4.16 *Over-fussy design*

10. *Does not allow statistical analysis.* Some graphical representations, as we have already indicated, do not enable the reader to undertake further analysis of the data. For example, with Figure 4.17, it is difficult to identify from the scale the exact number of units sold in each quarter. In the absence of this information, it then becomes difficult to go on to work out, for example, the combined sales for quarters 1 and 2, 3 and 4, and so on.

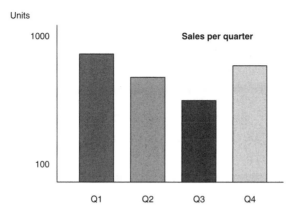

Figure 4.17   *The relationship between price and sales*

 ## Check 7: were there any interpretation flaws resulting in 'unsafe' decisions?

We conclude this chapter by looking at flaws in the overall *stance* that analysts might take to the survey data.

Feet of clay: failure to identify a key methodological weakness

The decision-maker should step back from the survey statistics and ask whether there are any fundamental flaws in the survey design likely to call into question the safety of his/her judgements. One example of such a flaw would be a survey with such a low response (or strike) rate that it does not present a representative picture of the wider population.

Conducted on the wrong agenda

One key question to ask about any survey is: was it conducted on the customer's agenda? Was a comprehensive programme of qualitative research conducted prior to the main survey in order to establish the key issues facing the respondent? Or was the research conducted about issues that exist only in the mind of those commissioning the survey? Another weakness with many surveys is that they fail to acknowledge the low salience to the respondent of the topic under investigation. For example, the thickness of Whizzo Cleaning Cloths will be important to the product manager, but something about which most of us do not feel passionate.

Naive story telling

It is important to establish whether the analyst had a grounded 'holistic' feel for the dataset, or whether the analysis was based on a superficial appreciation of the data. As Einstein said, 'the aim should be to simplify, but not to make things simplistic'. There are a number of tell-tale signs that will help the data user spot the naive interpreter of survey data. First, the decision-maker needs to be reassured that the analyst has not simply developed a 'plausible' story that does not stand up to more rigorous analysis. There are numerous illustrations of 'grand theories' being built around flawed inferences drawn from survey data. High suicide rates in Los Angeles were *explained* as being due to this sprawling urban centre being a depressing place in which to live. But later another analyst pointed out that the main reason why Los Angeles has such a high suicide rate is because of its high availability of inexpensive, anonymous, single hotel rooms that lend themselves to suicide. Another example is where researchers claimed that the reason why some mothers had Down Syndrome babies was because they had suffered stressful incidences – falls and so on – in pregnancy. In fact, it was subsequently learnt that stressful incidences during pregnancy has absolutely no link whatsoever to Down Syndrome. It is a phenomenon caused by a genetic chromosome deficiency. What happened was that women who had had a Down Syndrome baby – in their quest to explain what had happened – were more likely to recall in the research survey stressful incidences in their pregnancy than the 'control' sample of mothers who had 'normal' babies.

Under-analysis

The decision-maker needs to be aware of an analyst who has under-analysed the data. An example here would be failing to get to grips with variations by sub-group. For example, the 'suppresser' effect, to which we referred earlier, might not have been recognised. This could lead to grand theories then being developed around, for instance, regional sub-group differences, which are, in fact, a by-product of some other phenomenon, possibly varying levels of men and women living in the region, and so on.

Over-analysis

Surveys need interpreting in fairly broad brush-strokes. They can provide reliable insights, but the decision-maker should be alert to over-analysis. For example, a survey may provide a fairly robust guide to the proportion of Internet users who have experienced difficulties in accessing their Internet Service Provider. The survey may also provide some *topline* reasons of the difficulties that have been experienced. But it would be imprudent to take the short account of the actual difficulties experienced – possibly given in a short telephone interview – and to use these accounts as the basis for guiding the *detailed* remedial action the Internet Service Provider should take to improve its systems. The experienced survey researcher will know just how far to go with survey data, and not take it into the 'fantasy' zone by expecting too much detail from a survey interview.

No appreciation of how survey data 'work'

The seasoned survey researcher will know just how far to go with different types of survey data. He/she will know that respondents taking part in surveys do not have any sinister malevolent streaks. The idea that survey respondents are perverse and will give you a misleading response is simply not true. This may happen in the occasional opinion poll where respondents in a particular constituency plan to vote strategically; that is, come to some agreement about what pattern of voting will stop, or let in, a particular candidate. But with mainstream commercial research, when asked a question, on balance, people will give a straightforward answer. But, the experienced researcher will know that survey research is stronger in certain areas than others. For example, he/she will know that surveys do an excellent job in *classifying* people in terms of their key characteristics, such as age and gender and their usage of different products, and so on. The seasoned survey researcher will also know that asking questions about what people 'do' is, on balance, likely to produce reasonably reliable evidence. Why would most people not give honest answers to straightforward questions? Moreover, the experienced market researcher will know that surveys are stronger in some areas of attitudinal questioning than others. For instance, he/she will know that surveys are reasonably robust in assessing customers' attitudes towards *past and current experiences*. Ask an owner of, for example, an Audi A4 what he/she likes and dislikes about the car – the car that he/she has driven for the last six months – and you will generate extremely robust evidence. But the veteran of many survey research campaigns will know that taking that extra step – beyond asking people's attitudes towards concrete current and past experience – into the *hypothetical* world of 'what if' questioning, edges us into a set of much less robust findings. For instance, if an Audi motorist is asked whether he/she would continue buying an Audi if the price was doubled, and only a diesel model was available, then not surprisingly the responses to this type of 'out of the blue' questioning will need some careful interpretation.

Further evidence for the decision-maker about whether the survey researcher really understands how survey data 'works' will come from the way he/she looks at the interrelationship between behavioural and attitudinal questions in order to arrive at an estimate of likely future behaviour. He/she will not fall into the trap, for instance, of simply taking a percentage of individuals who respond to a hypothetical question, and use this as the base for forecasting the future. Here, the high profile given in the media to opinion polls (which actually make up a small percentage of all the survey work that is conducted in the United Kingdom) tends to promulgate the idea that research is about asking comparatively super-ficial topline 'what if' questions. Whereas, in fact, as this book has demonstrated, solid research is about building up an integrated picture of the interrelationship between how a person thinks about solid concrete experiences that have happened in the past and are happening to them now, and using this as the platform for an informed estimate of likely future behaviour (see Table 4.17) (remember Insight 7: the past is the only guide to the future).

The comparison in Table 4.17 of the 'perfect' and 'rotten' survey should, if nothing else, give the reader the energy to re-visit some of the points that we have made in this chapter about what constitutes good and bad survey research practice. The comparison between how good surveys can be, and what can go wrong when they are poorly designed

Table 4.17 *Examples of a 'perfect' and a 'rotten' survey*

The 'perfect' survey will	The 'rotten' survey will
• Follow a sampling procedure that does not bias the study in an unrepresentative direction.	• Ask questions that are not set in context and/or are not salient to the respondent.
• Be conducted with a sample size that allows meaningful conclusions to be drawn from the results.	• Have massive non-response bias that renders the results unrepresentative.
• Be designed so that the interview takes place with the appropriate respondent within a household (or business).	• Not be conducted with the targeted respondent who will consequently provide only partial, inaccurate or incomplete responses.
• Conduct the survey on the customer's, not the researcher's, agenda.	• Introduce numerous ambiguous and leading questions.
• Follow the questionnaire 'good practice principles' outlined above.	• Generate statistics that are treated as significant, although based on totally inadequate sample sub-bases.
• Be conducted using the appropriate data collection method.	• Make inappropriate use of a data collection method rendering certain parts of the dataset meaningless, e.g. asking prompted questions on a self-completion questionnaire.
• Make transparent any *sources of error* inherent in the survey process, so that these can be factored into the interpretation of the study.	• Be riddled with a series of minor inaccuracies, such as sloppy definitions of categories of response on the questionnaire that, taken together, destroy the integrity of the findings.
• Be analysed using the optimum analysis techniques, including ensuring that any 'suppresser effects' are detected.	• Be structured in a way that fails to demonstrate any understanding of the importance of a questionnaire being a blend of classification, behavioural and attitude questions.
• Employ holistic data analysis principles.	• Employ a pedestrian approach to the presentation, i.e. question-by-question answers to survey questions, rather than an integrated presentation that looks at the inter-relationship between all the data in the survey.
• Have been set up with the 'end in mind' and will therefore generate evidence that will impact directly on the decision-making process.	• Fail to set the survey data in the holistic context of other corroborating evidence and therefore draw naive conclusions.

and executed, is the difference between chalk and cheese. So it is worth investing time in knowing how surveys really 'work', so that appropriate interventions can be made to generate robust, rather than questionable data.

Designing Actionable Research

Overview

This chapter:

- sets out a seven-point guide to the steps to be followed in designing actionable research that will enhance the decision-making process
- this starts by establishing whether there really is a need for research
- looks at defining and refining the initial problem
- ensures that research is always designed with the decision-makers' end goals in mind
- summarises the techniques in the market research 'tool bag'
- provides a five-step guide to writing a market research brief.

FIVE

Designing Actionable Research

'Begin with the end in mind' – Stephen R. Covey.

This book is primarily about providing marketing personnel with the new skills and competencies that are necessary to make sense of the new type of marketing data arriving on their desks. But, linked to this goal, is the task of ensuring that any fresh research data being requested arrives in a form that meets the changing, more demanding, expectations of the twenty-first-century decision-maker. So in this chapter we provide guidance on what to do when commissioning a new piece of research. The chapter has been written for decision-makers and data users who must brief in-company market research specialists and/or external market research agencies who will then conduct projects on their behalf. We set out a seven-step checklist of procedures to follow in commissioning new research.

- *Step 1*: checking that you actually need to conduct research.
- *Step 2*: defining and refining the problem.
- *Step 3*: starting at the end: putting yourself in the end decision-maker's shoes and designing the study with this action in mind.
- *Step 4*: pinpointing the information gaps.
- *Step 5*: developing a fitness-to-purpose design.
- *Step 6*: deciding on your research design: choosing from the market research toolkit.
- *Step 7*: choosing an agency.

Step 1: is formal research the answer?

The starting point for designing a market research study to meet the decision-making requirements is to ask the fundamental question: is it realistic to consider the *formal* market research route? Another factor to take into account in deciding whether research is the answer is the observation made by David Ogilvy about *data-poor thinking*. He argued that thinking that takes place in a vacuum – without data – is of much less creative value than when data are available. This, of course, leads us into a difficult decision. Do we, when time and events are against us, opt for quality, first principles thinking, rather than conduct a rushed, ill-conceived market research study? Or, do we, following the Ogilvy point, collect some data – knowing that they are second best – on the grounds that they at least create a focal point for creative thought? On balance, it is probably true to say that it is better to have an approximate answer to a carefully thought out 'right question' than to have an exact answer to a vaguely thought out 'wrong question'. To help clarify thinking of this issue, it is helpful in deciding whether formal research is needed to look at the following five issues: not reinventing the wheel; the timetable; the budget; the practicalities; and the question of whether the research is going to meet the end decision-makers' expectations – its likely impact.

1. *Not reinventing the wheel.* It is obviously good practice to do a complete audit of what the organisation already knows so that the research budget is not wasted on researching a topic on which information already exists.

2. *Timetable.* It is futile to develop a major piece of market research that will take three months to conduct when the organisation must make its decision in a few weeks. Thus, the starting point for any putative research study should be the identification of the exact time by which a decision has to be made. It must be possible to implement the chosen research design in the agreed time-frame. It is important to ensure that the timetable allows sufficient 'front-end' quality thinking time. When time is tight it may be better *not* to proceed with the process of collecting new data, but to invest the time available in carefully thinking through all the angles from the standpoint of *first principles* and prior knowledge. Many disastrous market research studies have resulted from a sudden leap into fieldwork without any preparatory quality 'front-end' *thinking* time.

3. *Research budgets and costs.* Early on in the process of considering a possible study the initiator of the proposed research should be clear

about the budget that is available. Obviously, if only a limited budget is available, then this will severely curtail the range of market research evidence that can be collected. This is an obvious point but one that is often overlooked. It results in embarrassingly grandiose research designs being floated for low budget problems.

4. *Practicalities.* It is also important to size up the feasibility of the project that lies ahead. For example, if the computer department cannot generate the list of customers to be interviewed in the research for a month – and the results are needed in two weeks time – then clearly one needs to think again.

5. *Impact.* If the final results from the study are not going to be 'acceptable' to the decision-making audiences – that fail to make an impact – one needs to think again about whether conducting a formal market research study is the way forward. If the decision that eventually must be made is a high profile one that will be played out in the limelight, this will require highly credible evidence. But if the only research that can be conducted within the time-frame is unlikely to be sufficiently robust, it is probably *not* worth proceeding with a study that will only have a very low impact. In this situation it may be better to consider alternatives to formal market research, for example reviewing existing data in an internal staff *brainstorming* session.

So the key message is to check that the study can be conducted within the time-frame and budget, and ensure that there are no major practical hurdles *en route*. One must also be reassured that the proposed research study will fully meet the end decision-making audience's requirements. We started this chapter with a quotation from Stephen R. Covey's book, *The Seven Habits of Highly Effective People*. It reminds us of the importance, when we undertake a project, of beginning with the end in mind: *visualise* what you must be achieved at the *start* of any venture. Before commissioning new research one should be absolutely certain that it will deliver robust, politically acceptable information and actionable insights that will make the necessary 'impact'. The most essential question to ask prior to designing a market research study is: *'on completion of this project what do you expect to be able to do with the information it will generate?'* (see Tables 5.1 and 5.2).

Table 5.1   *A market research design from the House of Horrors*

- 10 000 postal questionnaires are sent to a representative sample of managing directors from UK companies. 1000 replies (10%) are received. The data, on the grounds that they are from a 'statistically robust sample of over 1000 managing directors', are used as the basis of developing a model of the personality traits associated with successful leadership. But of the 1000 replies, virtually all are from sole traders and managing directors of businesses employing less than five people. In short, the survey has failed to include the managing directors of the companies that employ the greatest proportion of the country's employees. The study, although based on a large number of interviews, is completely worthless.

Table 5.2   *A market research design from the Hall of Fame*

- In order to evaluate whether the International Boat Show is meeting the needs and requirements of exhibitors, visitors, the general public, and the media, a study combining qualitative and quantitative research is undertaken and subsequently analysed in an holistic way. The design involved research with the following categories: visitors were interviewed as they were going around the Boat Show, and a separate sample of visitors were interviewed after a couple of weeks when they had had a chance to reflect on the event. Exhibitors were also interviewed – qualitatively and quantitatively – at the event and again after one month, so they could comment on the exhibition after they had a chance to see what extra orders they had generated as a result of the Show.
- In addition, key members of the media were interviewed at the event. Furthermore, a detailed audit of all the PR and press coverage generated by the Boat Show was collated and analysed to see whether it demonstrated an improvement in terms of key criteria compared with previous years. Furthermore, the evaluation of the UK International Boat Show was compared with other Boat Shows around the world. This holistic analysis of this eclectic array of evidence generated both robust quantitative data on overall levels of satisfaction (both relative to previous years and other exhibitions) and also, in a qualitative fashion, pinpointed specific improvement action points for the organisers.

Step 2: defining and refining the problem

The old adage 'a problem defined is a problem half solved' is certainly true of market research. It is helpful to think of market research as being similar to medicine: a patient may *present* a problem to the doctor, but this may simply be a set of symptoms, or an incomplete account of what is actually wrong with the patient. The doctor's job is to talk to the patient, and get to grips with the *real* reason why the person is in the doctor's surgery. The same is true for the market *researcher*; the *presented* 'symptoms' are, in fact, often not the *real* problem. It is at this problem-definition stage when market researchers – whether they be in-house professionals or agency personnel – start to earn their crust. The professional researcher will – at this point – go into a process of 'total immersion': looking at the problem from every conceivable angle and perspective. Some tips on how to do this are given below.

- *Delimiting the project.* When beginning to design a market research study ensure that the proposed approach is manageable. Beware of the 'while you are at it' syndrome: attempts by those 'circling' around the project to add peripheral research objectives and questions that can destroy the character of a piece of research designed to address the *core* problem. If you were, for instance, looking at the market for four-wheel-drive cars, there may be a case for extending the focus of the study to include not only the private purchase market, but also the purchasing of such cars by businesses. But it is extremely unlikely that you will have a manageable project if you extended the study to look at major *bulk fleet* purchasing by organisations such as the United Nations. One tip when *delimiting* a study – that is, deciding on the boundary for, and priorities of, a research project – is to make sure that the way the boundary is drawn relates to the problem at hand. It is important not simply to define the scope of the study in a way that is convenient for the market researchers. Thus, in a study aimed at assessing attitudes towards a major tourist attraction, it may be tempting to exclude overseas visitors from countries that pose language difficulties in administering interviews, but this could exclude a key part of the target audience.
- *Prioritising.* Prioritising the order in which you will address the different research objectives is important. Thus, if the aim of the study is to establish the attitudes of a petrol company's customers towards introducing a customer loyalty card, this should receive the lion's share of the research resources. Feedback on overall attitudes towards the standard of service customers receive at their local garage – although important and related to the central topic – should be given a lower priority.

- *Context and salience.* One of the major limitations of many market research studies – as we have repeatedly stressed – is that they often involve asking questions that fall outside the respondent's 'frame of reference'. For example, the attitudes of small businesses towards banks will be heavily contingent upon whether they are currently 'borrowing' from the bank or are 'in credit'. In designing studies – and subsequently framing survey questions – it is important to pay particular attention to looking at the respondent's world through *his/her* eyes.
- *The fit with existing knowledge.* The chances are that much has already been written on the type of problem you are about to research. This means – at the problem-definition stage of your own upcoming project – try to identify frameworks and concepts that will help with the structuring of the research study. For example, simple ideas – such as the Boston Consultancy Group's notion of analysing an organisation in terms of the 'size of advantage it enjoys over its next competitor', and 'the number of opportunities this competitor has to overhaul your position' – could enhance the problem-refinement process.
- *Precisely defining words and phrases.* It is acceptable when first developing a problem to be *loose* with the way terms are used. But as the project progresses it is important to tighten up. For example, an *initial* plan to 'do a survey of UK businesses' will eventually need pinning down: do we want a study conducted with *all* of the 3.7 million businesses that exist in the United Kingdom, or is the real intention to concentrate on the UK's 1.6 million *VAT registered* businesses?
- *Clarifying ambiguity.* Any sloppy thinking must be addressed. For example, a study to be conducted for a local authority may seek to obtain *household views* on the standard of its recreation and leisure facilities. One person may interpret the word 'household' as meaning obtaining the view of the *head of the household*, but someone else may assume that in order to obtain the community's views on leisure services, then *all adults over 16* within each household should be included in the survey.
- *Unearthing critical assumptions.* Any critical assumptions that have been made in the problem-definition process must be brought out into the open and clarified. For example, a study on attitudes towards a

new super environmentally friendly type of organic farm produce could be set up on the underlying assumption that *all* people are concerned about healthy eating, but this would overlook the fact that *some* people still put pleasure ahead of health.

- *Sorting out objectives, questions and decision outcomes.* At the briefing stage of a project the aim is to encourage people to articulate the problem in whatever way they find most helpful. The research designer will find that this is often done in three distinct modes. First, there will be those who use the language of *research objectives*. For example, what is the customer's overall level of satisfaction with the standard of a newly installed customer Help Desk? Others will talk in terms of *possible questions* that could be asked in a survey. For instance, on a scale of one to seven, where seven is 'excellent' and one is 'poor', how would you describe the new Help Desk? Still others will articulate the problem in terms of *decision outcomes*. For example, on completion of the programme of research we must be in a position to decide (a) whether to leave the Help Desk as it is, (b) introduce various enhancements, or (c) scrap the entire concept and switch over to a new system. The market researcher's job is to be able to *translate* the 'objectives' of a study into 'survey questions' (that must be mean-ingful and salient to respondents), and then to be clear in his/her own mind about how the evidence generated from these questions will subsequently enable the 'decisions', that must be made at the end of the project to be addressed. Where confusion can set in is where a naive researcher, for example, takes a 'decision outcome' – 'Do you think the new Help Desk should be shut down, or not?' – and presents this as a survey question to a bewildered respondent for whom this type of decision-making is outside the frame of reference. In sum, it is necessary to be clear about the difference between 'objectives', 'ques-tions' and 'decisions', and ensure that the appropriate *translation* work has been done.

- *A final reality check.* Make sure that the study will meet the end data user's expectations. Ensure that you have not set in train an ambitious study that will in the end only disappoint. For example, it is extremely difficult to obtain data from surveys that allows us to plot the exact elasticity of demand for products. Market research is able to provide a good *steer* on price sensitivity, but it is extremely difficult to say, with absolute accuracy, that a price change from 1p to 2p will result in a drop of *x*% in sales, and so on. Care would therefore need to be taken in this example to manage clients' expectations – particularly if they are individuals who have been brought up in the traditions of the *pure* sciences and, as such (reasonably enough), are without any insights into how much can be achieved with *social science* methodology.

Step 3: start at the end: clarify the decisions to be made

Having understood the *real* problem rather than just addressing the problem *as presented*, the next step is to ensure the researcher has a clear picture of how – on completion of the study – the end decision-maker intends to use the data. 'Start at the end' by putting yourself in the decision-maker's shoes. Think 'future' histories: establish *now* how you visualise the conclusion of the project helping your end client. A key tenet of good market research design is always to fashion your market research solution with the action that the end decision-maker must take, based on the data, clearly in mind. The experienced market researcher will be able to close his/her eyes and think through all of the likely twists and turns that may take place in the course of completing a project and end with a clear picture of what the research is likely to be saying. These anticipatory skills are absolutely critical to the successful definition of a problem. Below we provide guidance on the issues to explore and questions to ask to ensure that you fully understand – in advance – the decisions that must be made based on your proposed market research study.

Doing your homework on the key decision-makers

It is good practice – as far as possible – to do some advanced homework on the key decision-makers. Think about those who will be involved in the decision. Establish whether there are *hares* in the decision team, who quickly assimilate information and rapidly form a picture of what is happening, and are comfortable making decisions on the spot. Or are they *tortoises* who are better skilled at assimilating complex and detailed information, and are adept at seeing the deeper issues underlying a problem? *Hares* will have much in common with one of the personality types identified by Dr Meredith Belbin – 'The Shaper'. Thus, they will be concerned about action and results, want to make things happen, have drive, and will always challenge inertia, incompetency and ineffectiveness. The *tortoise* will be similar to Belbin's 'Monitor Evaluator', with the skills of judgement, discretion, hard-headedness, and the ability to undertake dispassionate analysis in order to identify fair-minded approaches about even the most misguided of projects. Other taxonomies give us the following: the *snap* decision-makers who pride themselves on making fast and bold decisions; the *workaday* decision-makers who focus on the sensible practical aspects of the decision-making process; *analytical* decision-makers who like to master the logic of the situation; the *defensives* who prefer not to make a decision at all, and the *creatives* who enjoy taking decisions provided that they are continually breaking new ground. However, no one is perfect: the *hares* and the *creatives* will quickly get to the point, but could go for imprudent short-cuts and make rash decisions. Similarly, the *tortoise* and *defensives* will develop a patiently crafted, rounded view, but can get caught up with unnecessary detail, procrastinate, and be indecisive. It is worth investing time – possibly via short telephone interviews – in order to establish the position that the key decision-makers will take on the overall objectives of the project. This is an opportunity to pinpoint any individuals who have 'personal agendas' that may be slightly dissonant with the 'official' corporate perspective. Unless these underlying or hidden motivations are teased out it could mean that a well-crafted research study – unless tweaked and refined to the political circumstances – will ultimately fall on stony ground.

Checking out the decision process

Prior to designing a study try to build up a picture of how the decision process itself will work. Decisions may be made by a *formal* decision-making unit – containing 'initiators', 'information gatekeepers', 'influencers', and 'decision-makers', and so on – all meeting to make a classic *committee*-type decision. Alternatively, this may be a decision that has been delegated to a *task team* with particular skills and expertise. Or, it may be a decision where a particular individual – a lone ranger – has been given total responsibility for the decision. Understanding the decision-making structure – and the expectations of the decision-makers within whatever framework you establish will be in place – is critical to the process of designing the optimum research study. It will not be possible to have the luxury of this 'front-end' investigative work on all studies. But as a minimum – if access to some of the key decision-makers is difficult – the kinds of questions that key individuals might ask at the end of the survey should be anticipated, and the study structured to accommodate these issues. This will help you manage your end clients' expectations of the research process. It is often helpful to conjure up a mental picture of yourself presenting the final research evidence to the assembled decision-making team and then, based on this *visualisation*, take the appropriate pre-emptive action at the front end of the study to maximise the chances of the study successfully answering the questions that have been anticipated. Another useful tip is always to keep ongoing tabs on the political 'temperature' surrounding the decision that must be made on completion of the research project. This can be an extremely difficult task for the in-house market researcher, let alone the external agency supplier, but early feedback on any heightening of tension as the study progresses could give opportunities to steer around some of the impending problems.

Profiling the characteristics of the decision to be made

On the nature of the decision itself it is helpful to start by identifying the characteristics of the decision(s) to be made. This will pay dividends in deciding on the most appropriate research design. Below we list seven key characteristics of a decision, each of which could be influential in pointing to the research design in the most appropriate direction.

1. *What will it cost if you fail?* Try to establish the magnitude of the resulting losses should the project on which you are working fail. This may be measured as a failure to reach a revenue target, the impact on the 'bottom line', or the 'opportunity cost' of the failure. This analysis will immediately give you a feel for where you should

be heading with your research design. For example, if an organisation fails to hold on to its TV franchise this could lead to huge financial losses. Whereas if a new design for a newspaper does not catch on this may lead to a short-term loss in revenue, but would not necessarily put the newspaper out of business.

2. *Can you go back on the decision?* Determine the degree to which it is possible to change or modify the *initial* decision as the success or failure of the venture becomes apparent. For example, if a company decides to sponsor a particular sport, but there is a then a downfall of level of interest in this sport, there are numerous opportunities to adjust and tailor the decision in light of these changing circumstances. However, if a company buys a chain of grocery stores in an Eastern European country that subsequently goes 'bankrupt', it is difficult to go back on this decision by selling this asset.

3. *Is the clock ticking?* The decision timetable is a major factor in determining the kind of information that can be assembled to help the decision-maker. Decisions made against a 'ticking clock', with a 'drop down dead' deadline, are often played out with more heightened tensions than those that are less time critical.

4. *Is this going to change the world?* The extent to which the decision is a radical departure from the norm is another factor to take into account. For example, the decision a retailer might make about whether to open yet another store in the United Kingdom will generate different passions and expectations from a decision about whether or not to open its *first* ever overseas store.

5. *Can you keep it a secret?* The extent to which a decision is a 'private affair' that can be 'kept under wraps' by the organisation concerned, as opposed to being a decision that will be eagerly dissected by the world's media, is another factor to bear in mind in designing a research study. For instance, there will be a sharp difference between a decision on whether to change the organisation that currently holds the National Lottery contract – with all its attendant media hype – and a decision on whether to change the contractor that does a local authority's laundry.

6. *Does the decision come with any baggage?* Knowing whether there is harmony or dissenting viewpoints on the issue on which a decision is to be made is important. For instance, there is much 'baggage'

associated with the way the 'old' and 'new' wings of the Labour Party would broach the emotionally-charged issue of privatising the London Underground. This is in contrast to decision-making within, let us say, Virgin, where we understand that there is universal support for the 'dominant' bullish Richard Branson philosophy of expanding into many new fields.

7. *Will there be a domino effect?* Try to establish whether a decision is reasonably self-contained – that is, one whose outcomes – good or bad, can be 'ring-fenced' within a particular part of the business – as opposed to being a decision that, particularly if things go wrong, will have massive knock-on implications for the company as a whole.

Walking the decision-makers through hypothetical data

One way of ensuring that the research design that is about to be commissioned will produce the appropriate information for decision-making is to walk the decision-makers through some hypothetical data before the study has been conducted. We realise that this is not always practicable in every situation. But if it is possible it will pay dividends. It will significantly push up the chances of the eventual research results translating into helpful action. The process of getting managers to think about specific, albeit hypothetical, outcomes, well in advance of the actual findings, will help managers articulate their research needs. A further spin-off is the fact that the researcher will learn about how the decision-maker receives information. For example, having introduced the hypothetical data, the researcher could ask the following questions: What would happen if we got this result? Would you believe it? Would you make use of it? What else would you need to know to understand it better? What decisions and actions would this lead you to take? From this, the researcher could learn that the decision-maker is comfortable with (hypothetical) data that fall within the decision-maker's 'comfort zone', but is very uneasy with more unexpected results that take him/her into the unknown. A further benefit of providing hypothetical data is that this helps the decision-maker to develop decision criteria in advance of the arrival of the data. This means that decision-makers will be better prepared to interpret the final research results. This can lead to a shortening of the time between the research and the time when decisions have to be made. In short, the idea of taking the decision-maker through (hypothetical) data can make market research far more actionable.

Step 4: pinpointing the information gaps

It is clearly important, as part of the design process, for the researcher to establish how much, or how little, qualitative and quantitative information the organisation already holds on the topic under investigation. Clearly, this audit of what data currently exist is a platform upon which to base decisions about what new types of information to commission. At this point the designer will begin to get a feel for the amount of information that is required to deal with the problem at hand, and also what balance of qualitative and quantitative evidence is likely to be most appropriate to that decision.

Step 5: developing a fitness-to-purpose design

We now arrive at an absolutely core skill for the market researcher: the ability to structure the problem in hand. By this we mean the ability to see the 'shape' of the problem, and how this 'fits' with the solution. It is all about establishing how a combination of different research methods and techniques might together begin to create a body of evidence that will improve the chances of the client making the right decision. At this stage it is important for the research designer to go beyond seeing the problem in a fragmented or isolated way – simply as a series of individual questions that need answering – and to begin to conceptualise the way in which different types of evidence – information packages – can be woven together to solve the different components of the problem. In some ways this is an exercise akin to assembling the pieces of a 'jigsaw'. Approaching the task of establishing the overall approach to adopt in tackling a problem can be divided into a number of stages. We discuss these below.

Deciding on the overall approach: the 'classic' route or pragmatism

The first issue centres on whether the research designer sees the study being informed by the traditions associated with what we might term 'the classic school' of research methodology, or whether the approach is more suited to what we might label the more 'holistic-based' pragmatic school. The former could mean placing the emphasis on an experimental design that will pinpoint the impact of particular variables and provide statistically significant readings. The more holistic approach would seek to look at the way a combination of different pieces of evidence fit together to build our understanding and knowledge. For many commercial decisions it is not necessary to pursue the so-called 'classic' approach to research methodology. In many scenarios the extra time and money involved in achieving the 'council of perfection' research design is not warranted. In many scenarios it may be quite acceptable to provide evidence that, while not statistically significant, is sufficiently 'robust' to provide a clear 'directional steer'.

Deciding on the qualitative/quantitative mix

The next step is to decide on the exact balance of qualitative and quantitative evidence that is required to solve the problem. The idea of these two techniques being mutually exclusive 'foes' is largely unhelpful. It is more helpful to think of qualitative and quantitative research as being 'mutual friends': techniques that can be jointly deployed to help solve the marketing problem in hand. Invariably we will find with marketing issues that a research design that provides a blend of both qualitative and quantitative methodologies is extremely productive. Thus, it usually pays to undertake some qualitative research at the outset of almost any study. This is crucial in understanding the respondents' 'frame of reference'; it is essential to know where the particular issue being researched sits in their overall context. As a general rule, only accept the case for going *directly* to quantitative research if you are *absolutely* certain that you fully understand the customer's world.

Notwithstanding the fact there is usually a role for qualitative research, it is the case that the research designer must decide whether – *on balance* – a study is going to have more of a qualitative or quantitative emphasis. A typical scenario for qualitative research being the 'dominant' method would be one where the end client is familiar with the potential 'power' of qualitative evidence and is looking at a complex issue. This could be, for example, determining whether those who have recently bought a new computer-assisted digital camera can follow what are quite detailed instructions. This can be compared with a scenario in which quantitative research would be the ascendant method. For instance, this would be true of a government department – with a long history of using hard-nosed statistical evidence in order to support its decision-making – that must take soundings among motorists about the number of journeys travelled for different purposes before developing the next stage of its transport policy.

Deciding on the sampling method

In essence, the choices – as we have already touched upon – are twofold. There is the choice of conducting a probability sample, which means that we need a mechanism to ensure that each individual or firm in the sample has an equal (or known) chance of inclusion. The alternative is quota sampling, where interviewers are set quotas corresponding to the characteristics of the total population. As we have already discussed, the choice here, in the vast majority of commercial market research design decisions, will gravitate towards quota sampling. There will be special high-profile studies – often social research-based problems – that will require probability sampling, but for the vast majority of commercial problems quota sampling methods will suffice – provided various safeguards about the way the quotas are actually constructed are introduced – will suffice.

Deciding on the sample size

The following five factors need to be taken into account in deciding on the sample size for a particular research study.

1. *Required accuracy for total sample findings*. The greater the required precision, the larger the sample will have to be. As we have seen, the

sampling error reduces significantly up to approximately 400 interviews. After this point, the gains to be made become proportionally
less great. A survey statistic of 50% from a sample of 400 will be
accurate to within plus or minus 5% (at the 95% level of confidence).
However, had we thrown more resources at the sampling stage and
increased the sample to 1000, we would still only achieve an accuracy
of plus or minus 3.0%, i.e. the extra 600 interviews only reduces
accuracy by less than 2%.

2. *Accuracy required for sub-group analysis.* In many cases the reason
   for increasing the sample beyond what might be considered the
   optimum size of around 400 is not to gain greater precision in
   analysing the results of the *total sample*, but because the research
   analyst needs to look at results by key sub-groups, e.g. gender, age
   group, or socio-economic group. In these situations the research
   designer will often start with a general *rule of thumb* about how many
   interviews are needed in a particular sub-group, and then work up to a
   total sample size. Many researchers would argue that 100 represents
   the minimum number of interviews for the statistical analysis of a
   particular sub-group. However, if resources are limited, it is often
   necessary to reduce this ideal to 50 interviews per sub-group. This
   raises the question of the options open to the survey designer in terms
   of how they then elect to structure their sample to – on the one hand –
   be reflective of the overall population under investigation, while also
   maximising the number of interviews within any one sub-group. It is
   worth briefly addressing this issue. One approach here is to operate on
   an entirely *proportional* basis. Thus, if a sub-group represents 20% of
   the total population, and 100 interviews are allocated to this sub-
   category, we shall arrive at a total sample of 500. An alternative
   approach would be to employ *disproportionate* methods, whereby
   certain sub-groups are *over-* or *under*-represented. The difference
   between the *actual* and *representative* sub-sample would then be
   taken into account in the *weighting* process. This would ensure that
   the results for the total sample reflect a truly representative picture,
   and are not biased by the fact that certain sub-groups have been over-
   (or under-) represented. As we pointed out in Chapter 4, *core* overlapping evidence can be generated from individual sub-groups, which
   lessens the need for a larger sample.

3. *Prior knowledge.* Another factor in deciding on the size of the sample is an assessment of just how much is already known about the subject to be researched. Rarely will the research evidence alone be used as a basis for decision-making. The more the evidence can be placed in the wider context of 'prior knowledge' the less pressure there is on the research, and therefore the greater justification for smaller – rather than larger – samples. In short, where there is considerable breadth and depth of contextual evidence, some would argue that sample sizes can be reduced. In contrast, where very little is known about the survey topic, it would be prudent to invest resources in larger sample sizes. As a postscript to the above point, it should also be explained that larger samples are required when it is known that there is considerable variability in attitudes towards the phenomenon being studied. Thus, it follows that if we establish that there is comparatively little variability, then this tells us to conserve sampling resources. Conversely, where there is extreme variation in the phenomenon we are attempting to investigate, we would do best to invest sampling resources in making sure we have covered the waterfront.

4. *Coverage of the universe.* In the overwhelming majority of consumer research studies, the percentage of the population represented by the sample is not a factor that needs to be taken into account in arriving at the sample size. (This is a common source of error. Numerous organisations despatch market research briefs claiming that they must sample, for example, 20% of their customers, and so on, but in the vast majority of situations percentage coverage of the universe is *not* a relevant concept.) However, in certain business-to-business research studies where there is a *small universe*, the percentage sample coverage of this universe becomes a consideration in deciding on the sample size. In these situations the higher percentage coverage of the universe does work to reduce the sampling error. Thus, if there are 20 manufacturers of aeroplane engines in the world, and we successfully conducted interviews with 10 of them, then the fact that we have a 50% coverage of this *small universe* does reassure about the robustness of the sample. The same thinking does *not* apply when we are sampling the many millions of people that make up, for example, the UK customer base.

5. *Budget and logistics*. In last place – but perhaps it should have been first – is the available budget and the time available for conducting the interviews.

Deciding on exactly who is to be interviewed

In developing a fitness-to-purpose design it is important to be absolutely clear about *exactly* who is to be interviewed. This definition needs to go beyond simply pinpointing the demographic and socio-economic characteristics of the respondents to be sampled. Important decisions need to be made about the overall focus of the study: is this to be with 'users', 'potential users', or 'non-users' of the product or service under investigation? For example, who should we talk to in making decisions about how to develop the functionality of a mobile phone? This is a rapidly growing market, and it is predicted that, in the fullness of time, virtually everyone will have their own mobile phone. At present, there will be a sharp difference between a study conducted among people who have owned a mobile phone for some years, and a study conducted among individuals who have purchased a mobile phone over the last month or so. The former category will presumably now be quite committed to the new technology, whereas the latter category may still have certain reservations – and may even be embarrassed about using a mobile phone. In addition, it is important to be mindful of the opportunities to recruit individuals into a market research study based on their attitudes. For example, with the mobile phone example, it would be possible to ask a series of attitude statements designed to pinpoint individuals who are positive about communications and information technology, or alternatively, to focus the study among those who attitudinally declare themselves as being 'technophobes'.

Putting it all together: ensuring there is a fitness-to-purpose research design

The end point of the process of 'structuring' the problem in hand is to review whether there is a 'fit' between the eventual decision to be made and the information 'package' that you are suggesting. You must feel that

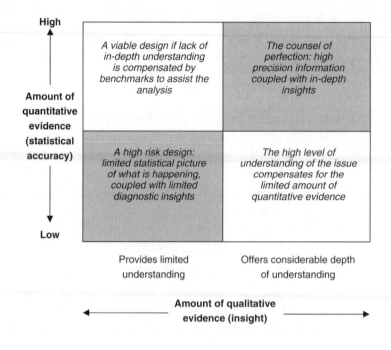

High

Amount of quantitative evidence (statistical accuracy)

Low

	Provides limited understanding	Offers considerable depth of understanding
	A viable design if lack of in-depth understanding is compensated by benchmarks to assist the analysis	The counsel of perfection: high precision information coupled with in-depth insights
	A high risk design: limited statistical picture of what is happening, coupled with limited diagnostic insights	The high level of understanding of the issue compensates for the limited amount of quantitative evidence

Amount of qualitative evidence (insight)

Figure 5.1   *Is the final information mix going to solve the problem?*

there is a fundamental compatibility between the amount, quality and type of evidence you will be assembling and the decisions to be made. If you feel at this point that there is a major dissonance in your own mind, then the market research project itself will be doomed. In Figure 5.1 we provide an overview of the way in which a review of different combinations of the *quantity* and *quality evidence* will create different types of study. Thus, this figure tells us that in the top right-hand part of the matrix we have the 'counsel of perfection': high levels of precision coupled with in-depth insights. This can be contrasted with a design that could be equally valid (this time in the bottom right-hand quadrant of the matrix) whereby, although there are limited amounts of data, this is more than compensated by the high levels of understanding afforded by the availability of various existing models and frameworks within which to interpret these data. Working with this kind of framework it should be possible to arrive at a conclusion about whether you feel comfortable that the 'research package' that you have designed will meet the decision-makers' needs.

Step 6: deciding on the research design

We now need to make a series of decisions about exactly which techniques and tools from the market research 'toolbag' we shall use in order to meet the information requirements. We only have limited space to address this detailed issue. What we can do is first provide an overview of the research design process: a look at the series of trade-offs that must be made. Then we provide a brief overview of the main contents of the market research toolbag.

Start with the ideal design and then trade down

Start by designing the *ideal* study; that is, the study that provides maximum robustness – a bias-free study with virtually no *sources of error*. This gives a starting point for then making a series of pragmatic (invariably downward) trade-offs. The research design process is essentially a five-way trade-off of the following:

1. *Precision.* Decisions need to be made about what level of accuracy and precision is needed on a particular issue.
2. *Depth of understanding.* What depth of understanding is required?
3. *Credibility.* The research design must be sensitive to the context in which the survey data will be used.
4. *Practicality.* Certain research approaches will simply not work due to various practicalities.
5. *Cost.* Clearly, a commercial research study must be evaluated against the benefits to be gained from the study.

In addition, all research studies must comply with the various Codes of Professional Conduct laid down for market research throughout the world. (In Europe, market researchers follow the ICC/ESOMAR and in the UK Market Research Society Codes of Conduct.)

Having conceptualised the *ideal* design and then traded down, the next step is to assess what *sources of error* have been introduced as a result of this trading down process. At point the conclusion may be that some of the trade-offs are too Draconian and have introduced far too many *sources of error* relative to the cost and/or time saving, and so on. You may wish to revisit your design solution and rethink certain aspects of the design. This idea of starting with the ideal and trading down will also help to sharpen up thinking about how you will interpret the final research data. If you have pinpointed an area where you know in advance you have a 'second-best' piece of data, then you have early warning of the need to factor this into your subsequent interpretation.

Selecting from the market research 'toolbox'

Deciding whether to opt for one method or technique rather than another is essentially a creative process, but it is possible to provide a few tips designed to ensure that quality thinking goes into the creation of the best possible research design. These are summarised below.

- *Think laterally.* Go 'outside of the box': free yourself from the details of the problem under consideration and spend some time (internally) brainstorming different angles and perspectives. For example, in a brainstorming session on assessing how the *Highway Code* might be laid out in a more user-friendly form, there would be merit in getting the views of non-English speakers. This would tell us to what extent icons, symbols and images – without the supporting text – are successfully communicating key messages.
- *Develop a challenging mind: keep reviewing the options.* A good research designer will 'not rest with the initial solution': he/she will continually be prepared to *agonise* over the problem and will keep going over different ways in which the design might be improved.
- *Always turn the problem on its head.* Do not rule out the unexpected – turn things around. For example, finding out how many people in the workplace have PC keyboard skills suggests a *workplace* study, but it may be possible to arrive at the solution via a *household consumer* omnibus (filtering out those who do not work).
- *Do not think in methodological stereotypes.* Qualitative research is often used extensively in support of larger-scale quantitative studies, but it can also provide a robust, 'self-contained solution to a problem'. Similarly, continuous research data usually monitors how well a product is performing, but the same data in the hands of a skilled

analyst can also be used diagnostically. Never assume that the typical way in which a method is used is the only way it can be deployed.

- *Think about combinations.* A combination of different research methods will often provide the optimum design solution. Qualitative and quantitative research are often blended together. Similarly with quantitative data collection methods, a mixture of face-to-face, telephone, and postal interviews will often best address the problem at hand.
- *Think about the order.* It is often the case that qualitative research precedes the quantitative phase of a study to feed into the development of a questionnaire, define respondents' *language*, and so on. But there will be situations where qualitative research conducted *after* the quantitative phase can be extremely helpful, providing diagnostic insights into some of the observations generated by the quantitative research. Always question the order in which different research methods are employed.

Your final methodological choices

We now arrive at the process of selecting from the 'market research toolbag'. This toolbag – a review of the main market research methods – appears as Appendix A to this chapter.

Step 7: choosing an agency

The primary purpose of this book is to help data users – those who must make judgements from data – to interpret the information in front of them. A secondary goal has been to provide advice on how to commission actionable research to plug any information gaps. And to complete this latter goal we arrive at the question of choosing a market research agency to carry out the new research. This is beginning to take us outside the main remit of the book. So what we have done is to provide, in Appendix B to this chapter, a detailed guide on how to prepare the market research brief that would be sent to agencies. This is the document the commissioner of research typically sends to agencies requesting the prepara-

Table 5.3 *Selecting a market research agency*

- *Likely impact on decision-making.* Will the agency be able to deliver actionable impactful results that will meet the end decision-maker's requirements?
- *Clear deep-thinking skills.* Has the agency demonstrated clarity of thinking and depth of understanding in responding to the research brief? Does it have the appropriate technical skills? Has it won any industry awards for distinctive or innovative thinking?
- *Experience and expertise.* What experience does the agency have in (a) your particular market and (b) dealing with similar kinds of methodological problems?
- *Resource platform.* Does the agency have the appropriate staff and other resources to undertake the project?
- *Project management.* Will the agency be able to manage the project effectively?
- *People chemistry.* What is the profile of the agency staff, and do you think you will be able to get on with the agency?
- *Quality standards.* Does the agency have Quality Assurance Standards in place, such as the Market Research Quality Standards Association (MRQSA) and/or ISO9001 or similar awards, covering the design and management of market research surveys?
- *Ethics.* Does the agency comply with the ICC/ESOMAR and The Market Research Society Codes of Conduct?
- *Value for money.* Is the agency providing you with value for money?
- *Contractual issues.* Is the way the agency does business compatible with your own needs and requirements?

---

tion of an appropriate research response (i.e. a research proposal). We supplement this by briefly providing a few 'tips' on what to look for when selecting a market research agency (see Table 5.3).

Appendix A: An overview of the market research 'toolbag'

Observation

- There are two main types of observation:

    - Where the respondents *are not aware* they are being observed; for example, observing, by approximate age and gender, how many cyclists use the prescribed cycle lane.
    - Where individuals *are aware* that their behaviour is being observed, e.g. a study to look at how people read national newspapers – do they start on the back page, go to a favourite section, start by scanning the headlines, etc.?

Client customer information

- Information held on the client's database about its customers – for example, supermarkets holding information collected as part of their loyalty scheme.

Marketing intelligence

- Various informal reports and information that are fed back from the salesforce and others within a company that provide up-to-date insights into what is happening in the marketplace.

Competitor intelligence

- This could be the result of a formal analysis of competitors, or more informal insights into what competitors are doing.

Integrated internal customer and survey datasets

- There is a growing trend towards integrating information held on the client/ customer database, with data obtained from external sources, and integrating these into an overall dataset.

New electronic information

- In addition, one needs to factor in information becoming available over the Internet.

Desk research

- Information that *exists* either in the public domain or within companies, which does not require the setting up of a new (or primary) market research study. The sources are vast, but include:

  - Previous market research reports that are held by a company.
  - Various data held in the public domain that profile the overall consumer and business populations (usually held in hard copy and electronic, on-line information formats).
  - There is also the opportunity for secondary data analysis – the reconfiguring of existing data in a way that addresses the specific problem being explored.

Ad hoc research

- Research commissioned on a bespoke, as-and-when needed, basis. This type of research can be broadly classified into the following approaches.

Qualitative research

- Here the emphasis is on exploring the underlying reasons why people behave and think as they do.
- The studies tend to be (although they do not have to be) smaller scale. The approach is response-orientated; that is, the answer to the last question given in the discussion will largely determine the next question asked by the researcher.

Quantitative research

- This will be large scale: respondents taking part will be asked the same question in the same way. This standardisation means it is possible to aggregate the results, and then look at variations in responses to these standardised questions, given by different sub-groups of the sample.

Specialist options

- To complete the picture, it is helpful to note various other specialist market research services that should be considered when thinking about a particular problem. These include:

  - *Mystery shopping*: where researchers – following the conditions for this practice laid down in the ICC/ESOMAR/MRS Codes of Conduct – sample various services. For example, calling up a telecommunications company's directory enquiry service and noting down, against pre-determined criteria, how well the *transaction* was handled.

Internet

- Internet users cannot of course be used as a proxy for the population at large. But if the goal is to obtain the views of Internet users – let us say on using the Internet to buy groceries – this medium offers potential. But there is still much to learn about the psychology of researching over the Internet.

Continuous: longitudinal research

- This involves collecting data from the same group of respondents, or from the same set of retail outlets, in a way that will provide a *time series* that is particularly helpful in looking at trends. Typical continuous services include the following:

Consumer panels

- Where a representative sample of consumers are contacted on a regular, perhaps monthly, basis and asked about the products they have purchased, and so on. The consumer panel allows shifts in attitudes and behaviour, including brand-switching behaviour, to be closely monitored by different demographic and socio-economic groups.

Retail audits
- Where a representative sample of retail outlets are contacted on a continuous basis, and the movement of consumer products into and out of the outlets is monitored.

Standardised services

- Here, we are referring to the existence of a survey *infrastructure* that can be quickly accessed, although different respondents will be interviewed each time. Examples include:

Omnibus surveys
- It is possible to place a small number of questions on a survey that is regularly conducted by a market research agency. (The clients placing the questions share the cost of the survey but only receive back the results of their own questions.)

Syndicated services
- There could be opportunities to buy into a syndicated survey that, for example, involves assessing companies' attitudes towards computer virus/ protection software packages.

Appendix B: A five-step guide to writing a market research brief

Client organisations wishing to undertake a market research study usually prepare a *market research brief* – a document that outlines their market research needs and requirements – and they send this to one, or more, agencies. The agencies then prepare a *research proposal* – a response to the research brief, explaining what research design they recommend to solve the problem, at what cost, and in what time frame. In this document we provide some tips on how to prepare a market research brief.

Step 1: taking the brief; doing your homework

An organisation's marketing team may present a 'problem' to their in-house market research specialists that may only be a symptom of a more fundamental issue. So the starting point for the preparation of the research brief is to get underneath the surface of the issue to identify the underlying problem. The market research specialist must make sure he/she fully understands the overall context in which the problem is located. He/she must also pin down the details of the problem: obtaining exact definitions of terms being used, and eliminating any ambiguity in the way in which the issue has been explained. At this stage, clarity of thought about the *'business' objectives* that need to be addressed following the market research project is critical. These need to be distinguished from the *'research' objectives* that the study is expected to answer. He/she should also be clear about the *'decisions'* the users of the research must make in pursuit of their business objectives. Step 1 involves listening, and intelligent questioning – getting to grips with the true nature of the problem.

Step 2: shaping the brief

The next stage is to start fashioning the project into one that is manageable and realistic. This may involve working in an iterative way: going back to the person who first gave the brief and seeking clarification on key questions. Watch out for the 'while you are at it' syndrome: the request for more and more information by the internal client, just because a survey is being done. This tendency must be kept in check so that the project does not grow in an unmanageable way. Ensure you manage the expectations of the person who initiated the study: communicate the fact that market research design is a 'trade-off' between the considerations listed below.

- How much precision is required?
- How much depth of understanding is needed?
- What are the practicalities involved?
- What is the timetable?
- What is the budget?

The project must also be conducted within the ICC/ESOMAR/MRS Codes of Conduct. At the end of this process make sure the internal client is aware of the trade-off that has to be made and is comfortable about what the end result of the project will achieve, i.e. manage the expectations of the initiator.

Step 3: deciding on the tender procedure

Some organisations will send their research brief to one agency with which they have developed a relationship. Others will prefer to put the project to a competitive tender. Typically, three agencies will be invited to tender. Agencies should be told that a tender is competitive.

Step 4: writing the research brief

We now arrive at the task of actually writing the research brief. A written brief is important because:

- it forces the internal client to articulate the problem,
- it forces the MR specialist to start considering some of the operational issues, and
- it helps the agency to formulate a precise response to a clear set of issues.

There is no one right or wrong way to write a brief, but most briefs will contain the following elements:

1. *Background.* There should be a comprehensive, yet succinct, review of the business issues that form the basis for the market research project. Summarise, for the agency, relevant previous research. Alert the agency to any political subtexts prevalent in the organisation and tell the agency where it can go for extra information. It is unhelpful to hold back data or insights to see whether the agency comes up with the same information. Providing as much relevant information as you can will help the agency develop a better quality proposal.
2. *Business objectives.* Clearly explain the business objectives of the project. For example, if a bank is considering undertaking a project among small businesses to assess their use of the Internet, explain that a key business objective is to decide whether the bank should use a software house or develop these electronic commerce skills in-house.
3. *Research objectives.* Provide a short summary of the overall aim of the research. Follow this with the detailed objectives. For example, with the electronic commerce project, establish the degree to which small businesses currently use the Internet for business transactions.
4. *Information requirements.* Supplement the above business and research objectives by listing, detailed information requirements. This should *not* be a never-ending 'wish list', but a considered check list of the information required from the study.
5. *Expected use of results.* This section – sometimes referred to as *decision outcomes* or *applications of the research* – tells the agency how the results of the study will be used. For example, with the electronic commerce example, tell the agency that the results of the study will be used to improve the functionality of the bank's current electronic commerce products.
6. *Action standards.* Share with the agency any action standards against which the decisions will be made. For example, let us say a new coffee is being considered. The action standard here will be: (a) is the new coffee preferred

to the current brand? and (b) is it preferred to a (specified) competitor? Only if the new product meets these two conditions will the new formulation be introduced.

7. *Useful information and critical issues.* Ensure that the research brief contains information critical to the agency in deciding on its approach, and providing an estimate of costs. For example, explaining to the agency whether it will be able to use customer lists for sampling purposes, or must 'free find' respondents, is important. In addition, information such as the location of the briefing meeting (whether this is central London or Northern Scotland), and how many presentations are required, and so on, is important.

8. *Approach to research.* In certain situations the client organisation will wish to indicate to the agency the methodology to be used. However, normally the client will just suggest methodological alternatives and encourage the agency to come up with its own recommendation, together with the rationale for this choice.

9. *Deliverables.* The brief should specify the exact deliverables that are expected from the agency. These may include:

- a verbal presentation (specifying the number of hard copies of the presentation required etc),
- a report (again specifying the number of hard copies required, together with whether electronic versions are needed, and so on), and
- other 'deliverables' include tabulations, attendance at various progress meetings and so on.

10. *Contact names.* The brief should specify the relevant contacts within the client organisation with whom the agency can speak when preparing the brief.

11. *Proposal submission details.* The brief should specify:

- when the proposal must be submitted,
- to whom, and where, it must be sent, and
- how many copies are required.

If the agencies will be required to produce a quality proposal, allow them sufficient thinking time. If possible a *minimum* of one week for the preparation of a proposal should be built into your timetable. If possible, give the agency up to two weeks, but much depends on the scale of the project.

12. *Timings.* Specify exactly when the research presentation and report are required. Also indicate any other critical timings, for example when the

fieldwork must be conducted. Do not place artificially tight, or unrealistic time constraints on the agency. This rarely makes for productive research.

13. *Budget.* There are two schools of thought. Generally agencies prefer to receive an indication of the budget. It gives them a clear guide as to the scope of the project required. Some clients, however, favour not 'specifying' the budget, letting agencies decide what research design is appropriate to answer the research objective.

14. *Agency selection criteria.* The brief should contain a statement of the criteria by which agencies will be selected: their experience working in a similar market; the quality of their personnel; the way in which critical issues have been addressed, and so on.

15. *Also map out the timetable for deciding on an agency and the procedures you will follow.* Will there be a shortlisting stage, or (for major projects) the need for the agencies to present their proposal, and so on?

Step 5: feedback to agency once the selection has been made

Provide the unsuccessful agency with feedback as to why it was not successful. This will help the agency enhance the quality of future proposals. For the successful agency, promptly provide – in writing – any amendments you would like it to introduce into the winning proposal.

C H A P T E R 6

Holistic Data Analysis

Overview

This chapter:

- explains the key principles of holistic data analysis: including the 'panorama' and 'triangulation' principles
- maps out the main elements of the holistic data analysis process: the interrogation of the evidence; contextualisation; analysis; and the application of information to the decision
- provides a 10-step practical guide to conducting holistic data analysis, introducing the concept of establishing the 'weight, power and direction' of evidence.

SIX

Holistic Data Analysis

'Far better to dare mighty things, to win glorious triumphs, even though chequered by failure, than to take rank with those poor spirits who neither enjoy much, nor suffer much, because they live in the gray twilight that knows not victory, nor defeat' – Theodore Roosevelt.

Finding the *truth* – identifying the themes and patterns in customer and marketing data – is a challenge. The solution rests less on the revealing of one big 'magical', leading edge, 'one-stop' statistical technique, and more in promulgating the notion that effective data analysis is about doing a series of small things well. This is the essence of the 'holistic' approach to data analysis that we have been advocating throughout this book. It is, we believe, the way forward in coping with today's world in which we have vast quantities of imperfect data drawn from a range of different sources. To start, it is helpful to review the key principles of the holistic analysis approach.

The key principles of holistic data analysis

Insight-based: the panorama and triangulation principles

The insights about the nature of research enquiry and marketing data articulated in Chapter 2 provide the platform for the holistic analysis approach. These insights are not meant to be distant, vague, abstract, philosophical ideas that are raised then forgotten and drift off into deep space. We started the book with these insights because we believe that, in the future, the intelligent analysis of data will require individuals to have reflected on some of these fundamental issues about the nature of investigation and data. In particular, ideas such as the 'panorama' principle (context is everything and everywhere) and the 'triangulation' principle (two pieces of evidence are better than one) are key elements of the holistic approach to data analysis.

Blurring the qualitative and quantitative divide

The holistic approach to data analysis also means feeling comfortable working with both qualitative and quantitative data. It is important to attack the myth that qualitative and quantitative research – and their subsequent analysis – are very different. There are, of course, differences between the two data collection approaches. But by the time we arrive at the analysis stage it is unhelpful to think of this analysis as being a battle between two arch enemies: the quantitative and qualitative approaches. Rather, we should be thinking of qualitative and quantitative research as mutual friends. Thus, it is helpful to take the view that:

- qualitative research can be analysed quantitatively, and that
- quantitative research can be analysed qualitatively.

Working with 'hard' and 'soft' measures of 'validity'

Another key principle of the holistic approach to data analysis is a preparedness to work with *soft* methodological concepts. Thus, with holistic analysis the notion of the 'believability' of data sits alongside, in quite a respectable way, the more formal concepts of the 'validity' and 'reliability' of data. Similarly, the holistic analysis approach embraces the fact that in today's business climate, we have to recognise the importance of taking into account management intuition and setting this alongside the more formal explicit evidence. All of this reflects the fact that it is not always possible to fall back on statistical interpretations of the evidence. Often the best that the data user can do is to assess how well the evidence squares with his/her own experience. This approach, as already touched upon earlier, squares with the whole notion of 'grounded theory': inspecting each piece of research evidence in relation to other theoretical information available on the topic to see whether the incoming evidence adds to our conceptual understanding.

The idea of taking softer measures of validity into account is also underpinned by the Bayesian approach to decision-making. Management hunches, to use the Bayesian jargon, can be seen as the 'prior prob-abilities', and the later survey data as the 'posterior probabilities'. What seems to have happened in the past is that the management intuition 'probability' becomes relegated, in this Bayesian balance, to play second fiddle to the survey data. It is assumed that the greater robustness and certainty of survey data will swamp the contribution of our 'prior beliefs'. This overlooks the important distinction between 'implicit' and 'explicit' knowledge.

Clients' intuitions may be steeped in implicit knowledge – everything from the body language of the last customer to whom they spoke, to their impressionistic understanding of market trends – in short, the host of hard and soft facts digested by clients in their day-to-day work. This is important because management hunch, intuition and knowledge – often difficult to articulate explicitly – could include facts which *genuinely* challenge the explicit findings of survey research. What is required is a method for identifying and drawing out precise, *implicit* client intuitions in order to place them in the Bayesian balance against *explicit* research findings.

Hybrid thinking

The other key feature of the holistic approach is that it is based on a hybrid form of thinking that sits between the conventional inductive and deduc-tive methods. We are now beginning to realise, as indicated earlier, that human beings are not, by nature, inductive thinkers. We tend *not* to observe and then, generalising from our observations, form a theory. We tend to edge – sometimes deductively – towards a partial 'theory'. We then modify this initial 'theory' in the light of various subsequent observations we make. Thus, the way we analyse is a hybrid between induction and deduction.

The main techniques underpinning holistic data analysis

Throughout this book we have been gradually building up a picture, not only of the fundamental principles that underpin the holistic approach to data analysis, but also of the various information processing, evaluation and analysis techniques that, taken together, characterise the holistic way of working with data. In essence, the various techniques can be categorised into the following four broad activities: interrogation, contextualisation, analysis, and application. We look at each in turn.

Interrogation

In today's information climate we must now find fast and efficient ways of interrogating less than perfect incoming information: we must know the key questions to ask to quickly establish the robustness of incoming information. This means going beyond the traditional approaches – checking the 'basic' methodological facts – to pinpoint any flaws that characterise the new genre of information that is landing on our desks (Figure 6.1).

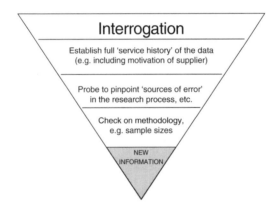

Figure 6.1   *Interrogation*

Contextualisation

Today, our contextualisation of incoming information must be more comprehensive than in the past. It needs to go beyond simply looking at recent similar product experiences to explore where the new data fit into what we know about the 'shapes and patterns' that characterise this particular market (Figure 6.2).

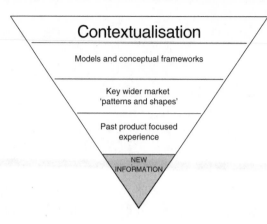

Figure 6.2   *Contextualisation*

Analysis

Holistic analysis stretches beyond the current checks made of the overall 'face validity' of the data (possibly supported with some statistical testing) to embrace concepts such as looking at the 'weight', 'power' and 'direction' of evidence. These are all analysis concepts we explain shortly. In addition, analysis should embrace a 'rounding up' of management hunch, intuition and judgements on the data under scrutiny. *Anecdotal* observations by the end data user are acceptable. Although there is a possibility that these reflect 'one-off', outlying observations, they may well be *archetypal* experiences that reflect the breadth and depth of the end data user's experience. Holistic analysis provides frameworks for helping to integrate the 'explicit' and 'implicit' information (Figure 6.3).

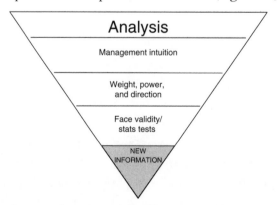

Figure 6.3   *Analysis*

Application

Here, under the holistic 'paradigm' we must go beyond simply setting out the options that are open to the decision-maker, and begin closely to interrogate the 'safety' of the evidence being used to support a particular business solution. Then, looking to the future, as strategic marketing information databases and knowledge management systems become even more sophisticated, we should have the benefit of monitoring, on an ongoing basis, just how effective different types of market and customer information *packages* have been in generating successful decision outcomes. So, in the future, we may be seeing the concept of *decision effectiveness memory banks*. This would reflect the growing importance that organisations now attach to being able to identify the precise connections between the decisions they have made and the outcome of these decisions. Then, having looked at the relationship between the decision and its effectiveness, the company would be able to put the spotlight on the extent to which the information that underpinned the decision was a contributory factor to the success or not (Figure 6.4).

Figure 6.4   *Application*

Putting it all together: holistic analysis summarised

Putting together the above four quadrants we arrive at an overall summary of the holistic analysis approach (see Figure 6.5). To recap, at

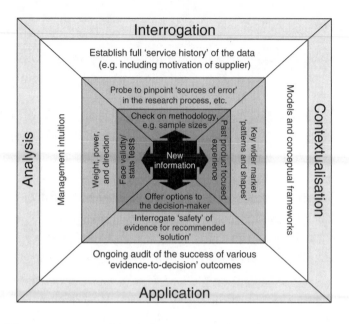

Figure 6.5   *A summary of the holistic approach to data analysis*

the centre of the figure there is a reference to new (incoming) information. The information here could refer to qualitative 'clues' that provide a starter for beginning to think creatively about a problem, through to large-scale survey data. This central square is surrounded by four quadrants, each of which refers to the four activities described above: 'interrogation' (looking at the robustness of the information); 'contextualisation' (looking at the information in its wider market context); 'analysis' (looking at the evidence and numbers); and 'application' (establishing what the evidence means for the decisions to be made). The main point being made in Figure 6.5 is that currently, under the *existing* market research 'paradigm', new information will receive the treatment shown by the part of the diagram with shading. Thus, typically, the analyst will check the survey sample size; look at market research reports for similar products; conduct some simple numerical tests on data; and then tell the decision-maker what options are open to him/her. We are arguing for a *new* holistic market research/information analysis paradigm – one that 'stretches' what market researchers currently do to embrace the various activities shown in the white parts of each quadrant of the figure. This new approach would mean there would be much less of a gap between the information and its application to the decisions that need to be made. In summary, the holistic approach is the difference between the activities shown by the dark shading and the activities that are embraced by the entire diagram.

To conclude our overview of the holistic approach to data analysis we should point out that the entire holistic approach – our whole box – will be in a constant state of change, reflecting the arrival of new information and cultural *paradigms*. For example, someone reading this chapter in 10 years time may be itching to re-write our robustness checks to better reflect changes in the way the Internet will affect the way we 'receive and process' information.

Ten-step guide to holistic data analysis

We now build on our overview of the key principles and techniques of holistic approach by providing a practical step-by-step guide on analysing data in a holistic fashion.

Step 1: clarifying the end decision-maker's expectations of the analysis

Not everyone reading this chapter will be the end decision-maker. There will be a number of individuals who are responsible for analysing data which will then be passed to an end decision-maker. Therefore as the first part of the analysis process we have included the task of ensuring that the analyst establishes to what level the end decision-maker expects the analysis to be taken. Below, we summarise the different levels to which a data analyst might be expected to take his/her interrogation of the data and subsequent interpretation.

- *Commenting on the robustness of the answers to survey questions/ objectives.* At its most minimalist an analyst might just be expected to provide a brief methodological comment surrounding a particular statistic. For example, if a survey showed that 30% of the customers were dissatisfied with a product, the analyst might point out that this survey statistic, given the sample size, is accurate to within say ±5%.

- *Absolute interpretation of findings.* At the next level, the analyst might be expected to provide an interpretation of the meaning of a statistic. For example, if 30% of holiday-makers disliked their holiday hotel, the analyst might add an interpretation along the lines of: *this seems high and should be a source of concern to the holiday tour company.*

- *Interpret findings in a normative context.* Moving along the spectrum, the analyst may go beyond simply providing an interpretation of the findings based on an 'absolute' assessment of the numbers and set the survey evidence in the broader context of what we already know about the market. For example, at this level, the analyst would go beyond simply pointing out that in 'absolute terms' 30% dissatisfaction with the hotel seems high, and set this statistic in the context of other available normative evidence. This, for instance, could tell us that – on the basis of various surveys conducted over the years – it is unusual to find more than 10% of customers being so disenchanted with their hotel.

- *Present options.* Next in our hierarchy, the analyst could be expected to review the options open to the decision-maker. For example – to continue the above hotel illustration – recommending the options of (a) dismissing all the existing staff and replacing them with new recruits, (b) introducing a major customer care training programme, or (c) lowering customers' expectations by reducing the cost of a room, and so on.

- *Recommend best solution.* At the next level, the analyst might be expected to go beyond simply providing options, and make a recommendation about what – based on the survey evidence (and also possibly his/her own experience) – he/she feel would be the *best* route to adopt. In the hotel example, the suggested solution might be totally to refurbish the hotel.

- *Decision facilitator.* Still further along the spectrum could be the expectation that the data analyst will be closely involved in the actual making of the final decision. This would mean setting the solution recommended by the data analyst (refurbishing the hotel) in the wider context of evaluating whether the cost of refurbishing the hotel would be better deployed on some other scheme, and so on.

- *Taking responsibility for decision outcomes.* At the top end of the expectations of the data analyst is the idea that he/she must take responsibility for the outcome of the decisions that are being made, remembering that good decisions can lead to bad outcomes and vice versa. So, given this, it could be that the data analyst is expected to 'follow through' the initial decision – monitoring to what extent changing circumstances are now influencing the effectiveness of the initial decision – and be prepared to advise accordingly in order to ensure that a successful outcome to the initial decision is achieved

Step 2: clarifying the analysis goals

Step 2 is the important task of clarifying the exact goals of the analysis about to be undertaken. There are two key points to make here.

- *Objectives, decisions and questions.* Start by revisiting the issue of classifying the 'research objectives' and 'decision outcomes' for the project. Be absolutely clear about both of these before embarking on your analysis. Remember what we said earlier about the three ways in which the aims of a project may be articulated: research objectives, survey questions, and decision outcomes. As we explained earlier, all these three modes of communicating the purpose of the study are helpful. But, this does mean that the data analyst must be clear in his/her own mind about the essential difference between these three styles of setting a 'goal'. Confused thinking on this issue will hinder the clarity of the analysis. For instance, presenting the final analysis as simply the answers to a list of survey questions is pedestrian and is unlikely to be well received. Professional analysts will have a clear idea about how they are going to group the various answers to different survey questions to produce a confirmation of evidence that addresses each of the research objectives. Following on from this, he/she will be clear on how he/she will then draw all his/her evidence together to answer the specific 'decision outcomes'.
- *Be alert to change.* In clarifying the analysis goals remember that the objectives and decision outcomes articulated in the *original* market research brief (and subsequent research proposal) may have changed since the study first started, such as a new competitor appearing. It also could be due to changing perceptions and expectations of the

end decision-maker about what the study was originally designed to achieve. The experienced analyst will make sure that during the course of the study, he/she keeps in contact with the end data users to see whether their expectations have changed, and manage this accordingly.

Step 3: clarifying what you already know

The next step in the analysis process is quickly to 'audit' all the existing evidence at your disposal. Critical to the holistic approach to the analysis of data is making sure you have a fully rounded understanding of how your problem 'nests' in various 'contexts' and builds on existing management intuition and knowledge.

- *Capturing what we know about the customer's world.* The data the analyst is looking at may well be about respondents' attitudes towards an electronic on-line version of their favourite yachting magazine. But it would be naive not to set this feedback in the wider context of previous statistics on what readers thought of *hard copy* versions.
- *Factoring-in implicit knowledge.* Internal company marketing information and management judgement should be *explicitly* brought into the data analysis and interpretation process, rather than sitting outside the primary research process. It is recognised that teasing out these management insights takes time; much of our implicit knowledge is locked away deep in our memory banks.
- *Embracing the competitor context; making use of marketing intelligence.* It is important to establish exactly what management think competitors might do in response to their organisation's own initiatives. For example, if management think that a key competitor will start a 'price war' if the company were to reduce its prices, it is important for the analysts to be aware of this, and to factor this into their interpretation of the research data.
- *Benchmarks.* It is also important before starting on analysis to see whether there is any relevant *normative data*, information that will help interpret the data and provide a standard against which to judge the current evidence. For example, as we have explained, fast moving

goods manufacturers will monitor, over the years, the relationship between the claimed level of purchase in a survey, and the actual subsequent take-up of that product in the marketplace.

- *Capitalising on theories, frameworks and models.* Some practitioners may be rather dismissive of so-called *academic* frameworks and theories. But these models and theories, when put into the context of the evidence from a study, can provide some important insights. For example, if you were undertaking a study aimed at assessing attitudes towards a rather dramatic 'wear a seatbelt or you could be disfigured for life in a crash' TV campaign, it would be helpful to know that 'cognitive dissonance' theory alerts us to the fact that some individuals when confronted with frightening messages – people flying through car windscreens – may not get themselves back into 'psychological equilibrium' by following the message of the campaign – i.e. fasten your seatbelts – but instead, in panic, reject *both* the problem and the solution and ignore the TV campaign completely.

Step 4: working from first principles and common sense

Our analysis should begin by drawing solely on first principles. Using common sense may seem obvious, but it has not become common practice. Do *not* undertake any advanced statistical tests at this stage in the process – simply ask the following seven questions.

- Did you expect this finding?
- Do you believe it intuitively?
- Are there any differences between the sub-groups that fit with your view of the world?
- When you start asking yourself questions about the data, do you find the data are internally consistent?
- Do any other data you know of support this finding?
- Would you feel confident explaining these findings to others (in the pub)?
- Do you feel that these findings are safe to use?

Today, with management science and information very much in the ascendancy, it is easy to allow common sense and first principles to take a back seat. But information without human insight and intuition is dangerous. For example, we now know that during the Cold War the West's secret services had precise *quantitative* (numerical) information about Russia's missile strength. But we have now learnt that our security gurus had no *insight* about how the Russian Military were thinking about the West. We simply *assumed* that they were getting ready to attack us. But we now know that the Russians were genuinely convinced that it was the Americans – through its Pershing and Cruise missiles – who were planning a 'first strike' on Russia. The West had made the mistake of concentrating on the mechanics of information collection, rather than accompanying this with trying to unravel the Russian 'psyche'.

Step 5: checking the quality of the data

The next step in the holistic process is to carry out some basic checks on the quality of the data. It could be argued that it is logical to do this *before* the common sense and first principles analysis that we have advocated above. Indeed, in some cases this would be prudent. On balance, however, the first reflex of the holistic analyst is to see whether the evidence squares with prior knowledge. This can provide a focus for then going back to check any figures about which you may be suspicious. There are three aspects to this quality-checking process. First, carry out some basic checks to establish the extent of any methodological 'error' in your survey data. Secondly, establish whether there are 'gaps' in your knowledge about the dataset that are likely to hinder your analysis of the problem. Thirdly, there are a series of common sense quality checks to conduct. Each is discussed below.

Sources of error checks

Start by asking the following questions. This will help to establish the degree to which there are any errors inherent in different aspects of the survey process:

- Are there any flaws in the overall survey design?
- What is the extent of (a) sample bias and (b) sampling error?
- Is there any interviewer bias/variability?
- Is there any questionnaire bias?
- Is there any respondent/politeness bias?
- Is there any coding variability?
- Is there any data preparation?

Check for gaps in your knowledge

- Are there any key pieces of contextual information that are missing, but if located could help you with your interpretation?
- Are you sure at what point in the questionnaire this idea was introduced?
- Do you have a feeling that further homework to explore some of the background to the data would pay dividends?
- Do you have any concerns that particular sub-groups, that could be of particular interest to a client, have not been analysed?
- Do you sense that the data miss issues that are being anxiously awaited by your end client?

Common sense quality checks

- Do you have any nagging queries about exactly how an item of data that appears on a table was defined?
- Are you not sure why certain questions in the survey were asked?
- Are you clear what each statistic is based on? (Is it the whole sample, or is it a filtered survey question that has not been asked of everybody?)
- Are you certain about the exact wording of the question that has been summarised on the computer table? (Would understanding the fuller question help you better understand the answer? If so, go and look this up.)
- Is it clear whether the information was asked on an unprompted or prompted basis?
- Were respondents allowed to give a multiple or single response to the question?

- Are you clear which way the percentages go? (In most tables the percentages go downwards, but in some tables percentages can go across.)
- Have the data been grouped and aggregated in a way that is confusing? Should you disaggregate them?
- Is it clear whether the response was to an open-ended or pre-coded question?
- Is there any suggestion that the table has been incorrectly specified? Some common errors include:
  - wrong filter
  - wrong base
  - failure to clarify the difference between the 'don't knows' and the 'not answereds'.

Step 6: data reduction; making the dataset manageable

Next, organise your data into a more manageable form that will aid the identification of the key storyline. There are two lines of attack here. First, it is helpful to draw on those statistical techniques that help us cut down on the amount of data in front of us. These include, of course, using various *measures of central location*. It could also include applying various *measures of variation* in order to summarise the way responses to a question are distributed. At this stage it is also helpful to apply one or two top line tests to establish the overall error margins within which a survey statistic needs to be interpreted, and to obtain a broad rule of thumb guide as to what differences between two survey statistics are required for this to represent a statistical difference. This should not override the point we made earlier about the importance following the holistic analysis approach of looking at the overall shape and pattern of data, rather than being locked into pure statistical tests of significance. However, it is clearly prudent to have a broad idea, when looking at a dataset, as to what kinds of differences are meaningful, as this is all part and parcel of the process of cutting through and reducing the data to those elements that have most meaning. So, in short, part of the data reduction process will involve using tried and tested, standard statistical techniques. This achieved, we then move on to the second line of attack, which is to reduce the data using common sense and first principles. Below, we provide 12 key data reduction principles. For each we provide a statement of the key principle and follow this up with a before and after example of the principle in action.

Principle No. 1. When appropriate round up statistical percentages:

Before	After
10.89	11
11.91	12
12.98	13
13.71	14

Principle No. 2. Ensure the title explains as much as possible about what type of respondent was asked what type of question:

Before		After	
Attitudes towards air travel		Level of agreement among regular businessair travellers towards three statements about flying	
	%		%
I enjoy flying	60	I enjoy flying	60
I have to fly although I		I have to fly although I	
don't enjoy it	30	don't enjoy it	30
I hate flying	10	I hate flying	10

Principle No. 3. As a general rule, the 'dominant' subject, e.g. brand, should be a 'row' and the sub-group variation, e.g. region, be a 'column':

Before			After			
Region	Soap buy		Soap buy	Region		
	Flux	Ramay		Total	North	South
Total	**50**	**50**		%	%	%
North	70	30	Flux	**50**	70	30
South	30	70	Ramay	**50**	30	70

Principle No. 4. Present tabular data in an easy to follow order, rather than in the order that has been generated from the computer print-out:

Before			After	
Favourite holiday location			Favourite holiday location	
	100 %			100 %
USA	20		Spain	40
France	30		France	30
Spain	40		USA	20
Italy	10		Italy	10

Principle No. 5. By reflex many will automatically place the percentage sign on the column, rather than the row, but sometimes this will be incorrect. Be precise about which way the percentages run:

Before			After		
Bought Whizzo by	Age		Bought Whizzo by	Age	
	Under 30	Over 30		Under 30	Over 30
	%	%			
Cash	20	80	Credit card %	80	20
Credit card	80	20	Cash %	20	80
Wrong			**Correct**		

Principle No. 6. Do not use the bases that were generated from the first iteration of computer print-out, think about what is best to make your point:

Before		After	
Total travel to Europe at least once a year	1000 %	Total travel to Europe at least once a year	1000 %
Awareness of French supermarket chains:		*Base*: All aware of at least one French supermarket chain:	200 %
● Champion	8	● Champion	40
● Intermarche	5	● Intermarche	25
● E. Leclerc	5	● E. Leclerc	25
● Casino	2	● Casino	10
Never visited France and/or aware of any French supermarkets	80		

Principle No. 7. By changing the order, and also possibly the grouping of rows, it is possible to make data clearer:

Before	
Location of last purchase	Total %
● London	20
● Birmingham	10
● North-East	15
● Newcastle	10
● South-East	25
● Midlands	20

After	
Location of last purchase	Total %
● South-East/London	45
● Midlands/Birmingham	30
● North-East/Newcastle	25

Principle No. 8. The grouping, and also changing of column order, can make data easier to follow:

Before			
Buy	Region		
	Midlands	North	South
	%	%	%
Daily	10	5	20
Weekly	30	25	35
Monthly	60	70	45

After			
Buy	Region		
	North	Midlands	South
	%	%	%
Daily	5	10	20
Weekly	25	30	35
Monthly	70	60	45

Principle No. 9. Grouping sub-groups and using an average can make it easier for the reader to understand row and column data:

Before				
% Read magazine	Age			
Region	20–29 %	30–39 %	40–49 %	50+ %
London	35	38	45	55
South-East	25	22	40	40
North-West	25	29	10	3
North-East	15	11	5	2

After		
% Read magazine	Age	
Region	20–39 %	40+ %
London		
South-East	30	45
North	20	5

Principle No. 10. Graphical design concepts such as (white) space and/or dotted lines can make data easier to understand:

Before			
		Children	
Goods purchased	Total %	Yes %	No %
Tea	92	91	93
Milk	90	89	91
Bread	94	93	95
Eggs	63	62	64
Cheese	42	41	43
Butter	54	53	55
Sugar	93	92	93
Bacon	35	34	36
Lamb	28	28	29

After			
		Children	
Goods purchased	Total %	Yes %	No %
Bread	94	93	95
Sugar	93	92	93
Tea	92	91	93
Milk	90	89	91
Eggs	63	62	64
Butter	54	53	55
Cheese	42	41	43
Bacon	35	35	36
Lamb	28	28	29

Principle No. 11. Sometimes it is legitimate to 'dump detail' and get over the main headline figure with a summary statistic:

Before	
Car owned	Total %
Mercedes	20
Audi	25
BMW	20
Citroen	15
Renault	10
Peugeot	10

After	
Own car made in	Total %
Germany	65
France	35

Principle No. 12. Sometimes a table will lack impact and a chart will lack detail, so a mixture of graph and table can pay dividends:

Before	
Car owned	Total %
Mercedes	20
Audi	25
BMW	20
Citroen	15
Renault	10
Peugeot	10

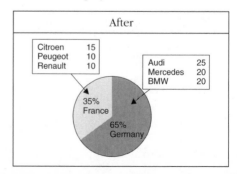

Increasingly, presentations are using *computer projection systems* which allow the idea shown above – mixing number and graphics – to be developed into sophisticated formats. These techniques are powerful and exciting. They help bring together a mixture of (reduced) data and imaginative graphics and allow the delivery of many of the above data reduction principles. The new technology includes being able to 'unfold' data line by line, row by row or column by column as the presentation progresses. It also includes the ability to use a 'spot-light' to show groupings of different categories of data. It is also possible to use techniques whereby various market segments shown in a pie chart 'open up' to reveal an embedded video clip of an 'archetypal' comment being made by someone from this segment. The options are almost endless.

Data reduction: putting it all together

In Table 6.1 we show how, by applying some of the simple data reduction principles outlined above, it is possible to move from a dataset that it is difficult to analyse, to one that allows us immediately to see the key trends. (The data in the table are fictitious and should not be used for decision-making!) (See Tables 6.2 and 6.3.)

Step 7: identifying the 'storyline'

We now arrive at the point in the analysis process where we must identify the overall 'storyline' inherent in the dataset: just exactly what are the data trying to tell us? It is helpful to break this task down into the following activities.

Dump detail: concentrating on the 'top line'

It is helpful to begin the analysis by concentrating solely on finding out about the 'top line' story. At this point, you will be analysing in broad strokes: you should not be afraid to dump detail in order to 'cut to the chase' and establish what the main storyline is all about. You must not be frightened to omit things. If you do not understand something in close

Table 6.1   Data reduction – putting it all together: the original presentation of the data

	Base sizes (no.)	Theatre	Classical concerts	Jazz concerts	Pop & rock concerts	Opera	Ballet	Contemporary dance
Visitors in 1994 to the theatre and concerts (percentage adults)								
Total UK adults 15+	4520	37.2	12.1	6.2	22.3	6.4	6.6	4.0
Male	2178	33.2	11.5	6.8	24.5	5.8	4.2	3.0
Female	2342	41.1	12.7	5.6	20.3	7.0	8.9	4.9
15–24	845	33.2	8.1	7.9	40.3	4.5	5.0	5.8
25–34	835	38.0	10.4	7.4	40.3	6.6	7.4	5.0
35–44	768	42.3	11.8	6.2	28.7	6.7	6.9	5.5
45–54	622	43.4	15.5	6.5	16.4	7.5	7.5	4.0
55–64	573	40.5	16.3	7.2	4.0	7.5	8.0	2.3
65+	877	28.3	12.0	2.7	0.8	6.0	5.4	1.5
AB	812	59.0	26.2	11.9	28.2	15.1	13.9	7.6
C1	1061	44.5	13.8	7.9	26.8	7.1	8.1	4.9
C2	1306	28.5	5.7	3.4	21.6	2.8	3.2	2.2
D	776	22.3	4.7	2.3	18.5	1.8	2.5	2.1
E	565	17.4	4.5	2.4	8.0	2.1	2.2	1.5

Table 6.2 *Data reduction*

- Putting it all together: original data with five improvements
- Rounding percentages
- Re-orientating the columns and rows of the table
- Ordering columns from high to low
- Grouping sub-groups
- Better labelling to make the table self-explanatory (and a postscript device to explain a statistic where there was particular variation)

Visitors to UK theatres and concerts in 1994 by gender, age and social class

All adults 15+	Total sample	Gender		Age			Social class			
		Men	Women	15–34	35–64	65+	AB	C1	C2/D	E
Base for %	4520	2178	2342	1680	1963	877	812	1061	2082	565
Visited following type of concert in 1994	%	%	%	%	%	%	%	%	%	%
Theatre	37	33	41	36	42	28	59	45	26	17
Pop & rock	22	24	20	40	18*	1	28	27	20	8
Classical	12	12	13	9	14	12	26	14	5	5
Ballet	6	4	9	6	7	5	14	8	3	2
Opera	6	6	7	6	7	6	15	7	2	2
Jazz	6	7	6	8	7	3	12	8	3	2
Dance	4	3	5	5	4	2	8	5	2	2

- Note the following variation within this sub-grouping: 55–64 years – 4%; 45–54 years – 16% and 35–44 years – 29%.
- Respondents could mention more than one theatre or concert visit. Some respondents made no visits.

Table 6.3 *Data reduction – putting it all together: this version involves focusing on the main points of difference*

Visitors to UK theatres and concerts in 1994

Base 4520	Total adults 15+ %	Visits greatest amongst
• Theatre	37	ABs: 59%
• Pop & rock	22	15–34 yrs: 40%
• Classical	12	ABs: 26%
• Ballet	6	ABs: 14%
• Opera	6	ABs: 15%
• Jazz	6	ABs: 12%
• Dance	4	ABs: 12%

detail, do not worry – it can be returned to later. Think of the task as being akin to how someone would tackle a jigsaw. There is little merit in devoting many hours to establishing that in the bottom left-hand corner of the jigsaw there is a particular breed of dog. What you need to know (to pursue the metaphor) is that by first quickly putting in the sky and other edging, i.e. the main parts of the jigsaw, you will establish that the jigsaw is about a man out walking his dog. Then return later to the details of what kind of man and what type of dog. In Table 6.4 we provide a technique that will help you identify the top line story in *survey* data.

Be prepared to 'shuttle'

Remember Insight 2: investigation is a circular not linear process. The reality of data analysis is that you must constantly 'shuttle' between the evidence and your initial interpretations. Start with the initial insights you have obtained from the survey evidence and then – on the basis of subsequent discussions with colleagues during the course of the analysis – go back to the beginning again to make absolutely certain that there is a 'fit' between the storyline (theory) you are developing and the facts at your disposal. The whole basis of 'hypothesis testing' in science is one example of this 'circular' process. Having identified the top line; be prepared to re-visit your initial 'take'. Specifically, it will be helpful to sharpen this iterative analysis process by addressing the following six issues:

Table 6.4 *A technique for quickly identifying top line survey findings*

A: *Take a copy of the survey questionnaire and enter the answers to each of the questions for the total sample.* Do *not* worry about how the results vary by different sub-groups within the population, such as by young and old, men and women, and so on. At this point you are simply concentrating on recording the overall *total sample* storyline.

B: *Organise your marketing objectives in priority order.* List all the issues that you expect the survey to answer, or address, in priority order, from *most* to *least* important.

C: *Identify which questions provide answers to each of the prioritised marketing objectives. Then physically cut out this question, together with its answer, and group these questions and answers under the respective marketing objectives.* You are now physically grouping the different questions and answers so you may find that the answer to question 2 goes alongside the answer to question 47 and question 27 in addressing marketing objective number 1 and so on.

D: *Immerse yourself in understanding the overall storyline.* Now, absorb what the top line story is telling you. If necessary, tell the story to yourself out loud and see whether you feel it is right.

E: *Only when you are familiar with the total storyline for the survey should you consider moving into an analysis of the variations by key sub-groups.*

- *Must, not nice, to know.* Have you concentrated on what are crucially relevant findings, and excluded other peripheral information? Have you concentrated on the 'must answer', as opposed to 'nice to know' issues? Have you made sure that you have not gone off on a 'frolic of your own'; that is, developed a 'storyline' based on a very partial preconceived view of the world?

- *The 'fog' factor.* Have you translated complex numerical arguments into simple, easy to understand language? Have you used devices, such as comparing and contrasting items of information, in order to make your point? Are your charts self-explanatory – that is, could someone look at the numbers and, without reading any text, come to the correct interpretation?

- *The blind alley.* Have you made sure you have not been driven up a blind alley by a freakish figure? Remember that *any figure that looks interesting is probably wrong*. If there is just one figure that underpins the whole line of the analysis on which you are about to embark, go back and check that this is not simply an incorrect figure.

- *I don't believe it!* Could you provide a sound rationale for the arguments you are advancing? Can you explain the data verbally to yourself without recall to complicated numerical arguments?

- *The 'pub' test.* An important litmus paper test to check whether your 'storyline' is becoming overly confused is to do the 'pub' test. Imagine you were explaining your analysis to the 'average bloke' next to you in the pub. Could you explain this to this person in a way that he/she would find credible, understandable and easy to follow?

- *End client's expectations.* Can you answer the questions that the client will inevitably ask you at the presentation? Are you close to answering all the key business questions?

Step 8: identifying the overall 'shapes and patterns'

Throughout this book we have referred to the importance of trying to find 'shapes and patterns' that run across datasets that will provide decision-makers with key insights, rather than just isolated, tactical observations about market behaviour. This is the process of finding *rhythms and themes* in the dataset.

It is part of the natural human condition to seek out consistent rhythms and patterns that exist in events and information. But amid this quest for symmetry – rather than irregularity – beware of opting for over-simplified, 'rounded-out' versions of reality. Living things do not like chaos. All organisms, from the very simplest single celled animals and plants upwards, are 'pattern detectors'. They love rhythmic cycles and predictability. Looking at this, at its most simplest, the scientific process is obviously about 'order'. The objectives of science are first to find out what there is out there (i.e. establish the 'furniture' of the universe); then find out how these things are related to one another; and then to establish how a change in one (or some) of these things causes changes in another. This achieved, scientists will then seek to make predictions about what will happen in the future to a thing (or group of things) based on what has happened to them in the past, and identify any novel intervening events we expect to occur. Thus, in sum, we are all 'pro-grammed' constantly to seek out 'consistent shapes and patterns'.

However, from time to time – in the world of marketing – the solution will require an off-the-wall, more anarchic look at the world. Did the zany Benson & Hedges advertising result from a 'conventional' analysis of smokers' information needs or something less considered?

Essentially, shape and pattern detection involves two mutually reinforcing sets of skills. First, there are the skills required to apply the key holistic concepts that we have begun to discuss, notably looking at the weight, power and direction of evidence. And secondly, there is utilising the power of statistical analysis to look at the shapes and patterns in data. Below, we look at each of these two key areas.

Applying key holistic analysis concepts

We have already introduced the notion of establishing the *weight, power* and *direction* of evidence. We now build on the points made previously to provide further detail on exactly how these holistic analysis approach concepts can be applied to the data analysis process.

 Weight of evidence By weight, we are referring to where the evidence stands on the following two dimensions:

- *Balance of opinion.* This provides a 'quantitative' assessment of how many individuals favour one option rather than another. (In a quantitative survey this would be statistically based and with a qualitative study based on 'counts' taken as part of the content analysis of transcripts, etc.)
- *Depth of feeling.* This was an insight into the *intensity of feeling* that people experience on this topic. (This could be based on a qualitative assessment of verbatim comments and/or on quantitative structured attitude questioning.)

When the inter-relationship between the 'balance of opinion' in favour of a particular initiative and the 'depth of feeling' on the issue are examined together, we start to build up a picture of the overall weight of evidence that would support or reject a particular initiative. This is shown in Figure 6.6, together with an example for each of the four quadrants.

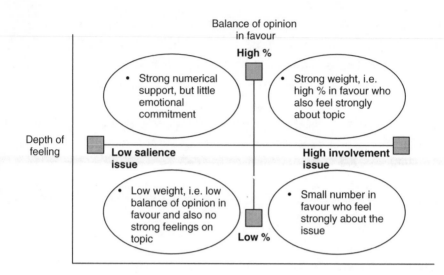

Figure 6.6 *The weight of evidence: the relationship between balance of opinion and depth of feeling*

- *Top right-hand quadrant.* An example of high numerical support combining with intense depth of feeling would be, following the death of Diana Princess of Wales, the *weight* of evidence in the United Kingdom in support of commemorating her life in various ways.
- *Bottom right-hand quadrant.* An example of where there could be a small numerical balance of opinion in favour of a particular point of view, but where the depth of feeling amongst this group is so strong that it becomes quite a potent force, is the media's initial view of the Millennium Dome. The majority of visitors seemed to be reasonably satisfied with the exhibits on offer, but once the media – with some venom – vented their feelings, then pressure mounted leading to the resignation of the CEO.
- *Top left-hand quadrant.* Here we find strong numerical support being coupled with little emotional commitment in favour of the decision. An example here might be attitudes towards a decision to do away with leaded petrol.
- *Bottom left-hand quadrant.* An illustration of a combination of low numerical support and low levels of salience might be (in England!) a decision to create more European Members of Parliament.

The power of the evidence   It is helpful to think of evidence as not just having 'weight', but also 'power'. This assessment of the 'power' of a piece of evidence, takes into account the following *explicit* and *implicit* elements.

1. *The explicit assessment.* This refers to what we know about this particular 'genre' of data. For example, is this data of a type whereby one single, free-standing observation leads us relentlessly to a logical conclusion, or is it the type of data that only makes sense when fitted into a time series and/or evaluated against a benchmark? Let us now look at this concept in more detail. Below, we provide a classification of different data types. Understanding the nuances of different categories of data – their power and limitations – is a key part of the holistic analysis of data.

- *Data as a 'clue'.* It is helpful, as we have already indicated, to think of data as a 'clue' in the investigative sense: as powerful food for thought in taking an investigation forward. Clues are the kind of data that can often be overlooked and relegated to the 'editing room floor' of data analysis. Winston Churchill once observed that people often 'stumble upon the truth, but get up, brush themselves down and continue as if nothing had happened'. For example, 3M were on the verge of abandoning Post-It Notes because it did not know how this 'new technology' could be applied when it decided to hand out batches of Post-It Notes to its office staff in order to obtain some 'clues' as to what people did with them. The rest you know!
- *Single (logical) observations.* There will be certain situations where only one observation is needed to arrive at a decision that action is needed. For example, if we establish that an (allegedly) child-proof medicine bottle was opened by one child in a (supervised) product packaging test, then this *single* observation alone tells us that we should take immediate action. Here, we do not need 'balance of opinion' type evidence: knowing what *proportion* of all children could repeat the feat is not the point.
- *Relative data.* Knowing where your data sit in relation to other readings and observations is clearly important. For example, knowing there are three points for a win and Tottenham Hotspur has obtained 30 points, tells you something. But knowing this places them 18th out of a league of 20, tells you more!

- *Time series data.* Data that can be set in the context of what went before are comparatively easy to interpret and are therefore a key part of the evidence armoury.
- *Norms.* Equally as powerful as the above are data for which there are clear yardsticks against which to evaluate the 'standing' of your own item of evidence.
- *Conceptual models.* Data that can be fitted into a 'conceptual model' that has been developed to explain how a particular market works will be more powerful than data that cannot be so classified. For example, we are all familiar with the idea of there being 'early' and 'late' adopters of products. But in the highly dynamic communications and information technology sector, this 'model' needs refining. We still have the early, go-ahead adopters and experimenters, and the tardy 'technophobes'. But today there is a new category – those who immediately go into the *watching brief* category. These are customers who will be wise enough to know that a piece of new technology is something that they will eventually need, but who will wait for key triggers – such as confirmation that a key competitor has taken the plunge and bought the new kit and/or that a trusted friend is providing reliable product reports – before purchasing themselves. The point we are making is that if information fits into some form of conceptual model of how a market 'works', this gives this item of evidence considerable power.
- *Predictive models and forecasts.* In some situations the decision-maker will be able to make use of a predictive model that will help him/her make reasonably reliable forecasts about, for instance, the likely take-up of a product at different price levels.

2. *The implicit assessment.* This tells us where our item of data fits into the wider context of what we already know about this topic after taking into account existing management 'prior knowledge'. In today's sophisticated world of management science it is tempting to take the view that what we intuitively know about something is somehow secondary to all statistical information *science*. But this is not the case. As we have already stressed, in undertaking *holistic* data analysis it is important to remember that your own implicit intuitions, hunches and prior knowledge on a particular issue can be just as important as the formal, explicit evidence.

It is not the case that what you hold in your head is somehow 'unworthy', and, as such, should be the poor relation to 'management science'. In the past people have tended to be rather dismissive of individuals who elect to explain their world via 'anecdotes' about apparently isolated incidents. But these so-called anecdotes may in fact represent genuine insights, rather than simply one-off experiences. In short, these observations may represent valuable archetypal experience – insights that need to be factored into our collective understanding. It must always be remembered that anecdotes – or more precisely archetypes – could be highly representative of a widely occurring factor or phenomenon. It thus becomes important in understanding a marketing problem to work hard to capture such implicit, intuitive knowledge. Put another way, 'knowing without knowing why' is totally acceptable. Below we look at two specific types of implicit knowledge, 'prior knowledge' and 'management hunch'.

- *Prior knowledge.* An important indicator of the potential 'power' of an item of information is, of course, where it sits in terms of our *prior knowledge* on the topic. Fresh primary evidence that can be set in the context of previous experience that might support a particular point of view will clearly carry more interpretative 'power' than data that exist in a relatively 'contextless' vacuum. By including prior knowledge in the formal analysis process the quality of understanding is significantly improved.
- *Management hunch.* Just because management hunch – what is in your head – is difficult to articulate explicitly, does not mean that this should not be respected as a genuine complement to more explicit marketing information. Translating implicit knowledge into a more tangible explicit form that can be accessed and analysed by others is a challenge, but, notwithstanding the potential difficulties, it is important to use these insights alongside the more 'scientifically collected' information. In sum, you know more than you think you do: respect your judgement and feel confident in factoring your hunches into the 'formal' evidence.

It is helpful to look at the inter-relationship between the two dimensions that make up the 'power' concept. Thus in Figure 6.7 we show how the power of a piece of data will be determined by what type of data this is. As explained, sometimes we only need one single logical observation in

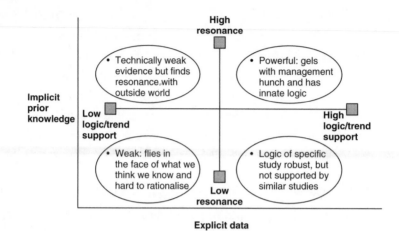

Figure 6.7 *The power of evidence: the relationship between implicit prior knowledge and the explicit data*

order to take action, but other times, we need data to be part of a wider trend. One can see from Figure 6.7 that data can be categorised as being high or low in logic and/or the support the data enjoy from being part of a trend (time series). The second power dimension is the extent to which the new evidence fits with prior and implicit knowledge on the topic. Does it generate a high or low resonance? We can now distinguish between data in the *top right-hand quadrant*, i.e. where management hunch gels with the innate logic of the evidence, and data in the *bottom left-hand quadrant* that are weaker because they fly in the face of what we think we know, and are hard to rationalise in terms of the logic of the argument.

Identifying the direction of the evidence   The direction of evidence concept again has two dimensions. First, there is the question of whether the data are high or low in terms of their *internal* directional consistency.

Do different parts of the dataset come together to reinforce the consistency of the story? Secondly, there is the issue of the *external* consistency of data – where do the data sit in regard to being supported, or not, by the pattern of other external evidence. Working with the inter-relationship of these two concepts, we can begin to think of data being 'directionally sound'

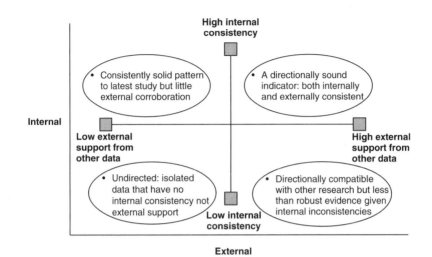

Figure 6.8   *The direction of evidence: the relationship between the internal and external consistency of data*

(both in terms of their internal and external consistency), as opposed to being 'undirected and isolated' (see Figure 6.8).

The power of statistical analysis

It is important, as we unfold the holistic data analysis approach, not to create the impression that we are setting up some kind of 'them and us', sectarian warfare between the disciplines of 'classic', statistical theory and some of the softer holistic (right brain) skills we have been introducing. This book is about striking the appropriate balance between logic and intuition. It is about learning how to use our experience to find the appropriate path between the logic of the hard evidence, and what our intuitive insights are telling us. In many scenarios, statistical analysis will be very much to the fore in helping, not only to test the robustness of particular items of evidence, but also in helping to pinpoint the key shapes, patterns and trends in complex datasets.

It is important for the holistic analyst – the bricoleur – to feel confident in utilising various statistical analysis techniques. It should be stressed that there is a fundamental difference between *mathematical* prowess, and the ability to understand and use *numerical* concepts. So, let us reassure the non-mathematical data analyst that it is possible to understand quantitative data with little more than basic numeracy. Understanding numbers does *not* require higher order mathematical skills (this would be a bonus).

So, in sum, it is important for the reader not to think that holistic data analysis is somehow a counterpoint to quantitative analysis. The whole point of holistic analysis is to combine the mutually reinforcing power of qualitative and quantitative analysis.

This is another massive topic of which we can only scratch the surface in this book. In Table 6.5 we provide a brief review – explained in conceptual terms – of some of the multivariate statistical techniques at our disposal to help reduce data to manageable proportions and pinpoint the fundamental shapes and patterns contained within the data.

 ## Step 9: conceptual model building

We have already highlighted the importance of the culmination of the data analyst's work being some form of 'conceptual model' that explains how customers behave and/or markets 'work'. We have explained that these conceptual models can sometimes be qualitatively based, but have particular power if they are developed with a combination of large-scale, 'hard' numerical data, supported by softer qualitative evidence and intuitive insights. Again, this is a massive topic and difficult to describe beyond making the point about the importance of making conceptual model building the culmination of the holistic analysis 'craft'. Specifically, in this book we have made various references to the value of developing conceptual models in order to help make sense of 'isolated' pieces of incoming marketing data. The term 'conceptual model' will mean differ-ent things to different people. But it is important to register the point that when we use the term, we are not simply referring to a general schemer that organises data. Neither are we necessarily referring to a full 'pre-dictive model'. By conceptual model we are referring to something that sits between these ends of the spectrum – a framework characterised by having some of the following elements:

- *Locates a problem in context.* A feature of the conceptual model is that it will position the data in a wider macro and historical perspective. So

Table 6.5 *A review of some multivariate techniques*

- *Factor analysis.* Factor analysis has two main objectives. First, to reduce a very large number of variables (i.e. statements to which a sample of respondents have given agreement/importance type responses) down to a manageable number of 'factors' which capture the essence of respondents' views on the subjects to which the original statements referred. Secondly, to prepare importance/agreement style datasets for further statistical analysis which require the datasets to comprise only entirely independent variables (such as in regression techniques or standardised means and variances as in cluster analysis). The basic technique underpinning factor analysis is correlation: a factor analysis starts by establishing the degree to which respondents' views on different statements coincide or overlap. Thus, if most respondents give very similar scores (high or low) to two different statements, there is a high, positive correlation between the statements; if respondents tend to differ in their scores, i.e. they give to two different statements, e.g. some scoring one very high, whilst scoring the other very low, others scoring both very high, etc., there is a low correlation between the two statements. And if they give equal, but opposite scores, to two statements, e.g. very high on one statement and very low on the other, there is a high negative correlation between the two statements.

- *Cluster analysis.* Whereas factor analysis is a way of grouping together variables (i.e. statements to which a sample of respondents have given agreement/importance type responses) to reduce the number of them we have to deal with, cluster analysis is a way of grouping the respondents themselves together (into clusters) on the basis of similarities between them in the scores that they gave to the statement. There are two main types of cluster analysis technique: hierarchical clustering, which is based on mathematical principles, whereby clustering choices and judgements are transparent, and iterative cluster analysis, which is a heuristic, rather than strict mathematical technique, whereby the clustering choices are more arbitrary and largely opaque. This technique needs validation, which may not always prove conclusive.

- *Trade-off analysis.* Trade-off analysis is one of the terms used to describe a broad range of techniques for estimating the value people place on the attributes or features which define products and services. Some of the better known techniques are discrete choice; choice modelling; hierarchical choice; card sort; SIMALTO trade-off matrices; preferences-based conjoint analysis; adaptive conjoint analysis; and pair trade-offs. The goal of any trade-off survey design is to assign specific values to the range of options buyers consider when making a purchasing decision. Armed with this logic, marketers can focus on the most important features of products or services, and design messages most likely to strike a chord with target buyers. To make this idea concrete, it is perhaps helpful briefly to outline two main methodologies – conjoint analysis and SIMALTO.

  - *Conjoint.* This stems from the term 'considered jointly'. In essence, respondents are asked to indicate strength of preference for different propositions, often against one another, each of which embodies different combinations of the attributes we are trying to measure. For example, we asked respondents to think about Holiday A (Spain, stay in apartment, with pool, chartered flights) and Holiday B (America, stay in a villa, no pool, scheduled flights). We asked respondents to tell us which holiday they preferred by choosing a number between one and nine. We could find that someone who did not mind at all

continues

Table 6.5 (*continued*)

which country they travelled to, but was looking for a pool and villa, might think that the two holidays were roughly equally attractive, except that the American holiday had scheduled, rather than chartered flights. This might make them slightly more likely to prefer Holiday B. Another person might so strongly prefer the idea of a holiday in Spain and hate the idea of a holiday in America, that this would mean they strongly prefer the Spanish holiday and so on. The point being that a whole range of holiday choices are presented to the respondent, with the analysis telling us which particular attributes are driving choice.

– *SIMALTO*. This stands for Simultaneous Multi-Attribute Level Trade-Off. The process is as follows:

- Respondents are presented with a grid of attributes, with levels of offer on each attribute ranging left to right (worst to best).
- An attribute level to the right-hand side of the grid is worth 'more than' a level to the left.
- The expected ideal level on each attribute is defined by respondents (they can choose any level).
- The unacceptable level is defined.
- The perceived positioning of different others is defined by reference to the grid.
- The respondent is then allocated a certain number of points to spend across the grid. This number is less than the total available. This means they are invited to trade off certain possibly desirable levels against others. This begins to establish the trade-off between (for example) price and functionality.
- The number of points is then reduced to force further trade-off. At each stage the attractiveness and likely-to-use measure for the whole offer is established. So it can be seen that if only 20 points were available to a respondent he or she would not be able to choose the best possible product (which requires 24 points) but must necessarily make trade-offs. The trade-offs become more demanding as points are removed from the budget. Thus, the SIMALTO approach has the merit of establishing the real individual trade-offs that people make (what they are prepared to sacrifice first, as well as establishing how important each individual attribute is to them).

an individual piece of data explaining why certain people may decide to cash in a savings plan before it has run its full term will be positioned in the context of developments in the overall economy, comparisons with other financial regular savings products, and also set in the context of trends in the lapsing of various types of saving plans over time. As part of this contextualisation, critical comparator data may also be drawn into the analysis. For example, we could look at whether there are any fundamental differences in attitudes towards saving products in the United States and Europe and so on.

- *Draws together and integrates all available primary and secondary evidence.* The second feature of the conceptual model is that considerable emphasis will be placed on ensuring that all the different types of evidence currently being collected to investigate the problem – desk research, secondary data analysis, qualitative research, quantitative evidence – will be drawn together. Specifically, the 'weight', 'power' and 'direction' of individual pieces of data will be assessed and then fitted together in a bricolage-like fashion to build an overall picture. Importantly, this process of drawing together the evidence will include *judgemental inputs*, bearing in mind the importance of factoring in implicit knowledge.

- *Pinpoints the key linkages and drivers.* A key feature of a conceptual model is that it will *attempt* to map all of the variables that theoretically need to be taken into account in studying a particular problem. In part, these variables will be pinpointed via the formal research, but also, in part, by other intellectual processes such as brainstorming different ideas, developing different scenarios about the future and so on. Having developed this overall map, attempts will then be made to establish the key drivers of particular types of behaviour and attitude. This may be achieved by working with the innate logic of different inter-relationships, or could involve various multivariate statistical and/or econometric techniques aimed at looking more precisely at the various cause-and-effect relationships. Thus, to pursue our example of people who terminate regular savings products prematurely, the conceptual model will be able to start explaining the way in which the macro-economic climate, age, income level, family circumstance, what might be happening in the media, and a host of other factors all come to play to shape and drive an individual's decision. It should be stressed that this activity may lead to the development of some form of 'predictive' model, but could well fall short of this by simply providing a framework that maps out the key influential factors, thereby allowing the decision-maker to make reasonably informed judgements about what might happen in particular circumstances.

- *Renewal.* The Counsel of Perfection calls for any conceptual model that has been developed to explain a particular phenomenon, not to be set in stone, but to be set up in a way that encourages people who are using the model continually to refine and develop it on the basis of incoming information.

Step 10: displaying the data; delivering actionable findings that meet decision-makers' expectations

The final part of the holistic approach to analysis is to ensure that the end product of all the analytical hard work manifests itself in the type of presentation that acknowledges the way busy decision-makers now take on board arguments and evidence. We have said that the holistic approach is akin to assembling a 'jigsaw'. But when the jigsaw is presented it is important that the audience cannot see the joins. What people want in today's time-urgent world is a clear explanation of what the *collective evidence* is telling them. People do not want ponderous, disjointed presentations of the various 'building blocks' of evidence. This observation certainly squares with the new evidence becoming available about how certain (particularly dynamic, highly effective and successful) people process the wealth of information in front of them. We are now realising that while apparently listening to a market research presentation, many 'high achiever' personality types will, in fact, be making certain judgements and decisions 'there and then', *on the run*, in 'real time'. These are people who do not go through the classic, linear 'building block', decision-making process, whereby they first listen patiently to the person presenting different elements of the argument, and then, at the end of the presentation – after reflecting on the evidence – eventually, in time, arrive at their decision. In today's pressured work environment many individuals will be *instantly* making judgements and decisions based on what incoming information is 'telling them'. This explains the restlessness of many individuals in 'classic' linear, building block type (market research) presentations. So it is important to provide a simple framework to help information users rapidly evaluate incoming information in a way that will help them make certain judgements and decisions 'on the run'. Below we provide an illustration of the old-fashioned 'building block' style presentation, and then compare and contrast this with the integrated attacking style which is required in the future.

Building block approach

The traditional way of presenting data is what we might call the *building block* approach. This is characterised in Figure 6.9. It involves assembling

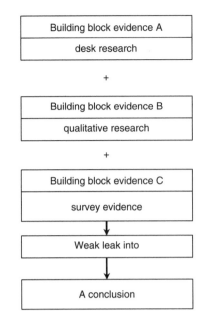

Figure 6.9   *The building block approach*

the different blocks of evidence, let us say the 'desk research', then the 'qualitative research', then the 'survey results', and so on. Following this, there would then be an often quite weak link from what these building blocks of evidence are telling us and the answers to the specific research objective.

An integrated attacking style

The above comparatively pedestrian 'building block' style to presenting research evidence can be contrasted with the far more concise and elegant *integrated attacking* style of presentation. One of the benefits of holistic analysis is that when presenting data you will be totally on top of all your evidence sources. You will fully understand all of the sources of error inherent in the survey process and also know exactly how different parts of the final argument have come together. In addition, you will have been through the process of piecing together and integrating evidence drawn from a range of different eclectic sources. This should put you in a strong position to pinpoint the key issues that need addressing in order to arrive at a particular conclusion. Thus, you should

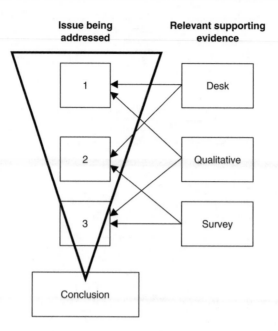

Figure 6.10   *The integrated attacking style of presentation*

be able to assemble the evidence in a far more attacking and integrated form than is normally the case with the building block approach. In developing an attacking style, there are various quantitative techniques that can help in displaying data in an 'attacking and pacy' way. For instance, there are various perceptual mapping and multi-dimensional scaling techniques that allow you to explain visually where brands and customers sit in an overall market context. These, and other techniques, can be quite powerful display tools. In Figure 6.10 we can see how this type of presentation starts by addressing key issue number one. In order to deal with this opening issue, the appropriate supporting evidence is drawn *selectively* from the desk research, qualitative evidence and the survey results. The presentation is therefore not 'driven' by the type of research being presented, but taken forward by focusing on the key issues. Moreover, only the most relevant and powerful evidence is *selected* to substantiate each point. We then move to issue two – operating in a similar way – relentlessly moving towards an end point, which is almost *self-concluding*, given the elegance and power of the ongoing argument.

The 'building block' approach to the presentation of an argument is something of which we have all been guilty. It is a kind of intellectual laziness. We will remember it from our college days. For example, if asked the question: 'Should Britain enter the Single European Currency?' our first reflex is to assemble and regurgitate *parrot fashion* our (or someone else's!) lecture notes on the 'history', 'geography', 'economics' and 'politics' of Europe, and so on. Having paraphrased all this rather general background material, we eventually reach the point where we have to make a massive leap forward in order to answer the actual question posed. But it is now that we realise that, at no point, have we tightly related the geographical and/or economic and/or political facts with which we were presented, to the critical question being posed about whether or not Britain should abandon the pound and embrace the euro. It is at this point that we make a rather pathetic attempt to link our facts to the answer. Here, a favourite is 'it follows quite simply of course that . . .', which, of course, immediately tells the seasoned campaigner that it does not. In contrast, the more integrated attacking style of presentation will immediately pinpoint the key issues which Britain must face up to in making a decision about joining the Single European Currency (such as, the implications of joining on our ability to control interest rates) and then provide all the arguments – drawing on economic and political evidence as appropriate – to support the point of views being presented.

Don't shoot the messenger

To put the finishing touches to the *perfect* presentation of your analysis, it is important to bear in mind that not all projects will have outcomes that are satisfactory from the standpoint of the end decision-maker. There will be situations where the key to a successful conclusion to a project will lie in carefully managing the presentation of *painful news*. A few tips on how to achieve this appear below.

- *Give early warning of results before the presentation.* You may have already presented hypothetical data, which will have given you a head start.
- *Ask (supportive) managers how they would recommend telling the news.* Make sure that you provide detailed accounts about the validity

and reliability and general robustness of the evidence, i.e. do not leave a door open that suggests that the 'bad news' can somehow be laid off because it is not based on solid evidence.

- *Present a balance of the 'for' and 'against' information.* Remember to reinforce the fact that managers can learn from failure as well as from success, i.e. tease out the positive constructive learning points. (Specifically, why not suggest viable strategies for coping with the problem by way of an added value dimension to your presentation?)
- *Emphasise what the research says the firm can do to improve a situation, rather than dwelling on negative situations.* There will be some good news – however slight – so always lead with this. This lessens the chances of the messenger being shot as soon as he walks in the door!
- *Help the audience recognise 'denial' symptoms.* It is quite commonplace for managers that are told by a market research agency that their initial ideas are flawed to go into 'denial'. This may first include denying that the market research agency has the necessary professionalism to make such a judgement. It could then move on to a grudging acceptance that the market research agency is right, but involve 'clinging on to straws' such as arguing that another research study, this time conducted with a slightly different type of respondent, may yield dramatically different results, and so forth. Given this tendency, it is helpful to (tactfully) remind the audience that this process of moving from absolute denial to partial denial to grudging acceptance and then acceptance of the research findings is quite common. But it is a process that needs managing.
- *Schedule an initial meeting to present the results* and another meeting to discuss its *implications.* Given the fact that in certain bad news scenarios clients will need to go through some period of 'grieving', while they gradually work through the 'denial' process, it is helpful to present the findings in two stages. The first to get over the evidence, and the second, following the denial phase, to get down to the practical and constructive task of what happens next.

Information-Based Decision-Making

Overview

This chapter:

- reviews organisational decision-making cultures that can influence the quality of decision-making
- explains the problems and difficulties organisations face when making information-based decisions
- looks at how different decision-making frameworks – including the 'Decision Evaluator' technique – can help the decision-maker more effectively apply evidence to the decision-making process
- reviews ways of ensuring that decisions, once made, are implemented in the spirit of what the research evidence is saying
- provides a summary of how to make optimum use of information when making, and implementing, decisions.

SEVEN

Information-Based
Decision-Making

'Once I have a feeling for the choices, I have no problem with the decision' – Lou Gerstner, IBM.

The inability to use information effectively is the Achilles' heel of many decision-making processes. When asked how they make decisions many managers will reply with: 'I weigh up all the evidence' or 'I look at the positives and negatives of the situation', and so on. But when decision-makers are pressed to describe in close detail the *exact* sequence of steps they follow to ensure they are making effective, high quality use of the information at their disposal, few managers tend to provide convincing answers. Some may be able to reel off the general 'textbook' approach: (a) define the problem and structure the nature of the decision to be made; (b) pinpoint the most important uncertainties associated with the decision; (c) review the information – hard and soft – that is available to help evaluate the problem; and (d) make the best possible judgement i.e. the one that will produce the most positive outcome for the organisation. But this utterly logical, disciplined – and difficult to refute – approach does not capture much of the 'messiness' of successfully using information for real-life business decision-making.

What we seek to achieve in this chapter is to provide some insights that will ensure more confidence in using information when making decisions. Our approach will not focus on mathematically-based decision models. This is because such approaches only account for a small proportion of marketing decision-making. Instead, we look at how doing a series of small and simple things can make all the difference in successfully applying information to decision-making. Of course, competency in handling information is only one side of the coin. Ultimately good decision-making involves wisdom. No amount of information, however good, will compensate for poor levels of judgement. However, we believe that much more can be done to minimise poor judgement. We start by looking at the way the culture in which decisions are made can affect our decision-making. By organisational culture we are referring to the lessons that a company learns during the course of its history – a set of assumptions that are considered to be valid because they have served that organisation well in the past.

Decision-making cultures

Organisational politics have a massive influence on how any one individual elects to make a decision within an organisation. This is a vast topic and space does not permit us to review all the different types of organisational cultures that could influence an individual decision-maker. Below, it is helpful to review briefly three key aspects of organisational decision-making cultures.

1. *The formal versus informal culture.* We all recognise that comparatively few decisions are taken in an objective, transparent, accountable way that fits in with the formal *written rules* for decision-making. We all realise that the way decisions are made within organisations will, in large measure, reflect a whole range of *informal* (unwritten) rules that characterise the way an organisation works. Here is not the place to catalogue all the informal practices that characterise organisational life, but they include such cultures as not being associated with failure, standing out from the crowd, meeting short-term (quarterly) results and making your boss look good!

2. *The empowerment versus blame culture.* It is also possible to position organisations on a spectrum that runs from a culture that seeks to empower people to make decisions through to one that seeks to blame individuals who make wrong decisions. The empowerment culture seeks to cascade decision-making power down the organisation. It engenders the idea of the company being a 'learning' organisation. Thus, learning from mistakes is seen as good practice. In contrast, where a blame culture exists, individuals will – because

they are living in a 'hire and fire' environment – be reluctant to experiment and take risks.

3. *Central control versus autonomy.* Organisations are also distributed along a spectrum running from, at one end, where more formal approaches to decision-making will operate, through to decision-making characterised by much more informality. For example, the classic formal 'decision-making unit' will involve an organisation having a group of individuals involved in the decision process, including the 'initiator' (the person who started the process); 'gate-keepers' (people who control the flow of information to the key decision-makers); 'influencers' (people who exert influence on the main decision) and the 'decision-makers' themselves (the people who have the most authority for the decision). We know that this type of formal decision-making often tends to be slower than more informal systems. We also know that there is little evidence to suggest that these formal decision-making units necessarily make for better 'quality' decisions. But they do have the advantage of being more likely to obtain reasonable buy-in to a particular decision, given the fact that different individuals within the organisation are invited to be part of the decision-making process. At the other end of the spectrum, in contrast, there could be autonomous focused 'decision task teams'. These will be comprised of experts in the field with particular technical expertise and/or project champions who have considerable authority and power to decide on particular initiatives. These task groups will be able to make quick and high quality decisions, but they do run the risk of not building a consensus of support for what they are doing, thereby possibly hindering the implementation of their decision.

Organisational decision minefields

Organisations often cultivate a dominant decision-making culture. This is seen as a focus that will push up the probability of defaulting to good, rather than bad, decision-making habits. However, notwithstanding the best of intentions, organisations – like people – can also develop bad decision-making habits. Below we provide a list of some classic organisational decision minefields.

Five organisational minefields

1. *An inward fear, not outward reward, culture.* Some organisations will make decisions in a *fear* culture. Individuals' decisions will be driven by the desire to 'protect their backs'. This will be in sharp contrast to organisations that play down failure and place the emphasis on the rewards that can flow from taking risks. Whether an organisation has inadvertently, or deliberately, inculcated a *'fear culture'* that limits decision-makers' horizons – rather than positively rewarding autonomous, risk-taking behaviour – is a separate matter. Either way, irrespective of how such a fear culture has grown up, the consequences invariably have negative consequences. Many organisations support added-value, customer-orientated initiatives in the good times, but when the going gets tough, they revert to being solely cost and product driven. In such a culture, *corporate myopia* can emerge. An organisation becomes preoccupied with fire-fighting and day-to-day sectarian warfare and thus becomes unwilling to recognise that it is facing a problem and take appropriate decisions. In this environment, people tend to assume that what they do is at the *centre of the universe*. Accountants think that business is all about money, marketing people think it is just about customers, and human resources people think it is only about staff relations. All of this is unhelpful, because what an organisation should be doing is not focusing on individual departmental problems, but looking at wider corporate goals.

2. *A failure to strike the right balance between risk and caution.* In today's *'just do it'* culture, there could be problems with organisations that are reluctant to invest in clear, deep thinking on the significance of the evidence and information with which they have been presented. In these companies, time spent on *clear deep thought* is seen as a sign of weakness in the macho, 'thinking is for wimps', 'do it now' business environment. At the end other end of the spectrum will be the *once bitten* phenomenon. Here, the trauma of a disaster can overly influence future decision-making. For example, a chemical firm's experience of an accident in which one of its Indian plants blew up, led the firm concerned to sell another plant that was close to an urban centre in Japan, even though this particular plant was

profitable and had an extremely good safety record. Another example where risk and caution are not in the right balance is where an organisation develops a *cost, rather than marketing-orientated approach* to decision-making whereby it is prepared to speculate to accumulate. This stands in sharp contrast to organisations that feel that they must *first* secure revenue – possibly through various cost-saving initiatives – *before* being prepared to invest in the future. Furthermore, organisations that have not quite got the risk/caution balance right tend only to search for an 'acceptable' decision, rather than striving for the 'optimum' one. In this scenario, only broadly acceptable (what the economists call *'satisficing'*) solutions that carry favour with the majority of individuals within the company are considered. This can stand in the way of inculcating a culture of constantly pursuing excellence and striving towards the optimal solution. In sum, some organisations fail to strike an appropriate balance between the need for entrepreneurial risk-taking and caution. It is generally accepted that there will be organisations that have to be *risk averse* in their approach to decision-making. For example, a public sector organisation – which is accountable to the taxpayer – will, reasonably enough, tend to default to a fairly risk-averse stance in decision-making: the emphasis will be on minimising the exposure to loss, while attempting to secure maximum benefit. This can be contrasted with a rapidly expanding mobile phone supplier, where entrepreneurial risk is something that the shareholders have perhaps come to accept in such a fast-moving dynamic market. But the balance can go too far in a particular direction – whether it be towards caution or risk.

3. *Fear of change and defaulting to the safety zone.* According to Darwin, the ability to change to different circumstances – rather than having the highest levels of intelligence or strength – is the key to survival. This is something that many organisations fail to comprehend. Thus, in looking at decisions, many companies will *preserve the status quo*. This tendency means that some organisations will be reluctant to call for a review of the *full* range of decision alternatives open to them and, in so doing, will skew their decision towards keeping things as they are now. A variant of the above is the tendency of some organisations to *anchor in the comfort zone*. This

refers to an organisational culture that – having called for various options to be examined – places far too much reliance on easy to understand, often recently experienced options, rather than having the confidence to branch out and genuinely explore the nuances of more ambitious, different, newer, potentially advantageous options. There are other organisations that, owing to their ability to change, develop a strategy of *following, not leading.* These are organisational cultures that focus on imitating or copying what its competitors (or near competitors) are doing in the marketplace. The culture in these organisations may include a policy of hiring individuals from competitors and quizzing them on what their former employer is doing. It is a culture that reflects a lack of confidence – a 'catch up' approach to decision-making. A particularly difficult situation, where change should, but does not take place, is when organisations will not let go costs already 'sunk' into a venture. This tendency to *hang on to sunk costs* means that companies become overly influenced in their current decision-making by their past investment. They see pulling out of a venture as an admission of failure. This is why we find in some organisations a tendency for projects to drag on forever: no one is willing to step in, stop it and carry the can, and set off in a more productive direction.

4. *A failure to question and challenge during decision-making.* Other decision minefields are organisations that do not continually challenge and question information and any assumptions that are being made. One feature of this is where organisations rely on *dodgy* 'rules of thumb'. This is where individuals, as part of the decision-making process, will make use of organisational norms that no one now questions. These routines and procedures become ones that individuals within the company come to rely upon, almost without thinking, when making decisions. For example, the price of a new product always has to be 'the direct costs incurred times three' to cover the overhead. The above phenomenon can lead to certain features of a project or initiative becoming 'normalised'. Then what happens is that this failure to *challenge the norm* means that over time an unchallenged norm gradually becomes accepted as true even though it is not. This is the type of thinking that leads to a series of increasingly poor decisions being made – the so-called 'doom loop'. This is a

phenomenon that can – in extreme circumstances – lead to actual disaster. For example, the Challenger Space Shuttle tragedy was due to an O-ring deficiency that had become 'normalised', such that regular occurrences of the fault in trials and tests were dismissed, accepted, and eventually not seen as 'real' faults at all. Another type of laziness that can infect the decision process is the tendency for *group think*. This is where an idea gains a critical mass of acceptance and becomes an accepted truth. Some individuals may feel they should question the dominant group view, but no one does. Then what happens is that after disaster has struck, such as the abandonment of the London Stock Exchange's Taurus computer project, individuals maintain that they themselves always thought the project would fail, explaining that they only went along with the plan because they thought this is what their fellow group members wanted.

5. *Poor decision timing and being oblivious to changing circumstances.* With decision-making, as with comedy, timing is of the essence. Poor timing lies behind a number of poor business decisions. What can happen is that anxiety sets in and an organisation *procrastinates*, delaying key decisions until it is too late. Similarly, while organisations are debating what to do, there can often be a massive *paradigm shift* in the environment that totally overtakes the decision. For example, a decade ago or more, while IBM was keeping a watching brief on the future trends in 'mainframe' computer usage, the 'personal computer' arrived on the scene with a vengeance.

Why we find decision-making difficult

One of the reasons that individuals find decision-making difficult is that we are all still learning to live with information ambiguity. We have not been brought up in an educational environment that has given us the skills to handle uncertainty. We warm to *puzzle-solving*, but feel apprehensive about *problem-solving*. 'Puzzle-solving' is about identifying the correct solution and then, subsequently, not having to worry about any attendant uncertainty. (You will have either made the right decision or not.) Problem-solving is where, even when what is considered to be the 'optimum' decision has been made, a residue amount of uncertainty surrounding the 'solution' remains. 'Grown up' organisations have people who feel comfortable about the uncertainty surrounding the solution chosen to a particular 'problem'. These are individuals who are not looking for simple 'black-and-white' solutions, with 100% cast iron guarantees of success; they are sanguine about carefully weighing up the different shades of grey, and weights and hues of evidence, and are comfortable about 'optimum' business solutions that, even after they have been made, are never going to be totally anxiety-free.

A particular problem is that, as human beings, our learning from past experiences seems to be far from optimum. The research evidence tells us that most people tend not to classify and categorise their past experiences systematically such that lessons can be easily learned for the future. We tend to be selective in what we remember. Big, recent, top of mind events tend to make the biggest impact, while other, potentially just as valuable, smaller, less dramatic happenings can easily be ignored. Similarly, the passage of time distorts what we learn from different events. We also tend to be more sensitive to losses than gains when making decisions, and to veer towards incoming arguments that support our (prejudiced) existing view of the world, rather than evidence that gives us a fresh perspective. We also know that if we are asked to make decisions in the public spotlight – and also in scenarios that involve frequent (public) assessment – we tend to veer towards caution, rather than adventure. But to be set against this, although often cautious, we often feel uncomfortable with inaction. For example, how many times following a big review of company procedures do we come to the conclusion that the best course of action is to take no action whatsoever. This means that many of us have a 'chameleon' approach to decision-making. We can be cool and rational most of the time, but can easily – given the emotional pressures of a particular scenario – revert to a totally out-of-character approach. Below we build on the above summary of what recent evidence seems to be telling us about some of the human frailties associated with decision-making.

Human decision mindtraps

- *Our memory and recall plays tricks.* One reason why we find decision-making difficult is that *we remember little of what we experience*. The human brain has a huge capacity but is little used; we have rich experiences of the 'moment', but for many of us, only pale, unclear outlines remain of these previous encounters. In addition, our learning from past experiences can be distorted by timing delays. As time goes by misperceptions and *noise* creep into our recollections of what past experiences have taught us. Given the fragile nature of our memory, we find that *first impressions* can powerfully influence our thinking. The human mind tends to give disproportionate weight to the *first* information it receives. Thus, initial impressions (and data) will 'stick'. This means an innocuous or an insidious comment about someone's capabilities will all stay in the memory, to the exclusion of other (lower down the running order), but possibly more important robust information. We also are influenced by *big dramatic events*. We tend to be over-influenced by events that leave a dramatic impression, putting to the back of our minds smaller, less noteworthy, but potentially significant experiences. Thus, we will recall major behaviour-shaping experiences, but tend to under-recall more subtle experiences that could generate insightful observations.

- *Selective perception*. In addition to our memory playing tricks, human beings also have a tendency to be highly selective when we 'pull down' information and experiences. For example, as might be expected, we all tend to see things more acutely when it relates to our own personal or professional interest. If you are a football fan, amid the morass of news and sports bulletins you will tend to hang on to references to your local team, with changes to the line-up of the English Synchronised Swimming Team going completely over your head. In addition, there is a tendency for us to want to *confirm our prejudices*. We tend to seek out information that confirms the hypotheses we rely upon to make sense of our world. We often ignore or avoid information that contradicts our familiar, favourite 'working hypotheses'. This means that we often fail to question incorrect beliefs; we have a 'mindset' that is not 'readjusted' by new incoming information. Instead of learning from past mistakes, we often build on them. There is also a *favourability skew* at work. This is a tendency to work harder to seek out information that supports our own beliefs and views rather than actively to seek out evidence that contradicts our views. In addition, when there is only a modest 'upside', but a massive 'downside', to a decision we will usually gravitate towards avoiding the downside. In short, people are more sensitive to losses than gains.

- *Big brother is watching.* As human beings, we also tend to learn to behave in a particular way in certain scenarios. For example, not surprisingly, when individuals perceive themselves to be in a *goldfish bowl* – making decisions in the public spotlight – they will behave differently than when in private. In the public gaze we are usually more cautious than if making a more private decision. Similarly, we learn to behave slightly differently when our decisions are being *regularly assessed*. The more frequently the success of an individual's decision-making is assessed, the less likely it is that this individual will be prepared to take a risk.

- *Mind games.* Another feature of the human brain is that we are prone to getting involved in *second-guessing* mind games. A classic example of this was the US Admiral who, while at sea in the Pacific Ocean, warned his bosses about the likelihood of a Japanese attack on Pearl Harbour. He was right, but was ignored. From then on, in order to make sure his voice was heard, the Admiral used to treble the size of any Japanese Fleet he spotted, knowing that his bosses would discount a large part of his intelligence report as scare-mongering. But once we start going down this treacherous second-guessing 'mind games' road, we can end up with all sorts of distortion.

- *The chameleon factor.* A further issue is that it is difficult for us to know what kind of person we are when it comes to decision-making because we change our colours. On balance someone may be a dominant, rational, cool-headed individual who avoids risks, but emotion can often kill our self-control. Thus, in certain situations, given the emotional pressures of the moment, we will sometimes act in an overly cautious (but more usually over-risky) manner. In sum, people act inconsistently, switching between being 'risk-takers' and 'risk-avoiders', depending on the situational factors in play at any particular time.

Applying information to decision-making

We have established that making decisions is difficult: organisational decision-making cultures can work against us, and we as individuals tend not to devote much energy to learning the lessons of the past. But, in addition, when it comes to techniques to help us apply information to decision-making, we find that in this field we have also made little headway. One problem is that, as indicated, many of the available (mathematical probability-based) decision-making models just do not reflect the world in which the majority of business decision-makers live. These models tend to set up 'puzzle-like', black-and-white scenarios, rather than reflecting the many shades of grey that characterise the typical business problem and its solution. In this chapter we provide a simple technique for helping the decision-maker make maximum use of marketing information. Different people respond to information in different ways. Below we review some of these differences.

What we do when presented with information

- *Flawed information processing strategies.* As explained in Chapter 2, when we looked at 'good information habits', few individuals come to information with an organised strategy for how they are going to cope. Thus, the first problem we find with the use of information for decision-making is that our approach is often erratic. For example, one strategy for coping with *information overload* – being faced with too much information – is to reduce every problem to a choice between two alternatives. Thus, a 'death by dichotomy' culture builds up whereby an individual is always only looking at two easy-to-grasp, but not necessarily the best, options. Another problem is that some people are reluctant to look at the detailed complex evidence underpinning an option. This can lead to only user-friendly, but perhaps *artificially simplistic*, information being used as the basis for decision-making. In short, for the small number of options we do look at, we tend to *over-simplify* the information we have available using already far too limited alternatives. Another flaw is in *availability drift*. This means that we tend to give more weight to information that is readily available. Our reflex is to ask 'what information do I have?' rather than 'what information do I need?'. Because you have something it does not mean that you should give it a greater emphasis than something you do not have. Sometimes, the focus on available information can escalate to the point where we are obsessed with *unearthing more and more information* to validate a decision, rather than intelligently utilising the information we have. Another information-processing weakness is the tendency to believe that – having set up an elaborate project – the outcome should always be *change, rather than maintaining the status quo*. In some cases action could be the right decision, but in others the best solution could be to change nothing. But we find this difficult to do.

- *Figure phobia*. Many individuals will feel nervous when confronted with statistics. They perhaps do not appreciate that all that is required to look at many statistics is basic 'numeracy', rather than more profound mathematical skills. This means that some tend, given their *fear of numbers*, to gloss over critical calculations on which business decisions can rest. This uncertainty with numbers can lead to some individuals placing an *over-reliance* on 'black box' techniques. Thus, we find people basing decisions on black box, statistically-based decision-making techniques that they do not really understand, but nevertheless use because they seem to offer some quasi-scientific comfort and validity.

- *Uncomfortable with subjectivity*. To compound the above tendency, some will feel uncomfortable – even nervous – with arguments based on qualitative evidence. This *nervousness about qualitative evidence* can mean that too much reliance is placed on quantitative evidence. At the heart of this nervousness is probably *discomfort with subjectivity*. For instance, some individuals are comfortable about factoring concrete measurable variables into decisions, such as time, distance, weight, volume and so on, but find it difficult to embrace more 'subjective' estimates and forecasts of a particular event happening. There are still many people who are unable to cope when their brain receives two apparently counter-veiling types of signal – logic and intuition. They find it difficult to operate in a holistic way, balancing out their more rationale left-side and more intuitive right-side brain skills.

- *Lack of confidence with uncertainty*. Some individuals, when faced with what they consider to be a confusing mixture of qualitative and/ or quantitative data, can become extremely unsure in coping with the kind of uncertainty that is typical in business. These are not problem-solvers. In order to extricate themselves from this uncomfortable mental state they often clutch at the flimsiest of evidence and information, treating this as an unshakeable fact that they hope – pray – will replace uncertainty with a definite solution. However, they can end up by making decisions that are based on falsehoods, rather than robust evidence.

Decision-making frameworks

Against this backdrop of certain human frailties when it comes to information-based decision-making, we now move on to a practical framework that should make the decision-making task easier. It is called the 'Decision Evaluator' technique. We have reviewed many of the existing decision-making frameworks and, in an eclectic fashion, borrowed some of the best ideas and rejected those that do not seem to relate to the world of business. As explained, some of the more mathematically-based decision models have made little headway in the real business world because they fail to cope with some of the complexities of modern business life. However, there are some mathematically-based techniques that are entirely consistent with the holistic philosophy of this book. For instance, one of the best known techniques is the idea of setting up a *decision tree*. This graphic representation of the options that flow from a particular decision has been helpful in shaping our thoughts on our Decision Evaluator technique. Similarly, the idea of identifying particular scenarios, and undertaking a strengths, weaknesses, opportunities and threats (SWOT) analysis of what might happen in each of these different scenarios has been informative. This type of *scenario planning* has its origin in 'thinking the unthinkable' – that is, breaking free from current mental blocks and attempting to pinpoint what were hitherto totally unthinkable scenarios and working out what might be achieved in such eventualities. The notion of *game theory* has also been helpful. Essentially game theory is about making predictions about the way people, or organisations, will behave in order to pursue their own best interests. Thus, game theory is not strictly about providing a solution to particular problems, but rather a tool for getting people to think clearly about the future. Game theory can help decision-takers review the merits of the alternative strategies open to them in considering decisions. It provides a focus for considering the implications of their decision for themselves, their customers and their competitors. The Decision Evaluator technique we have developed also draws together many of the holistic analysis principles we have discussed. It acknowledges the fact that much business decision-making is less of a science and more of an art, and recognises that decision-making requires not only rigorous analysis of harder data, but must also build in softer, less tangible aspects, such as intuition and experience.

The Decision Evaluator technique

In essence, this sets up a kind of 'decision pros and cons balance sheet' that guides us in interrogating the evidence and evaluating the 'safety' of the judgements and decisions we must make. The starting point is to make sure that you have carried out the various checks of the robustness of your evidence outlined in Chapter 2 of this book. A brief recap of these appears in Table 7.1.

Once you are sure about the robustness of the evidence, the Decision Evaluator technique divides into three steps. Each of these is discussed below. But before we move on to discuss this, it is important for the reader to appreciate that this technique is a conceptual framework, rather than a prescriptive tool. Thus, we expect the reader to absorb the general ideas behind the approach, then tailor these to his/her particular circumstances.

 ### Step 1: categorising the evidence (set up a decision balance sheet)

One of the main benefits of evaluating market research evidence, in the form of the Decision Evaluator (or similar) technique is that it looks at the evidence in an entirely different context from the conventional market research presentation. With the latter, the emphasis is on the audience absorbing the main storyline from the presentation, while at the same time reassuring itself about the professionalism with which the market research study was carried out and assessing the general robustness of the evidence, and so on. However, by going into a different gear –

Table 7.1   *A summary of our 12 key robustness checks*

1. *The believability check.* Apply common sense checks. If it does not square with your beliefs, go away and check further.
2. *Twymans' Law.* Remember, if it is particularly interesting, it is often wrong, so again go away and check.
3. *Internal consistency checks.* Is the item you have from your study internally consistent with other readings taken from the same study?
4. *The underlying assumptions.* Think closely about what assumptions have been made by the person analysing the results.
5. *The professionalism check.* If there are a number of silly errors, the chances are that this is a tell-tale sign of a study that is more fundamentally flawed.
6. *He would say that wouldn't he?* Check whether the supplier of the information had any particular angles or perspectives for presenting the arguments in the way it did.
7. *Chinese whispers.* Be mindful of the way evidence can be 'embellished' to the point where it will change its meaning.
8. *Spin.* We live in soundbite culture: there is a growing tendency to present 'on-message', simplified accounts of the 'truth'.
9. *Norms and benchmarks.* What can our past experience of conducting surveys on similar markets tell us about our new survey statistic?
10. *Corroboration.* Are there other sources of evidence – following the triangulation principle – that will help verify the piece of evidence in front of you?
11. *Back to the core evidence.* It can be helpful to think about each of the different elements that make up the research process and be absolutely clear about all the sources of error that could have crept into the process. So if you have got any doubts or worries, go back and demand to see the original transcripts or questionnaires underpinning a particular piece of evidence that was instrumental to building a particular argument.
12. *Confirmation.* Why not feed back the conclusion you have drawn on the evidence to the organisations that are responsible for supplying the information and see whether they agree with your slant.

setting up a 'decision workshop' environment – it is possible to involve the market research team and decision-makers in the process of looking at the *safety* of different information-based decisions. There will be different ways of doing this, but one useful technique is to set up evidence in a kind of 'balance sheet'. Specifically, this involves the following.

- *Assemble the 'for' decision evidence.* Start by assembling the evidence that would build the strongest possible case to support a decision in favour of the proposition under consideration. Let us take as an example the decision whether or not to invest in a new portable electronic on-board map that motorists could use instead of using a hard copy road atlas. Here, the evidence to support going ahead with this new product would be prioritised by the analyst/decision-maker and at the top of the list would be the evidence that provides the most powerful case. This would be followed by the next most powerful and so on.

- *Assemble the 'against' decision evidence.* Next, assemble the evidence that could be deployed to build the case against investing in the venture (i.e. on-board portable map), again drawing on all available sources of evidence and intelligence. List the evidence from the most powerful opposition case alongside that which is less persuasive. You now have a kind of 'for' and 'against' decision 'balance sheet'.

In essence, the Decision Evaluator technique sharpens the focus of the decision-maker by bringing an almost barrister-like, adversorial role to the evidence. In effect, the analyst/decision-maker selects the evidence that he/she feels would allow them – as the prosecutor – to 'win' the case. This can then be repeated, but this time going through the process assuming the role of the defence lawyer who would select the evidence that he/she would help them to best defend the case. In short, the purpose of our approach is to ensure that the decision/judgement that you are making stands up in 'court'.

Step 2: testing your decision to destruction

Having arranged the evidence that argues the best case 'for', and also the strongest case 'against' the venture under scrutiny, the next step is to test each item of evidence to *destruction*.

- *Assume you have 'perfect' knowledge.* Review the evidence you have assembled to support the 'for' decision and envisage having available perfect information, i.e. all the information that in an ideal world you would like to make your decision (but that you probably do not have in practice). Now ask whether there could be any incoming information that could dramatically challenge or weaken the argument you are advancing here under the 'for' decision. This approach could similarly be employed to interrogate the 'against' decision.

- *Think from the customer's perspective.* Now let us change tack and put the spotlight on your current and potential customers. There are a number of techniques for testing your decision from the customer's perspective. One example is to *role-play* the *customer from hell.* Ask the person who is championing the project to role-play the seller of the product or service, and ask, let us say, the head of the market research team to play the 'customer from hell'. Work through all aspects of the product/service offering to see how well it performs in this 'nightmare' scenario.

- *How do you really feel?* Next, imagine spinning a coin. If the coin comes down heads, your organisation is committed to the 'for' decision. If it comes down tails, it is committed to the 'against' decision. Go through this process and list down all of your *immediate* thoughts and feelings on hearing which way the decision has gone. This approach can put you 'in touch' with how you really feel about the 'for' (and 'against') decisions. It is a way of making sure that the more deep-seated, intuitive, implicit feelings and knowledge of the decision-making team are brought out into the open and put firmly into the decision-making equation. This process of getting in touch with one's true feelings about the decision can involve reviewing some of the organisational 'minefields' and decision 'mindtraps' raised above. For example, are you sure you are being sufficiently 'dangerous' and risk-taking with your decision-making, and are not falling into the 'comfort zone'? But equally are you sure that your decision is not being made in an overly emotive way?

- *The strategic ladder test.* It is often argued that 80% of business success is explained through 'strategic excellence'. This means that in 20% of cases a strategically flawed decision can be made to 'fly' by using tactical excellence. But, on balance, the key to successful decision-making is first to make sure that 'the ladder is leaning against the right wall'. It is therefore worthwhile reviewing the evidence you have assembled for (and subsequently against) a particular decision to see whether the evidence represents sound strategic thinking. So check whether your support for a decision hinges on big assumptions being made about the initiative being driven through by tenacious tactics, rather than being likely to succeed by dint of elegant strategy.

- *In the decision hot seat.* Another suggestion on how to test the safety of your likely decision is to snap out of thinking of yourself as playing out a 'business role' within the sophisticated world of management science, and to shape up to your decision as if you were *using your own money*. It can be quite a salutary lesson to dig deeply into your psyche and ask yourself whether, if it was your own mortgage money riding on the venture, you would go ahead in the form that you are proposing!

- *Get the view from the 'third corner'.* To supplement the above perspective, we suggest you also obtain a view from what we have labelled the 'third corner'; that is, from the perspective of 'stake-holders' in your organisation. These should include not only customers, but also employees, shareholders, key industry opinion formers, industry journalists working in your area, and a whole host of others who have an influence in the field in which you are working. Understanding the problem from this 'outside' perspective could pay dividends.

Step 3: testing your decision in critical scenarios

At step 3 we borrow from the tried and tested principles of 'scenario planning' and game theory and use some of these techniques to test the decision in different situations that might result from the decision. Try to *anticipate* how your decision will be received in different customer and market scenarios.

- *The uncontrollables.* Test the decision to be made in the context of the so-called 'uncontrollables' that could impinge on the decision. For example, it is worth inspecting whether any changes in the exchange rate in a key export market and/or the political stability of countries in which major investments are being considered are likely to impinge on the actions that will flow as the result of your decision.

- *Second-guessing the competition.* It is helpful to introduce some techniques in order to see how well the decision will stand up given different assumptions about how the competition might respond to the decision. Let us take the example of the introduction of a new product or service. One approach is to think about the concept of the *Counsel of Perfection competitor*, that is, the competitor – assuming no constraints or difficulties – who would be able to introduce the *perfect* product or service. That is, set up in your mind the world's most formidable competitor. It is a company that, in reality, you are unlikely to face, but for testing purposes it is helpful to establish just how well your proposed new product or service venture would stand up if such a perfect competitor were to arrive on the scene. It may also be helpful to step down one rung on the Counsel of Perfection ladder and this time think of a more realistic *best of class* competitor. Do some homework on the market and identify the 'best' competitor in your product class. Then review your putative decision in the light of your observations about this best of class competitor. In sum, it is helpful to observe examples of best possible practice in the area in which you are to make an entry and then to do a detailed 'compare and contrast' on different aspects of your offer, relative to the competitor. For example, if you were thinking of opening up a chain of hotels, take one element of the process – let us say booking a room – and see how your booking-in procedures compare with, let us say, Claridges in the West End of London.

- *Sensitivity analysis*. First, ask the project 'champion' to define all the elements that make up your product or service offer, then, for each element, describe the range of variants that might be considered. For example, if one element is to provide a *helpline*, at one end of the spectrum this could be a 'seven days a week, 24 hours a day service', but on the other hand it could be a 'five days a week, 9–5 offer'. Secondly, ask the market research agency, based on the available evidence *and* its own experience, to pinpoint to what extent the venture is likely to fly or fail, depending on whether the 'top' or 'bottom' end of the range of variations on each particular element is the variant selected.

- *Identifying internal advocates and terrorists*. Taking the best decision or making the best judgement does not necessarily equate with producing the best decision *outcome*. There have been many cases where an apparently good decision has faltered because of the internal difficulties associated with implementing the new idea. Thus, it is worth building 'balance sheet' checks into the Decision

Evaluator, equivalent to the 'customer from hell', but this time, with the worse possible *internal* 'enemy' in mind, namely your most strident critic within your organisation. Then try to anticipate all the objections or difficulties that this person (terrorist) may raise about your proposed decision and its implications for your company. To avoid paranoia setting in, it is also helpful to do the same exercise but this time from the counterpoint of anticipating what your most fervent ally and supporter within the organisation would say about your proposed decision and its likely outcome. This 'ambassador' would presumably give you a certain amount of 'latitude', in just the same way as your arch critic would do you no favours. Finding a path between these two perspectives will possibly be what actually happens in practice.

- *The dynamics: coping with change.* A feature of virtually all business markets is that they are in a state of constant flux. Given this, it is important to remember that you are not making the decision in an ivory tower as a theoretical economist where you can make all sorts of assumptions. It is not acceptable to fall back on the rather lame excuse that the decision was overtaken by events. In the world of business, there is the expectation that the decision-maker will put in place certain techniques to, as far as possible, anticipate some of these likely changes. Therefore, it will pay dividends to employ simple techniques such as envisaging what the reaction to your decision might be in five years time, based on best possible assumptions about what the world might look like at this time.

- *Visualisation: future histories.* As explained, Covey, in *The Seven Habits of Highly Effective People*, tells us that effective people 'start at the end' – they visualise exactly how the result of a decision or action they are embarking upon will pan out. Therefore to conclude the final step of the Decision Evaluator approach it is worthwhile attempting to visualise all aspects of the decision you are about the make – how it will first be introduced, how it will then be progressed, leading through to 'visualisation' about the final impact of the decision. If the entire beginning-to-end decision-making process passes this visualisation test, without generating any anxieties or concerns, then it probably bodes well for the decision you are about to make. But if this process of visualisation throws up nagging doubts and worries, you perhaps need to return to some of the evidence you have assembled for (or against) the decision, to see whether you might want to revise it.

We are aware that our own ideas on the Decision Evaluator technique will not be ones that will, in their entirety, always be applied in their most rigorous form. In many situations such an approach will be too time-consuming. But we believe that it is important that information providers start thinking about offering frameworks, along the lines of the Decision Evaluator, that will help decision-makers to make informed judgements.

Implementing marketing decisions

It is important not just to think of decision-making as resolving a specific choice or course of action at a particular moment in time, but as an ongoing commitment. Barker in *How to Become a Better Decision-Maker* writes:

> 'Making a decision is more than choosing what to do. It involves making a commitment, however small: rationally and emotionally. Furthermore, it involves making a commitment on behalf of others – particularly in a work or family situation – and asking them to commit to your commitment.'

In other words, effective decision-making is not just about the quality of the choice that is made about competing options. It is also important to ensure that the decision is appropriately executed. There are many examples of good decisions followed by poor implementation. This is a particularly important area. Many of the alleged failures of market research do not centre on totally technically inadequate pieces of research, but rather on the way in which the evidence was interpreted. The Edsel car is a case in point. The popular folklore is that the Edsel was the most heavily market researched vehicle of its day, yet it turned out to be a failure. The Edsel is often dragged out of the cupboard by the media when they want to imply that market research does not work. But a close inspection of the facts tells a different story. First, the Edsel was not particularly well researched. There was some name testing, but there was little research done on the overall style and design of the car. Secondly, when it came to implementing the limited amount of research that was conducted it seems that grave errors were made. For example, in the 'name' research 'Edsel' did comparatively badly compared with the other names that appeared in the test (Rover, Jupiter, Arrow, Ariel, Ovation, Dart and Mars). Nevertheless, Ford made the decision that the car would be named after Henry Ford II's father. In addition, the limited research that was conducted on the overall design of the car did suggest problems, but this did not lead to any substantive re-thinking about the style of the car. So the problem with the Edsel was poor research but also a failure to take appropriate action on the evidence that was available.

Given the importance of ensuring that information-based decisions are properly implemented, below we provide a clear set of prescriptions to ensure that there is not a slip between the market researchers' presentation of the evidence and the execution of the final recommendations. We consider this to be part of what holistic data analysis is all about. The aim here is not to turn market researchers into management consultants. However, today it is generally recognised that if market researchers are to improve the chances of market research recommendations being effectively actioned and implemented they must work in closer partnership with their clients than has perhaps been the case in the past. Below we discuss six reasons why some very good decisions can be followed by less than optimum implementation.

Naive starting point

One reason why there may be difficulties in implementing a set of research findings centres on the fact that the research may have been interpreted in a very naive way that does not provide sufficient 'clues' for the decision-maker about the likely difficulties ahead. One problem is the danger that the researcher – in an attempt to please – will create too much order out of what is essentially a chaotic scenario. Once any form of market research or evaluation project has been mounted, there is enormous pressure on the analyst to present a rounded, logical, plausible account of what the research and evaluation are telling us. This is only to be expected. Decision-makers do not want to be confronted with a mountain of confusing, contradictory evidence. Thus, analysts' attempts to identify the *central* storyline in data are, on balance, to be commended. However, there is a danger that in certain situations much of the 'messiness' surrounding a particular storyline is eradicated from the final presentation. This can have the detrimental effect of not providing the decision-maker with a sufficient grasp of some of the bumpy terrain that he/she must navigate in completing his/her journey. For example, it seems clear that in the future there will be considerable reliance on e-commerce trading. But it would be over-simplistic to paint a picture of future retailing that does not include healthy competition between 'conventional' and electronic methods of purchasing.

Asking the research to do too much

One reason why implementing research findings is problematic is because the original research is being 'stretched' too far. As we have already explained, any research design is going to be a compromise between the 'ideal' information set and what it is practicable to achieve within the budget. But sometimes the fact that final research design involves a trading down from the 'ideal' is forgotten. One problem is where the *concept* that was tested in the research is – for various practical reasons – different from the final *product* to be introduced into the marketplace. This can lead to the researchers being asked to answer all sorts of questions about a product they actually know little about. They may offer a view to be helpful, but in practice the evidence they have at their disposal to make such judgements relates only to the original concept, not to the soon to be introduced product. Clearly, the lesson here is to ensure that there is not too big a gap between the concept being tested and the product to be put into the marketplace. But where there is such a gap, one needs to be careful about over-interpreting available evidence. Another problem centres on a research study being set up on a comparatively broad canvas in order to look at more general trends and issues in the marketplace, but at a later point the research team being asked questions at a level of specificity that is beyond the research. For example, a study may pinpoint that readers of a magazine found it difficult to 'navigate' their way around the publication. But the research may not have probed in detail on exact design solutions for dealing with this issue. Then what can happen is that at the market research presentation the researchers are quizzed about possible ways of solving this 'navigation' problem, eventually getting cajoled into offering a specific comment that is not necessarily firmly rooted in what the (general) evidence is saying. So this is another difficulty in successfully implementing research findings.

Time delay between the research and its implementation

Another problem is where there is a long delay between the presentation of the evidence/the decision to go ahead, and the start of the project. This is a fairly self-evident point. We all know that time clouds much of the detail of a debate. Thus, there can often be difficulties in situations where a project starts some considerable time after the original decision to launch a product was made. In addition, of course, the longer the time delay between the research and the start of the project, the greater the likelihood that the marketplace will have changed in a way that cannot be anticipated by the research team. Clearly, this can seriously affect the successful implementation of market research evidence.

Departing from the original research recommendations

It is helpful to think in terms of the decisions to be made based on market research falling into the following three categories: 'red'; 'green' and 'amber'. There will be some situations in which the market research study will provide a clear 'no-go red light'. Equally, there will be some situations where the outcome of the study is a 'sure-fire green light' winner – situations where the idea is so powerful that even if the organisation put its worst person on the case, and that at all stages of the execution there are 'screw ups', the idea would still float. The reality is that the majority of market research studies fall into the 'amber light' category: it is not a 'no-go red', but neither is it a 'sure-fire green light' winner. The research is telling us that if certain improvements are made to the proposition tested in the research, then the 'amber light' could be 'coaxed to green'. But the critical issue then becomes to ensure the qualifying conditions attached to the main research conclusions are adhered to. For example, the Sinclair C5 electric car was an example of a product that fell into the 'amber light' category. The research evidence showed that there was some interest in the concept of an electric-powered car. But the research showed that it was *not* a product that should be introduced on a *mass* market basis; introducing the C5 onto UK roads would not work. The research suggested that introducing the C5 in protected environments, such as large warehouses, golf courses and the like, was the way forward. But what happened was that this critically important qualification to the recommendation that the car should be launched was ignored. So an 'amber light' was interpreted as a 'green light', and the product was in fact introduced onto the UK roads (not a protected environment), which eventually led to failure. So, it is important to manage these amber light situations. It is true that in this book we have argued that it is important to include management judgement in the interpretation process. But if this totally overrides the key message coming out of the explicit research evidence, then clearly this can lead to major implementation difficulties.

Every action produces a reaction

One further reason why there are often difficulties in the implementation of market research evidence is that not enough is done to understand the way the marketplace is likely change in the event of the introduction of a new product or service. For example, Marks & Spencer, in response to complaints that their designs are rather lacklustre, may introduce a range of innovative ideas, but only to find that competitors, such as Gap, have become even more creative. Given this, it is important to identify the actual and potential strengths and weaknesses of competitors. You need to know where they are likely to attack you, where your opportunities for counter-attack are, and how, if at all, you can influence their behaviour. All of this will help to ensure that the market research study leads to successful implementation.

Gaining support for the decision

Another reason why there can be difficulties in implementing a decision centres on the fact that insufficient work may have been undertaken to help the organisation come to terms with the need for change. One cannot assume that because an organisation has made the 'right' decision, it automatically follows that everyone within an organisation will be 'on side' in support of this decision. It is therefore important to take the following steps to ensure that good decisions are properly implemented.

- *Inadequate buy-in.* One problem with the execution of what was – at the time – a sensible decision, centres on the fact that many project managers make decisions with little attempt to involve others in the decision process. This approach may offer the advantages of saving time and resources, but it neglects the importance of obtaining 'buy-in' to a decision ahead of its implementation. A decision that is presented as a *fait accompli* will often fail.
- *Failure to appoint a 'champion'.* Ventures managed by a committee invariably fail. What is needed is a 'make it happen' champion. Whether or not a company is able to commit to a project a *champion* – who will be given appropriate staff support, financial and other resources to make the venture a success – is critically important. It is here that many of the stories about the (alleged) failures of market research begin their life. Thus, we believe that many of the (apocryphal) stories of market researchers failing to predict the failure of a product are *not* due to the market research evidence being incorrect, but due to the company not having a *champion* – a highly capable, intelligent and well-resourced person or team who can dot the i's and cross the t's of the decision. Let us suppose that a market research study showed that a customer loyalty scheme would be an outstanding success, *provided* it offered customers 'professional, classy and substantive' rewards (such as free membership of a major travel organisation), but the company end up offering customers a plastic carriage clock. Here it would hardly be surprising if the scheme were to 'bomb'. This is not the fault of market research; it is the result of the failure to appoint a champion who is capable of making an informed interpretation of the original 'amber light' scenario and then following this through to action.
- *Balanced teams who are rewarded.* Successful implementation is not just about having a project champion. It is also important to ensure

Agency market researchers have become accustomed, following a presentation, for the CEO to claim that he/she 'already knew that'. But, in fact, all that these 'wanna be' clairvoyants are really saying is that he/she was aware of *all* of the issues raised by the market research study. But there are no prizes for this. People should not be running an organisation if they are not aware – at least in outline – of all the issues that are facing their customers. The more pertinent question should be: was the CEO able to put all the issues of which he/she was aware in the correct priority order as perceived by the customers? And going beyond this, was the CEO clear about customers' 'depth of feeling' on *each* of these topics. In other words, could the CEO go beyond simply citing the issues, to prioritise them, and then talk authoritatively about which of these factors *drive* customers' attitudes? If the CEO could successfully *prioritise all of the issues* from the *customer's* perspective and explain exactly *how each factor motivates the customer*, then maybe the company should not have commissioned a market research study. But in the authors' experience this is extremely rare. So are there any market researchers brave enough to ask their *end client* (before the start of the study) to write down and place in a sealed envelope *all* the issues that will come out of the study, in the right priority order, expressed with the right depth of feeling? Then, following the presentation the envelope could be opened. The deal is that if the CEO is right in every detail – issues, priority and depth – the market researcher has to pick up the tab for the study. But if all the CEO can do is list the issues (unprioritised with no feel for the depth of feeling) then the market research agency wins and the CEO must double the agency's fees!

Figure 7.1   *The envelope test: establishing whether or not research has really made a contribution*

that the champion for the project is supported by a team of individuals. The ideal team will include seasoned professionals who are aware of much of the complexity, but also other less experienced individuals who can bring fresh ideas and perspectives. Let us take an analogy. Let us say we are developing a new navigation system to help amateur yachtsmen. Here, the ideal team would include a novice yachtsman who has never even crossed the channel, through to a 'salty dog' who has repeatedly crossed the Atlantic. In addition, the team will include individuals with strong 'left-brain' logical skills (let us check out the new functionality of the electronics) plus more intuitive 'right-brain' thinkers (in the event of a failure can we still use the charts manually).

So, in sum, what we are saying that it is critically important to manage the end decision-makers' expectations of what research can achieve. Market research suppliers may be tempted to employ the envelope test (Figure 7.1) as a way of demonstrating that their research has met expectations and made a contribution.

Good practice decision and implementation guide

We conclude by providing in *summary form* a series of tips designed to improve the quality of decisions made from information, and also to help ensure that these judgements and decisions are successfully implemented.

Creating the optimum decision-making culture

- *A 'think big', proactive, 'can do' culture.* Organisations that are expansive, bold and imaginative tend to engender a confidence in their staff that often translates into a positive and professional approach to decision-making. This creative, 'think positive' culture helps people dig themselves out from under the myopia of internal tradition, and look at things freshly and differently. Doing things differently is not necessarily the right approach in every case, but at least in this positive decision-making environment, change and innovation will always be given a fair hearing.
- *Remove a 'fear of failing' culture.* No one is immune to errors of judgement. Innovation and experimentation should be encouraged. So building on the above, a culture of learning through new experiences, rather than being blamed for failure, should be encouraged where individuals may express any dissenting viewpoints free from any recriminations
- *Vision grounded in reality.* Some organisational decision-making exists in an ivory tower. Others are much too close to the street. The optimum approach is to be sufficiently distant to develop creative visions but, at the same time, be grounded in 'street-wise' experience. In addition, always listen to the 'Cassandra' in your organisation. (Cassandra was able to foretell the future but was fated by Apollo never to be believed.) Those who have knowledge about, or suggestions on, problems or changes – but have only a limited voice or power within an organisation – should still be involved in decision-making. We now know that well ahead of its eventual collapse some people in Barings Bank were already warning about the dangers of giving Nick Leeson too much autonomy. But no one listened to them.

Making effective use of information

- *Apply the seven insights into 'information wisdom'.* The insights explained in Chapter 2 of this book should be a starting point for negotiating the 'information maze'.
- *Follow the 'good information habits guide'.* Effective decision-makers will have developed good information habits (see Chapter 2) that enable them to sort vast amounts of information under pressure in 'real time' in an effective way. They will develop techniques to help them quickly to zero in on key 'must know' data (key milestones, triggers and other critical indicators).
- *Create the right information platform.* When starting a project ask the question, 'Do I have the information I need to make a decision?' If not, then good practice dictates that the missing information should be secured (following the good practice guideline outlined in Chapter 5 on Designing Actionable Research). At this point it seems obvious, but many decisions will be flawed because they are based on the information that is available rather than on the information that is needed.
- *Whole brain thinking.* Cultivate the holistic approach to information: use experience to balance the 'logical' and 'intuitive' elements to any decision. Be open to the holistic concepts of the 'weight', 'power' and 'direction' of evidence and learn how to blend these with statistical tests.
- *Do not let history repeat itself.* Learn from the past. Try to work towards having a clear picture of how effective different information 'packages' have been in delivering different types of decisions in the past. This will allow you to avoid the well charted organisational decision-making minefields.

Making sound judgements and choices

- *Develop a tolerance for ambiguity.* Good decision-makers can live with ambiguity, uncertainty and grey areas. It might not always be possible to arrive at the optimum choice. Sometimes you may have to 'satisfice' (that is, find an acceptable rather than 'perfect' outcome). But you need to feel comfortable about living with the consequences of this less-than-perfect choice. Be prepared to agonise. Just when you think you have got it right, remember that you are solving a problem, not a puzzle. There is always going to be a residue amount of uncertainty. Be prepared to live with this over a period of 24 or 48 hours and revisit your decision. Always check out underlying assumptions and keep asking questions about the decisions to be made.

- *Know and challenge yourself and be curious.* It is important to know what kind of decision-maker you are: are you a tortoise or a hare? (And, having established this, do the same for other members of the decision-making team.) In addition, develop curiosity. Good decision-makers will be not only be creative and imaginative, but be prepared to explore every angle. Try to learn from others who are facing similar decisions. There could be important metaphors, analogies and comparisons that could help. Effective decision-makers are 'grasshoppers'. They are able to go from one decision to another whilst still allowing as many alternatives as possible to be explored for each. Good decision-makers will continually be challenging themselves. There is an old adage, that when it is exactly right, it is good enough. When you think you have made the decision, ask yourself a series of *what if* questions to see whether you can improve it still further.

- *Employ clear deep thinking and logical reasoning.* First, at the outset of any research project you should develop a clear set of decision action standards. These are statements about what you intend to do given different outcomes to, for example, a survey of customers. This will provide a focus for mapping out the alternatives upon which a decision is required. In addition, develop disciplined decision frameworks to encourage clear deep thinking and logical reasoning about the evidence. The Decision Evaluator technique, explained earlier in this chapter, is helpful in this context because it looks at the *safety* of information-based decision-making.

- *Consult others.* Seek information and opinions from a variety of people, especially those who may disagree with you. Avoid anchoring them to your ideas; you want freshness, not a reflection of your own ideas. So do not disclose leading information that reveals your own opinion too soon. You do not want 'group think' outcomes. It is helpful to think in terms of having a 'devil's advocate' – someone you can trust to argue against, i.e. the decision you are contemplating. Also ask yourself how various people – a role model, another company or industry – would deal with this problem. Could you get what you are proposing past Jeremy Paxman?

- *Be decisive.* It is important to make active choices. Sometimes the best strategy is to do nothing and wait. But only do this if you have actually been through a proactive evaluation process. Do not get into a situation where decisions are made out of inertia, or by default. Face up to problems; do not procrastinate. Also, do not fall into the trap of letting past mistakes – a commitment to earlier ill-fated schemes – lower your confidence in making decisions this time around. But avoid over-confidence.

- *Continued renewal of decision-making skills.* There is another adage that tells us to repair the roof when the sun is shining and we are not under pressure. Continually review your skills for sharpening your decision-making. Success is all about adapting to change: do not use yesterday's decision-making approaches for today's problems.

Ensuring your decision is properly implemented

- *Anticipation.* Think future histories: think through the decision from the beginning to the end by developing the 'visualisation' technique. Put yourself in your customers' shoes. How are they likely to react to this decision? Pinpoint any problems or hurdles and take anticipatory proactive action.

- *Obtain buy-in and build consensus for the research.* It is crucial to get top level buy-in for the findings of the market research study. It is important not to overwhelm managers with detail. If decision-makers become overwhelmed and impatient with market research they might reject much of its wisdom. Impart only the 'need to know' not 'nice to know' information. A helpful tip in getting buy-in to a decision is to get a video tape of the CEO talking about the research findings and how they are going to be implemented. Keep your research presentations action-orientated, create a sense of urgency and always tailor your presentation to the audience. Try to tell the story through the eyes of the customer. Always go for impact and make sure you speak the decision-maker's language. Communicate with action as well as words. Video clips of people in stores are all likely to have an impact. Use different media to get your message across. Everybody also needs to be kept 'on message'; subtle differences in wording can create huge differences in the audience's take from the same presentation. We know that right-brain intuitive thinkers learn best by listening to archetypes (anecdotes and stories). In contrast, left-brain thinkers like logically reasoned arguments. The solution is to provide a mixture of both in your presentation.

- *Ensure that there is an energetic champion in charge of a balanced team.* Put high energy, positive thinkers with responsibility and authority on the project to 'make it so'. Always make sure you have a team of people working to your champion. This person must make sure he/she shares his/her decision-making reasoning with the team. It is important in building the team not to exclude key individuals. Remember, old 'dogs' (senior members of the organisation) have an important role to play in modifying new tricks. Experienced people with grounding in the problem are a useful foil to the 'young turks' who are driving the initiative forward.

- *Link the success of the project with rewards.* It is important to ensure that employees within an organisation are aware of what the company is trying to accomplish and why. Incentives brought in to help implement a strategy must be seen as realistically achievable, with the appropriate amount of resource being provided to encourage likely success. Any monitoring of progress towards achieving goals and targets must clearly be seen to be equitable, fair and realistic. In addition, any barriers to the likely achievement of goals and targets need to be worked out in advance. It can often be helpful to put the targets that you have laid down into the context of benchmarks achieved by other competitors. It is also helpful to ensure that people can see the links between what it is they are being assessed on, e.g. levels of customer satisfaction and so on, and their own rewards.

- *Do not be too proud.* If you have made a bad decision that can still be overturned – do it.

We believe that if the next generation of knowledge workers acquire the holistic analysis skills and new information competencies outlined in this book, then we will have gone a long way towards improving the quality of information-based decision-making and finding the wisdom *inside information.*

Bibliography

Barabba, V.P. & Zaltman, G. (1991). *Hearing the Voice of the Market: Competitive Advantage through Creative Use of Market Information*. Boston: Harvard Business School Press.

Barker, A. (1996). *How to Become a Better Decision Maker*. London: Kogan Page.

Baumard, P. (1999). *Tacit Knowledge in Organizations*. London: Sage.

Belbin, M. (1993). *Team Roles at Work*. London: Butterworth–Heinemann.

Claxton, G.L. (1997). *Hare Brain, Tortoise Mind: Why Intelligence Increases When You Think Less*. London: Fourth Estate.

Collins, J.C. & Porras, J.I. (1997). *Built to Last: Successful Habits of Visionary Companies*. New York: Harper Business Press.

Covey, S.R. (1990). *The Seven Habits of Highly Effective People*. New York: Simon & Schuster.

Davenport, T.H. & Prusak, L. (1998). *Working Knowledge: How Organizations Manage What They Know*. Boston: Harvard Business School.

Davidson, H. (1997). *Even More Offensive Marketing: An Exhilirating Action Guide to Winning in Business*. London: Penguin.

Dearlove, D. (1998). *Key Management Decisions: Tools and Techniques of the Executive Decision-maker*. London: Financial Times/Pitman Publishing.

Ehrenberg, A.S.C. (1974). *Data Reduction, Analysing and Interpreting Statistical Data*. London: Wiley, Interscience Publications.

Fishbein, M. (ed.) (1967). *Readings in Attitude Theory and Measurement*. New York: Wiley.

Glaser, B.G. & Strauss, A.L. (1967) *The Discovery of Grounded Theory: Strategies for Qualitative Research*. Chicago: Aldene.

Goldsmith, W. & Clutterbuck, D. (1997). *The Winning Streak Mark II: How the World's Most Successful Companies Stay on Top through Today's Turbulent Times*. London: Orien Business Books.

Harvard Business Review (1999). *Breakthrough Thinking*. Boston: Harvard Business School Press.

Kaplan, R.S. & Norton, D.P. (1996). *Translating Strategy into Action: The Balanced Scorecard*. Boston: Harvard Business School Press.

Kelly, G.A. (1955). *Psychology of Personal Constructs Vols I & II*. New York: Norton.

Marsh, C. (1982). *The Survey Method: The Contribution of Surveys to Sociological Explanation*. London: George Allen & Unwin.

McDonald, C. & Vangelder, P. (ed.) (1998). *ESOMAR Handbook of Market and Opinion Research*, 4th edn. Amsterdam: ESOMAR.

McMaster, M.D. (1995). *The Intelligence Advantage. Organising for Complexity.* Isle of Man: Knowledge-Based Developments Co. Ltd.

Nonaka, I. & Takeuchi, H. (1995). *The Knowledge-Creating Company.* Oxford: Oxford University Press.

Porter, M.E. (1980). *Competitive Strategy: Techniques for Analyzing Industries and Competitors.* New York: Free Press.

Seale, C. (1999). *The Quality of Qualitative Research.* London: Sage.

Stewart, T.A. (1999). *Intellectual Capital.* London: Nicholas Brealey.

Sveiby, K.E. (1997). *The New Organizational Wealth: Managing and Measuring Knowledge-based Assets.* San Francisco: Berrett-Koehler.

Taffinder, P. (1998). *Big Change: A Route-map for Corporation Transformation.* Chichester: Wiley.

Tibballs, G. (1999). *Business Blunders: Dirty Dealing and Financial Failure in the World of Big Business.* London: Robinson.

Tuck, M. (1976). *How Do we Choose?.* London: Methuen.

Index